Language and Symbolic Power

Language and Symbolic Power

Pierre Bourdieu

Edited and Introduced by
John B. Thompson

Translated by Gino Raymond and
Matthew Adamson

Polity Press

First published 1991 by Polity Press
in association with Blackwell Publishers Ltd.

First published in paperback 1992
Reprinted 1994, 1997

Editorial office:
Polity Press
65 Bridge Street, Cambridge CB2 1UR, UK

Marketing and production:
Blackwell Publishers Ltd
108 Cowley Road, Oxford OX4 1JF, UK

ISBN 0-7456-0097-2
ISBN 0-7456-1034-X (pbk)

A CIP catalogue record for this book is available from the British Library.

Typeset in 10¹/2 on 12pt. Times New Roman
by Wearside Tradespools, Fulwell, Sunderland
Printed in Great Britain by
Athenæum Press Ltd, Gateshead, Tyne & Wear

Contents

Preface

Most of the material in this volume appeared in French in a book entitled *Ce que parler veut dire: l'économie des échanges linguistiques* (Paris: Librairie Arthème Fayard, 1982). However, this English volume differs in certain respects from the original French book; two short essays have been left out, and five other pieces have been added. Hence *Language and Symbolic Power* is to some extent a new volume which does not have a direct counterpart in French. The original French book is itself a collection of essays, some of which are slightly modified versions of articles which had been published previously. Full bibliographical details of each chapter are given below.

1 'The Production and Reproduction of Legitimate Language', written in summer 1980, was originally published as 'La production et la reproduction de la langue légitime', in *Ce que parler veut dire*, pp. 23–58.

2 'Price Formation and the Anticipation of Profits', written in summer 1980, was originally published as 'La formation des prix et l'anticipation des profits', in *Ce que parler veut dire*, pp. 59–95.

   Appendix to Part I, 'Did you say "Popular"?', was originally published as 'Vous avez dit "populaire"?', *Actes de la recherche en sciences sociales*, 46 (March 1983), pp. 98–105.

3 'Authorized Language: The Social Conditions for the Effectiveness of Ritual Discourse' was originally published as 'Le langage autorisé. Note sur les conditions sociales de l'efficacité du

discours rituel', *Actes de la recherche en sciences sociales*, 5–6 (November 1975), pp. 183–90, and reprinted in *Ce que parler veut dire*, pp. 103–19.

4 'Rites of Institution' (transcript of a lecture given at a conference on 'Rites of Passage Today' at Neuchâtel in October 1981) was originally published as 'Les rites d'institution', *Actes de la recherche en sciences sociales*, 43 (June 1982), pp. 58–63, and reprinted in *Ce que parler veut dire*, pp. 121–34.

5 'Description and Prescription: The Conditions of Possibility and the Limits of Political Effectiveness' was originally published as 'Décrire et prescrire. Note sur les conditions de possibilité et les limites de l'efficacité politique', *Actes de la recherche en sciences sociales*, 30 (May 1981), pp. 69–74, and reprinted in *Ce que parler veut dire*, pp. 149–61.

6 'Censorship and the Imposition of Form' was originally published as 'Censure et mise en forme', in *Ce que parler veut dire*, pp. 167–205. This text is a revised version of two sections of a long article originally published in 1975 under the title 'L'Ontologie politique de Martin Heidegger', *Actes de la recherche en sciences sociales*, 5–6 (November 1975), pp. 109–56. The entire article was subsequently revised and expanded by Bourdieu and published as a short book bearing the same title: Pierre Bourdieu, *L'Ontologie politique de Martin Heidegger* (Paris: Minuit, 1988), published in English as *The Political Ontology of Martin Heidegger*, translated by Peter Collier (Cambridge: Polity Press, 1991). A number of minor alterations have been incorporated into the essay which appears in this volume.

7 'On Symbolic Power' was originally published as 'Sur le pouvoir symbolique', *Annales*, 32/3 (May–June 1977), pp. 405–11. An English translation of a slightly different version of this essay was published as 'Symbolic power', translated by Colin Wringe, in D. Gleeson (ed.), *Identity and Structure: Issues in the Sociology of Education* (Driffield: Nafferton Books, 1977), pp. 112–17. The essay has been retranslated for this volume.

8 'Political Representation: Elements for a Theory of the Political Field' was originally published as 'La représentation politique. Éléments pour une théorie du champ politique', *Actes de la recherche en sciences sociales*, 36–37 (February–March 1981), pp. 3–24. Some of the illustrative material in the original French article has been deleted from the English version that appears here.

9 'Delegation and Political Fetishism' (based on a lecture given to the *Association des étudiants protestants de Paris* on 7 June 1983) was originally published as 'La délégation et le fétichisme politique', *Actes de la recherche en sciences sociales*, 52–53 (June 1984), pp. 49–55.

10 'Identity and Representation: Elements for a Critical Reflection on the Idea of Region' was originally published as 'La force de la représentation', in *Ce que parler veut dire*, pp. 135–48. This text is a modified version of an earlier essay, 'L'Identité et la représentation. Éléments pour une réflexion critique sur l'idée de région', *Actes de la recherche en sciences sociales*, 35 (November 1980), pp. 63–72. In this translation, the earlier title has been retained.

11 'Social Space and the Genesis of "Classes"' was originally published as 'Espace social et genèse des "classes"', *Actes de la recherche en sciences sociales*, 52–53 (June 1984), pp. 3–12. An abridged version of this text was presented as the *Vorlesungen zu den Geistes- und Sozialwissenschaften* at the University of Frankfurt in February 1984; a slightly different version appeared in English under the title 'The social space and the genesis of groups', translated by Richard Nice, *Theory and Society*, 14 (1985), pp. 723–44.

The 'General introduction' and the introductions to parts I and II were first published in *Ce que parler veut dire*, pp. 7–10, 13–21 and 99–101 respectively.

The 'General introduction', the introductions to parts I and II and chapters 1–6 were translated by Gino Raymond. Chapters 7–11 were translated by Matthew Adamson.

J.B.T.
Cambridge, June 1990

Editor's Introduction

As competent speakers we are aware of the many ways in which linguistic exchanges can express relations of power. We are sensitive to the variations in accent, intonation and vocabulary which reflect different positions in the social hierarchy. We are aware that individuals speak with differing degrees of authority, that words are loaded with unequal weights, depending on who utters them and how they are said, such that some words uttered in certain circumstances have a force and a conviction that they would not have elsewhere. We are experts in the innumerable and subtle strategies by which words can be used as instruments of coercion and constraint, as tools of intimidation and abuse, as signs of politeness, condescension and contempt. In short, we are aware that language is an integral part of social life, with all its ruses and iniquities, and that a good part of our social life consists of the routine exchange of linguistic expressions in the day-to-day flow of social interaction.

It is much easier, however, to observe in a general way that language and social life are inextricably linked than it is to develop this observation in a rigorous and compelling way. The contemporary intellectual disciplines which are particularly concerned with language have been illuminating in this regard, but they have also suffered from a number of shortcomings. In some branches of linguistics, literary criticism and philosophy, for instance, there is a tendency to think of the social character of language in a rather abstract way, as if it amounted to little more than the fact that language is, as Saussure once put it, a collective 'treasure' shared by all members of a community. What is missing from such perspectives is an account of the concrete, complicated ways in which linguistic practices and products are caught up in, and moulded by, the forms of power and inequality which are pervasive features of societies as they actually exist. Sociologists and sociolinguists have been more concerned with the interplay between linguistic practices and concrete forms of social life; but in their work there is a tendency – though this is by no means without exception – to become preoccupied with the empirical details of variations in accent or usage, in a way that is largely divorced from broader theoretical and explanatory concerns. When social theorists have turned their attention to language they have not neglected these broader concerns, but all too often they have run roughshod over the specific properties of language and language use in the interests of developing some general theory of social action or the social world.

One of the merits of the work of the French sociologist Pierre Bourdieu is that it avoids to a large extent the shortcomings which characterize some of the sociological and social-theoretical writing on language, while at the same time offering an original sociological perspective on linguistic phenomena which has nothing to do with abstract conceptions of social life. In a series of articles originally published in the late 1970s and early 1980s, Bourdieu developed a trenchant critique of formal and structural linguistics, arguing that these disciplinary frameworks take for granted but fail to grasp the specific social and political conditions of language formation and use. He also began the task of elaborating an original, innovative approach to linguistic phenomena, an approach that aims to be both theoretically informed and sensitive to empirical detail. The theory that informs Bourdieu's approach is a general *theory of practice* which he has worked out in the course of a long and prolific career, spanning more than thirty years and twenty volumes of research and reflection.[1] Armed with the key concepts of this theory, Bourdieu sheds fresh light on a range of issues concerned with language and language use. He portrays everyday linguistic exchanges as situated encounters between agents endowed with socially structured resources and competencies, in such a way that every linguistic interaction, however personal and insignificant it may seem, bears the traces of the social structure that it both expresses and helps to reproduce.

The material brought together in this volume includes Bourdieu's most important writings on language, as well as a set of essays which explore some aspects of representation and symbolic power in the field of politics. My aim in this introduction is to provide an overview of this material and to outline the theoretical framework which guides Bourdieu's approach. For his critical analysis of orthodox linguistics, and the alternative account of linguistic phenomena which he offers, are effectively an application to language of a range of concepts and ideas elaborated elsewhere. I shall begin by summarizing briefly his critique of formal and structural linguistics, as well as his appraisal of the theory of speech acts developed by Austin. I shall then discuss some of the main concepts and assumptions of Bourdieu's own theoretical framework, focusing on those aspects which are most relevant to the analysis of language use. In the third section I shall broaden the discussion to consider Bourdieu's views on the nature of politics and political discourse, which are the concern of the final set of essays in this volume. My aim is to provide a sympathetic exposition of some themes in Bourdieu's work, not a critical analysis of his views. There are, of course, various aspects of Bourdieu's work which could be questioned and criticized, and indeed which have been questioned and criticized in the literature, sometimes in ways that are thoughtful and probing, at other times in ways that display more than a hint of wilful incomprehension.[2] But these are issues which I shall not pursue here.

I

As a thinker whose formative milieu was the Paris of the 1950s and early 1960s, Bourdieu is more aware than many of the intellectual impact of certain ways of thinking about language. Bourdieu followed closely the development of Lévi-Strauss's work and incorporated some features of Lévi-Strauss's method – in particular, his emphasis on the analysis of relations and oppositions – in his early ethnographic studies of kinship structures and matrimonial strategies among the Kabyle of North Africa.[3] But Bourdieu became increasingly dissatisfied with Lévi-Strauss's method, which gave rise to insoluble theoretical and methodological problems.[4] He was also somewhat sceptical of the fashionable trend called 'structuralism', which was rapidly gaining ground among Parisian intellectuals in the 1960s and which reflected, in Bourdieu's view, an overly zealous and methodologically uncontrolled application of the linguistic principles worked out by Saussure and others. The misadventures of structuralism alerted Bourdieu at an early stage both to the inherent limitations of Saussurian linguistics and to the dangers of a certain kind of intellectual imperialism, whereby a particular model of language could assume a paradigmatic status in the social sciences as a whole.

Hence, when Bourdieu undertakes a critique of the linguistic theories of Saussure and others, he is seeking *also* to counteract the influence of linguistic models in other domains of social and cultural analysis. Bourdieu is adamantly opposed to all those forms of 'semiotic' or 'semiological' analysis which owe their inspiration to Saussure: these forms of analysis are purely 'internal', in the sense that they focus exclusively on the internal constitution of a text or corpus of texts, and hence ignore the social–historical conditions of the production and reception of texts. Moreover, such forms of analysis commonly take for granted the position of the analyst, without reflecting on this position, or on the relation between the analyst and the object of analysis, in a rigorous and reflexive way. As a result, semiotic or semiological analyses may express, to a significant but largely unexamined extent, the position of the analyst in the intellectual division of labour.

It is important to emphasize that, in distancing himself from the various kinds of internal analysis which are commonly employed in the study of literary texts and cultural artefacts, Bourdieu is not seeking simply to *supplement* these kinds of analysis with an account of the social–historical conditions of production and reception: his position is both more radical and more original than this. Unlike authors such as Lévi-Strauss and Barthes, who took over certain concepts originally developed in the sphere of linguistics and sought to apply them to phenomena like myths and fashion, Bourdieu proceeds in an altogether different way. He seeks to show that language itself is a social–historical phenomenon, that linguistic exchange is a mundane, practical activity like many others, and that linguistic theories which ignore the social–historical and practical character of language do so at their cost.

Bourdieu develops this argument by examining some of the presuppositions of Saussurian and Chomskyan linguistics. There are, of course, many important differences between the theoretical approaches of Saussure and Chomsky – for instance, Chomsky's approach is more dynamic and gives greater emphasis to the generative capacities of competent speakers. But there is, in Bourdieu's view, one principle which these theoretical approaches have in common: they are both based on a fundamental distinction which enables language to be constituted as an autonomous and homogeneous object, amenable to a properly linguistic analysis. In the case of Saussure, the distinction is that between *langue* and *parole*, that is, between 'language' as a self-sufficient system of signs and 'speech' as the situated realization of the system by particular speakers. Chomsky draws a somewhat similar distinction between 'competence', which is the knowledge of a language possessed by an ideal speaker–hearer in a completely homogeneous speech community, and 'performance', which is the actual use of language in concrete situations.[5]

Bourdieu's objection to this kind of distinction is that it leads the linguist to take for granted an object domain which is in fact the product of a complex set of social, historical and political conditions of formation. Under the guise of drawing a *methodological* distinction, the linguist surreptitiously makes a series of *substantive* assumptions. For the completely homogeneous language or speech community does not exist in reality: it is an idealization of a particular set of linguistic practices which have emerged historically and have certain social conditions of existence. This idealization or *fictio juris* is the source of what Bourdieu calls, somewhat provocatively, 'the illusion of linguistic communism'. By taking a particular set of linguistic practices as a normative model of correct usage, the linguist produces the illusion of a common language and ignores the social–historical conditions which have established a particular set of linguistic practices as dominant and legitimate. Through a complex historical process, sometimes involving extensive conflict (especially in colonial contexts), a particular language or set of linguistic practices has emerged as the dominant and legitimate language, and other languages or dialects have been eliminated or subordinated to it. This dominant and legitimate language, this *victorious* language, is what linguists commonly take for granted. Their idealized language or speech community is an object which has been *pre*-constructed by a set of social–historical conditions endowing it with the status of the sole legitimate or 'official' language of a particular community.

This process can be examined by looking carefully at the ways in which particular languages have emerged historically as dominant in particular geographical locales, often in conjunction with the formation of modern nation-states. Bourdieu focuses on the development of French, but one could just as easily look at the development of English in Britain or the United States, of Spanish in Spain or Mexico, and so on.[6] In the case of French, much of the historical groundwork was carried out by Ferdinand Brunot in his monumental study, *Histoire de la langue française des origines à nos jours*.[7] Bourdieu draws on Brunot's work to show how, until the French Revolution, the process of linguistic unification was bound up with

the construction of a monarchical state. In the central provinces of
the *pays d'oïl* (Champagne, Normandy, Anjou, Berry), the languages and dialects of the feudal period gradually gave way, from the
fourteenth century on, to the dialect of the *Ile de France*, which was
developed in cultivated Parisian circles, promoted to the status of
official language and used in a written form. During the same period,
regional and purely oral dialects were relegated to the status of
patois, defined negatively and pejoratively by opposition to the
official language. The situation was different in the *langue d'oc*
regions of southern France. There the Parisian dialect did not take
hold until the sixteenth century, and it did not eliminate the
widespread use of local dialects, which existed in written as well as
oral forms. Hence a situation of bilingualism developed, with
members of the peasantry and lower classes speaking local dialects
only, while the aristocracy, bourgeoisie and petite bourgeoisie had
access to the official language as well.

As Bourdieu shows, the members of the upper classes had
everything to gain from the policy of linguistic unification which
accompanied the French Revolution. This policy, which was part of
Condillac's theory of the purification of thought through the purification of language, would give the upper classes a *de facto* monopoly of
political power. By promoting the official language to the status of
the national language – that is, the official language of the emerging
nation-state – the policy of linguistic unification would favour those
who already possessed the official language as part of their linguistic
competence, while those who knew only a local dialect would
become part of a political and linguistic unit in which their traditional
competence was subordinate and devalued. The subsequent normalization and inculcation of the official language, and its legitimation
as the official language of the nation-state, was not just a matter of
political policy: it was a gradual process that depended on a variety
of other factors, such as the development of the educational system
and the formation of a unified labour market. The production of
grammar books, dictionaries and a corpus of texts exemplifying
correct usage is only the most obvious manifestation of this gradual
process of normalization. Perhaps more importantly, with the establishment of a system of educational qualifications possessing a
standardized value independent of regional variations, and with the
unification of a labour market in which administrative positions
depended on educational qualifications, the school came to be seen
as a principal means of access to the labour market, especially in
areas where industrialization was weak. Thus, by the combined

effect of various institutions and social processes, people speaking local dialects were induced, as Bourdieu puts it, 'to collaborate in the destruction of their instruments of expression'.[8]

If linguistic theories have tended to neglect the social–historical conditions underlying the formation of the language which they take, in an idealized form, as their object domain, so too they have tended to analyse linguistic expressions in isolation from the specific social conditions in which they are used. In the work of Saussure and Chomsky, the isolation of linguistic analysis from the social conditions of use is closely linked to the distinctions drawn between *langue* and *parole*, competence and performance, and hence Bourdieu presses his critique further by asking whether these distinctions do justice to what is involved in the activity of speaking. In the first place, it seems clear that speaking cannot be thought of, in the manner suggested by Saussure, as the mere realization or 'execution' of a pre-existing linguistic system: speaking is a much more complex and creative activity than this rather mechanical model would suggest. In the case of Chomsky's theory, however, the issues are more complicated, precisely because Chomsky sought to take account of creativity by conceptualizing competence as a system of generative processes.

Bourdieu's objection to this aspect of Chomsky's theory is that the notion of competence, understood as the capacity of an ideal speaker to generate an unlimited sequence of grammatically well formed sentences, is simply too abstract. The kind of competence that *actual* speakers possess is not a capacity to generate an unlimited sequence of grammatically well formed sentences, but rather a capacity to produce expressions which are appropriate for particular situations, that is, a capacity to produce expressions *à propos*. Bourdieu's argument does not require him to deny that competent speakers possess the capacity to generate grammatical sentences; his main point is that this capacity is *insufficient* as a means of characterizing the kind of competence possessed by actual speakers. For actual speakers have a *practical competence*, a 'practical sense' (a notion to which we shall return), by virtue of which they are able to produce utterances that are appropriate in the circumstances; and this practical competence cannot be derived from or reduced to the competence of Chomsky's ideal speaker.[9] Thus actual speakers are able to embed sentences or expressions in practical strategies which have numerous functions and which are tacitly adjusted to the relations of power between speakers and hearers. Their practical competence involves not only the capacity to produce grammatical utterances, but *also* the capacity to make oneself heard, believed, obeyed, and so on. Those who speak must ensure that they are entitled to speak in the circumstances, and those who listen must reckon that those who speak are worthy of attention. The recognition of the right to speak, and the associated forms of power and authority which are implicit in all communicative situations, are generally ignored by the linguist, who treats the linguistic exchange as an intellectual operation consisting of the encoding and decoding of grammatically well formed messages.

It is with this limitation of Chomskyan linguistics in mind that Bourdieu turns to a different body of writing on language, namely, to Austin's work on speech acts. In some respects, Bourdieu's approach to language is quite similar to that developed by Austin and other so-called 'ordinary language philosophers' in the 1940s and 1950s.[10] Consequently, Bourdieu's appraisal of Austin's work is more sympathetic than his analysis of Saussure and Chomsky. In singling out a class of 'performative utterances', such as 'I do' uttered in the course of a marriage ceremony or 'I name this ship the *Queen Elizabeth*' uttered while smashing a bottle against the stem of a vessel, Austin stressed that such utterances are not ways of reporting or describing a state of affairs, but rather ways of acting or participating in a ritual; that they are not strictly true or false but rather 'felicitous' or 'infelicitous'; and that for such utterances to be felicitous they must, among other things, be uttered by an appropriate person in accordance with some conventional procedure.[11] This implies, according to Bourdieu, that the efficacy of performative utterances is inseparable from the existence of an *institution* which defines the conditions (such as the place, the time, the agent) that must be fulfilled in order for the utterance to be effective. Bourdieu is using the term 'institution' in a way that is both very general and active (a sense conveyed better by the French term *institution* than by its English equivalent). An institution is not necessarily a particular organization – this or that family or factory, for instance – but is any relatively durable set of social relations which *endows* individuals with power, status and resources of various kinds. It is the institution, in this sense, that endows the speaker with the authority to carry out the act which his or her utterance claims to perform. Not anyone can stand before a freshly completed ship, utter the words 'I name this ship the *Queen Elizabeth*' while flinging a bottle at its stem, and thereby succeed in *naming* the vessel: the person must be *authorized* to do so, must be vested with the requisite authority to carry out the act. Hence the efficacy of the performative utterance presupposes a set of social relations, an institution, by virtue of which a particular individual, who is *authorized* to speak and *recognized* as such by others, is able to speak in a way that others will regard as acceptable in the circumstances. It follows that the myriad of symbolic devices – the robes, the wigs, the ritual express-ions and respectful references – that accompany occasions of a more 'formal' or 'official' kind are not irrelevant distractions: they are the very mechanisms through which those who speak attest to the authority of the institution which endows them with the power to speak, an institution which is sustained, in part, by the reverence and solemnity which are *de rigueur* on such occasions.

While Bourdieu praises the speech-act theorists for calling atten-tion to the social conditions of communication, he thinks that Austin, and especially some of the authors influenced by him, have not fully unfolded the consequences of this view. They have not fully appreciated the implications of the fact that the conditions of felicity are primarily *social* conditions: hence there is a tendency in the literature on speech acts to resort to analyses of a purely linguistic or logical kind. Part of the problem lies in the work of Austin himself. Austin refers, rather vaguely, to 'conventional procedures' which must be followed for the felicitous utterance of a performative; and later, when he shifts to the terminology of 'locutionary', 'illocution-ary' and 'perlocutionary' acts, he suggests that illocutionary acts (the act performed *in* saying something) can be distinguished from perlocutionary acts (the act performed *by* saying something) by the fact that illocutionary acts employ 'conventional means'. But never does Austin examine in detail the nature of these conventions; never does he consider carefully what it might mean to treat these conventions as *social* phenomena, implicated in sets of social rela-tions, imbued with power and authority, embroiled in conflict and struggle. Austin therefore left the way open for others to think about speech acts in purely linguistic terms, oblivious to the social charac-ter of the conditions of felicitous use. To think about speech acts in this way is to forget that the authority which utterances have is an authority bestowed upon language by factors external to it. When an authorized spokesperson speaks with authority, he or she expresses or manifests this authority, but does not create it: like the Homeric orator who takes hold of the *skeptron* in order to speak, the spokesperson avails himself or herself of a form of power or authority which is part of a social institution, and which does not stem from the words alone.

It is in this context that Bourdieu expresses reservations about the

way in which another major social thinker, Jürgen Habermas, tries
to build upon the work of speech-act theorists. Habermas argues
that, in exchanging speech acts, individuals are implicitly raising
certain 'validity claims', such as truth and correctness; and that some
of these validity claims can only be redeemed or made good in an
'ideal speech situation', that is, a communicative situation in which
participants are motivated to accept or reject a problematic claim on
the basis of reasons or grounds alone.[12] Although Bourdieu does not
engage extensively with Habermas's work, it is clear that the way in
which he wishes to pursue the insights of speech-act theorists is quite
different from Habermas's account. Whereas Habermas seeks to
show that the analysis of speech acts discloses a 'rationally motivat-
ing force' at work in communicative exchange, Bourdieu is concerned to demonstrate that whatever power or force speech acts
possess is a power or force ascribed to them by the social institution
of which the utterance of the speech act is part; and hence the notion
of an ideal speech situation, in which the rational character of
communicative exchange would be unhindered by social constraints,
is a notion which is based, in Bourdieu's view, on a fictitious elision
of the social conditions of language use. This line of argument, which
echoes criticisms that others have made of Habermas's work,
certainly has some plausibility. One may have doubts about Bourdieu's own account of speech acts – one may wonder, for instance, if
he is not relying too heavily on those occasions in which the
utterance of speech acts is clearly part of some recognized social
ritual, like a marriage or a baptism, as distinct from those occasions
in which individuals engage in relatively unstructured face-to-face
interaction, like a banal and casual conversation between friends.[13]
But it cannot be denied that, by focusing on the institutional aspects
of language use and probing them with an astute sociological
imagination, Bourdieu has highlighted some of the social conditions
of language use in a way that is largely absent from the existing
literature on the theory of speech acts.

II

Bourdieu's writings on language offer more than an illuminating
critical perspective on the work of Saussure, Chomsky, Austin and
others: they also put forward a new approach to language and
linguistic exchange. This approach is essentially a development of
the theoretical framework that he has worked out in other contexts.

To understand this approach, it is therefore necessary to take account of Bourdieu's other theoretical work, that is, the key concepts and assumptions of his theory of practice.

Bourdieu's theory of practice is a systematic attempt to move beyond a series of oppositions and antinomies which have plagued the social sciences since their inception. For anyone involved in the social sciences today, these oppositions have a familiar ring: the individual versus society, action versus structure, freedom versus necessity, etc. Bourdieu's theoretical approach is intended to bypass or dissolve a plethora of such oppositions. When he develops his approach, however, he generally begins with a broad dichotomy, expressed at the level of epistemology or the theory of knowledge, between 'subjectivism' and 'objectivism'. By 'subjectivism' Bourdieu means an intellectual orientation to the social world which seeks to grasp the way the world appears to the individuals who are situated within it. Subjectivism presupposes the possibility of some kind of immediate apprehension of the lived experience of others, and it assumes that this apprehension is by itself a more-or-less adequate form of knowledge about the social world. What Bourdieu has in mind here are certain forms of 'phenomenological' and 'interpretative' sociology and anthropology, such as the phenomenological sociology developed by Alfred Schutz.[14] By 'objectivism' Bourdieu means an intellectual orientation to the social world which seeks to construct the objective relations which structure practices and representations. Objectivism presupposes a break with immediate experience; it places the primary experience of the social world in brackets and attempts to elucidate the structures and principles upon which primary experience depends but which it cannot directly grasp. The kinds of analyses developed by Lévi-Strauss and by some versions of structural linguistics are examples of objectivism in this sense.

Bourdieu's view is that both subjectivism and objectivism are inadequate intellectual orientations, but that the latter is less inadequate than the former. The chief merit of objectivism is that it breaks with the immediate experience of the social world and is able thereby to produce a knowledge of the social world which is not reducible to the practical knowledge possessed by lay actors. In Bourdieu's view, the break with immediate experience is an essential prerequisite for social-scientific inquiry, a break which is made all the more difficult by the fact that the social scientist is also a participant in social life and hence is inclined to draw upon everyday words and concepts in analysing the social world.[15] If objectivism rightly emphasizes the break with everyday experience, it suffers from shortcomings of its own. The main shortcoming of objectivism is that, by failing to reflect rigorously on its own conditions of possibility, it cannot grasp the link between the knowledge it produces and the practical knowledge possessed by lay actors; or, to put it another way, it cannot grasp the link between the objective relations and structures it elucidates, on the one hand, and the practical activities of the individuals who make up the social world, on the other. Thus, from the perspective of objectivism, the practical activities of individuals can appear as nothing other than the application of a rule, or the realization of a model or structure, which has been elucidated or constructed by the analyst. Practice is turned into a mere epiphenomenon of the analyst's own constructs. Bourdieu's view, persuasively argued, is that this perspective is irremediably flawed as an account of practice. His alternative theory of practice is an attempt to move beyond objectivism without relapsing into subjectivism, that is, to take account of the need to break with immediate experience while at the same time doing justice to the practical character of social life.

The key concept that Bourdieu employs in developing his approach is that of *habitus*. The term is a very old one, of Aristotelian and scholastic origins, but Bourdieu uses it in a distinctive and quite specific way. The habitus is a set of *dispositions* which incline agents to act and react in certain ways. The dispositions generate practices, perceptions and attitudes which are 'regular' without being consciously co-ordinated or governed by any 'rule'. The dispositions which constitute the habitus are inculcated, structured, durable, generative and transposable – features that each deserve a brief explanation. Dispositions are acquired through a gradual process of *inculcation* in which early childhood experiences are particularly important. Through a myriad of mundane processes of training and learning, such as those involved in the inculcation of table manners ('sit up straight', 'don't eat with your mouth full', etc.), the individual acquires a set of dispositions which literally mould the body and become second nature. The dispositions produced thereby are also *structured* in the sense that they unavoidably reflect the social conditions within which they were acquired. An individual from a working-class background, for instance, will have acquired dispositions which are different in certain respects from those acquired by individuals who were brought up in a middle-class milieu. In other words, the similarities and differences that characterize the social conditions of existence of individuals will be reflected in the habitus, which may be relatively homogeneous across individuals from similar backgrounds. Structured dispositions are also *durable*: they are ingrained in the body in such a way that they endure through the life history of the individual, operating in a way that is pre-conscious and hence not readily amenable to conscious reflection and modification. Finally, the dispositions are *generative* and *transposable* in the sense that they are capable of generating a multiplicity of practices and perceptions in fields other than those in which they were originally acquired. As a durably installed set of dispositions, the habitus tends to generate practices and perceptions, works and appreciations, which concur with the conditions of existence of which the habitus is itself the product.

The habitus also provides individuals with a sense of how to act and respond in the course of their daily lives. It 'orients' their actions and inclinations without strictly determining them. It gives them a 'feel for the game', a sense of what is appropriate in the circumstances and what is not, a 'practical sense' (*le sens pratique*). The practical sense is not so much a state of mind as a state of the body, a state of being. It is because the body has become a repository of ingrained dispositions that certain actions, certain ways of behaving and responding, seem altogether natural. Bourdieu speaks here of a bodily or corporeal 'hexis', by which he means a certain durable organization of one's body and of its deployment in the world. 'Bodily hexis is political mythology realized, *em-bodied*, turned into a permanent disposition, a durable way of standing, speaking, walking, and thereby of feeling and thinking.'[16] The importance of bodily hexis can be seen in the differing ways that men and women carry themselves in the world, in their differing postures, their differing ways of walking and speaking, of eating and laughing, as well as in the differing ways that men and women deploy themselves in the more intimate aspects of life. The body is the site of incorporated history. The practical schemes through which the body is organized are the product of history and, at the same time, the source of practices and perceptions which reproduce that history. The continuing process of production and reproduction, of history incorporated and incorporation actualized, is a process that can take place without ever becoming the object of a specific institutional practice, explicitly articulated in language. The latter presupposes the development of a certain kind of pedagogic institution which is not present in all societies, and which in our societies is generally associated with the educational system.

The habitus, and the related notions of practical sense and bodily hexis, are the concepts with which Bourdieu seeks to grasp the generative principles or schemes which underlie practices and perceptions, works and appreciations. But when individuals act, they always do so in specific social contexts or settings. Hence particular practices or perceptions should be seen, not as the product of the habitus as such, but as the product of the *relation between* the habitus, on the one hand, and the specific social contexts or 'fields' within which individuals act, on the other. Bourdieu uses different terms to refer to the social contexts or fields of action: 'field' (*champ*) is his preferred technical term, but the terms 'market' and 'game' are also commonly used, in ways that are at least partly metaphorical. A field or market may be seen as a structured space of positions in which the positions and their interrelations are determined by the distribution of different kinds of resources or 'capital'.[17] One of the central ideas of Bourdieu's work, for which he is well known among sociologists of education, is the idea that there are different forms of capital: not only 'economic capital' in the strict sense (i.e. material wealth in the form of money, stocks and shares, property, etc.), but also 'cultural capital' (i.e. knowledge, skills and other cultural acquisitions, as exemplified by educational or technical qualifications), 'symbolic capital' (i.e. accumulated prestige or honour), and so on. One of the most important properties of fields is the way in which they allow one form of capital to be converted into another – in the way, for example, that certain educational qualifications can be cashed in for lucrative jobs.[18]

A field is always the site of struggles in which individuals seek to maintain or alter the distribution of the forms of capital specific to it. The individuals who participate in these struggles will have differing aims – some will seek to preserve the status quo, others to change it – and differing chances of winning or losing, depending on where they are located in the structured space of positions. But all individuals, whatever their aims and chances of success, will share in common certain fundamental presuppositions. All participants must believe in the game they are playing, and in the value of what is at stake in the struggles they are waging. The very existence and persistence of the game or field presupposes a total and unconditional 'investment', a practical and unquestioning belief, in the game and its stakes. Hence the conduct of struggle within a field, whether a conflict over the distribution of wealth or over the value of a work of art, always presupposes a fundamental accord or complicity on the part of those who participate in the struggle.

The terms used by Bourdieu to describe fields and their properties – 'market', 'capital', 'profit', etc. – are terms borrowed from the language of economics, but they are adapted for the analysis of fields which are not 'economic' in the narrow sense. This is a point on which Bourdieu can be easily misunderstood. The reader may get the impression that, when Bourdieu uses these terms to analyse forms of interaction which are not strictly economic transactions, he is treating these forms of interaction *as if* they were economic transactions *and nothing more*; that is, one may get the impression that Bourdieu's approach involves a kind of economic reductionism. There may well be some genuine difficulties with Bourdieu's use of economic terminology, but it is important to see that his position is more complicated and more sophisticated than the charge of economic reductionism would suggest. His view is that the practices we describe today as 'economic' in the narrow sense (e.g. buying and selling commodities) are a sub-category of practices pertaining to a specific field or cluster of fields, the 'market economy', which has emerged historically and which displays certain distinctive properties. But there are other sub-categories of practices which pertain to other fields, such as the fields of literature, art, politics and religion; and these other fields are characterized by their own distinctive properties, by distinctive forms of capital, profit, etc. Hence Bourdieu does not wish to reduce all social fields to the economy in the narrow sense, nor to treat all types of practice as strictly economic transactions. On the contrary, he wishes to treat the economy in the narrow sense as one field (or cluster of fields) among a plurality of fields which are not reducible to one another. Within fields that are not economic in the narrow sense, practices may not be governed by a strictly economic logic (e.g. may not be oriented towards financial gain); and yet they may none the less concur with a logic that is economic in a broader sense, in so far as they are oriented towards the augmentation of *some* kind of 'capital' (e.g. cultural or symbolic capital) or the maximization of *some* kind of 'profit' (e.g. honour or prestige). So, for example, if we want to understand why a peasant family buys a second yoke of oxen after the harvest, on the grounds that they will be needed for treading out the grain of an allegedly plentiful crop, only to sell the oxen before the autumn ploughing when they would technically be most useful, we have to appreciate that the purchase of the oxen is a way of augmenting the family's symbolic capital in the late summer when marriages are negotiated.[19] The purchase of the oxen and their conspicuous display is a strategy of bluff that obeys an economic logic in a broad sense (the augmentation of symbolic capital and the maximization of symbolic profit), without being economic in the narrow sense of financial or material gain.

Bourdieu therefore assumes a fundamental link between actions and interests, between the practices of agents and the interests which they knowingly or unknowingly pursue, while at the same time he rejects the idea that interests are always narrowly economic. 'Even when they give every appearance of disinterestedness because they escape the logic of "economic" interest (in the narrow sense) and are oriented towards non-material stakes that are not easily quantified, as in "pre-capitalist" societies or in the cultural sphere of capitalist societies, practices never cease to comply with an economic logic':[20] this is the core assumption of Bourdieu's theory of the economy of practice. It is a substantive assumption, in the sense that it makes a certain (and by no means uncontroversial) claim about the basic character of human action. But it is also, and perhaps more importantly, a heuristic principle, in the sense that it calls upon the researcher to elucidate the specific interests at stake in the practices and conflicts which take place in particular fields. For the *content* of interests cannot be determined abstractly. What interests are, that is, what they amount to in any particular instance of action or struggle, can be determined only through a careful empirical or historical inquiry into the distinctive properties of the fields concerned. Hence if one wishes to understand the interests at stake in literary or artistic production, one must reconstruct the literary or artistic field in relation to the fields of the economy (in the narrow sense), politics, etc.; and one may find that, the greater the autonomy of the literary or artistic field, the more agents within these fields will be oriented towards non-pecuniary and non-political ends, that is, the more they will have a specific 'interest in disinterestedness' (e.g. 'art for art's sake').[21] The fact that literary or artistic production appears as disinterested, as a haven for gratuitous activity that is ostentatiously opposed to the mundane world of commodities and power, does not mean that it is interest-free: on the contrary, it means only that it is able more easily to conceal its interests beneath the veil of aesthetic purity.

There is a further qualification that should be added to this schematic account of Bourdieu's theory of practice. While agents orient themselves towards specific interests or goals, their action is only rarely the outcome of a conscious deliberation or calculation in which the pros and cons of different strategies are carefully weighed up, their costs and benefits assessed, etc. To view action as the outcome of conscious calculation – a perspective implicit in some forms of game theory and rational action theory[22] – is to neglect the fact that, by virtue of the habitus, individuals are *already predisposed* to act in certain ways, pursue certain goals, avow certain tastes, and so on. Since individuals are the products of particular histories which endure in the habitus, their actions can never be analysed adequately as the outcome of conscious calculation. Rather, practices should be seen as the product of an encounter between a habitus and a field which are, to varying degrees, 'compatible' or 'congruent' with one another, in such a way that, on occasions when there is a lack of congruence (e.g. a student from a working-class background who finds himself or herself in an elite educational establishment), an individual may not know how to act and may literally be lost for words.

In developing his approach to language and linguistic exchange, Bourdieu applies and elaborates the ideas that make up the theory of practice. Linguistic utterances or expressions are forms of practice and, as such, can be understood as the product of the relation between a linguistic habitus and a linguistic market. The linguistic habitus is a sub-set of the dispositions which comprise the habitus: it is that sub-set of dispositions acquired in the course of learning to speak in particular contexts (the family, the peer group, the school, etc.). These dispositions govern both the subsequent linguistic practices of an agent and the anticipation of the value that linguistic products will receive in other fields or markets – in the labour market, for example, or in the institutions of secondary or tertiary education. The linguistic habitus is also inscribed in the body and forms a dimension of the bodily hexis. A particular accent, for instance, is the product of a certain way of moving the tongue, the lips, etc.: it is an aspect of what Bourdieu calls, following Pierre Guiraud, an 'articulatory style'.[23] The fact that different groups and classes have different accents, intonations and ways of speaking is a manifestation, at the level of language, of the socially structured character of the habitus. Differences of this kind are well known and have been amply documented by sociologists, sociolinguists and social historians. A less obvious index of the differentiation of articulatory styles may be found in the ways that particular classes or the respective sexes are associated with particular conceptions of the *mouth*. This is easier to illustrate in French than in English. In French there is a distinction between a closed, pinched mouth (*la bouche*) and a large, open mouth (*la gueule*). Individuals from working-class backgrounds tend to draw a socially and sexually overdetermined opposition between these terms: *la bouche* is associated with the bourgeois and the feminine (e.g. 'tight-lipped'), whereas *la gueule* is associated with the popular and the masculine (e.g. 'big mouth', 'loud mouth'). One can see that, from this viewpoint, the adoption of the articulatory style of the upper or middle classes may appear to some individuals from working-class backgrounds as a negation not only of their social identity, but also of their sexual identity. Working-class male speakers can adopt the dominant articulatory style only at the cost of a double negation, involving both the renunciation of their class habitus and the acquisition of dispositions which are perceived as effeminate. Bourdieu suggests that this may help to explain the fact, observed by Labov and others,[24] that working-class women display a greater tendency to adopt prestigious forms of speech than working-class men, while the latter tend to take the lead in developing new vernacular forms of expression.

Linguistic utterances or expressions are always produced in particular contexts or markets, and the properties of these markets endow linguistic products with a certain 'value'. On a given linguistic market, some products are valued more highly than others; and part of the practical competence of speakers is to know how, and to be able, to produce expressions which are highly valued on the markets concerned. This aspect of the practical competence of speakers is not uniformly distributed throughout a society in which the same language, such as English or French, is spoken. For different speakers possess different quantities of 'linguistic capital' – that is, the capacity to produce expressions *à propos*, *for* a particular market. Moreover, the distribution of linguistic capital is related in specific ways to the distribution of other forms of capital (economic capital, cultural capital, etc.) which define the location of an individual within the social space. Hence differences in terms of accent, grammar and vocabulary – the very differences overlooked by formal linguistics – are indices of the social positions of speakers and reflections of the quantities of linguistic capital (and other capital) which they possess. The more linguistic capital that speakers possess, the more they are able to exploit the system of differences to their advantage and thereby secure a *profit of distinction*. For the forms of expression which receive the greatest value and secure the greatest profit are those which are most unequally distributed, both in the sense that the conditions for the acquisition of the capacity to produce them are restricted and in the sense that the expressions themselves are relatively rare on the markets where they appear.

Bourdieu offers a vivid example of this dynamic. The example is from the town of Pau in Béarn, a province in southern France from which Bourdieu himself comes and where a local dialect, Béarnais, is spoken. The occasion is the official celebration, in September 1974, of the centenary of the birth of a Béarnais poet, Simin Palay. A French newspaper published in the province reported an event that 'greatly moved' the audience who 'applauded at length': the event was that the mayor of Pau addressed the audience in 'good quality Béarnais'.[25] Why should a group of people whose native language is Béarnais feel greatly moved by the fact that the mayor of their town addresses them in Béarnais on the occasion of honouring a Béarnais poet? Such a response is possible, argues Bourdieu, only in so far as they tacitly recognize the unwritten law which imposes French as the only acceptable language on official occasions. The mayor of Pau employs a *strategy of condescension* by which, in the very act of negating symbolically the objective relation of power between the two languages which co-exist in this market, he draws symbolic profit from this relation. He is able to draw profit from the hierarchy between the languages because everyone recognizes the unwritten law and knows that, as mayor of a large town, he has all of the qualifications which guarantee his competence in the dominant language. By virtue of his position he is able to negate symbolically the hierarchy without disrupting it, to transgress the unwritten law and thereby exploit the hierarchy to his advantage in the very process of reaffirming it. What is praised as 'good quality Béarnais' when issued from the mouth of the mayor would have been accorded a quite different (and no doubt much lower) value had it been uttered by a peasant who spoke mere fragments of French.

As this example illustrates, in reproducing linguistic expressions speakers take into account – in varying ways and to differing extents – the market conditions within which their products will be received and valued by others. The speaker's assessment of the market conditions, and the anticipation of the likely reception of his or her linguistic products, operate as internalized constraints on the very process of production. Individuals implicitly and routinely modify their expressions in anticipation of their likely reception – in the way, for instance, that adults alter their vocabulary and tone of voice when speaking to children. Hence all linguistic expressions are, to some extent, 'euphemized': they are modified by a certain kind of *censorship* which stems from the structure of the market, but which is transformed into *self-censorship* through the process of anticipation. Viewed from this perspective, phenomena of politeness and tactfulness, of choosing the right word for the right occasion, are not exceptional phenomena but are simply the most obvious manifesta-

tion of a situation common to all linguistic production. Tact is
nothing other than the capacity of a speaker to assess market
conditions accurately and to produce linguistic expressions which are
appropriate to them, that is, expressions which are suitably euphemized.

Mechanisms of censorship operate not only in the production of
everyday oral discourse, but also in the production of the scholarly
discourses found in written texts. Here as elsewhere, when Bourdieu
speaks of 'censorship' he is not referring to the explicit activity of
political or religious organizations seeking to suppress or restrict the
diffusion of symbolic forms. Rather, he is referring to a general
feature of markets or fields which requires that, if one wishes to
produce discourse successfully within a particular field, one must
observe the forms and formalities of that field. This is just as true of
the scholarly fields of literature, philosophy and science as it is of the
mundane markets of everyday social interaction. Bourdieu takes the
philosophical discourse of Heidegger as an example. Heidegger's
work is particularly interesting precisely because the language is so
arcane, so preoccupied with distinctions, allusions and rhetorical
effects – in a word, so euphemized. What Bourdieu tries to show is
that the style and form of Heidegger's prose is a product of the
mechanisms of censorship and strategies of euphemization associated with his position in a specific philosophical field, itself related in
determinate ways to the literary, political and broader social fields of
Weimar Germany. Part of the distinctiveness of Heidegger's work is
that it borrows many words from ordinary language – *Sorge* (care),
Fürsorge (solicitude), *Sozialfürsorge* (social assistance), etc. – and
introduces them into a philosophical field from which they had
previously been excluded. But at the same time, these words are
fundamentally transformed by a process of euphemization, through
which they are adapted to the forms and conventions of philosophical discourse. In this way, Heidegger's work acquires the appearance
of autonomy, the appearance of a self-sufficient body of texts which
call for internal exegesis, while simultaneously alluding to and
concealing its dependence on ordinary language. It is this distinctive
combination of loftiness and simplicity, or ordinary words ennobled
by the forms of philosophical respectability, which defines, in
Bourdieu's view, the specificity of Heidegger's language. The difference between Heidegger and the more forthright exponents of the
'conservative revolution', such as Ernst Jünger and Möller van den
Bruck, can thus be seen as a difference primarily of *form*, linked to
their different positions within the fields characteristic of the Weimar

period. By carefully reconstructing these fields and analysing the mechanisms and strategies associated with Heidegger's location within them, it may be possible to shed some fresh light on Heidegger's work while steering clear of the rather polemical opposition between those critics who charge him with an apologetics for Nazism and those who seek to redeem him at any cost.[26]

Irrespective of whether one is considering the oral discourse of everyday life or the scholarly discourse of written texts, it is important to see that systematic discrepancies may arise between linguistic markets and the forms of censorship associated with them, on the one hand, and the capacities of individuals from differing social backgrounds to produce linguistic expressions appropriate to those markets, on the other. As a result of such discrepancies, individuals from differing social backgrounds are able to relate to linguistic markets, as well as to themselves as producers for these markets, in differing ways. Bourdieu illustrates this point by considering some of the typical speech practices of individuals from different class backgrounds when they find themselves in formal or official situations (an interview, a classroom discussion, a public ceremony, etc.).[27] Individuals from upper-class backgrounds are endowed with a linguistic habitus which enables them to respond with relative ease to the demands of most formal or official occasions. There is a concordance or congruence between their linguistic habitus and the demands of formal markets. It is this congruence which underlies the confidence and fluency with which they speak: their confidence merely attests to the fact that the conditions in which they are speaking concur fairly closely with the conditions which endowed them with the capacity to speak, and hence they are able (and know they are able) to reap symbolic benefits by speaking in a way that comes naturally to them. Hence, on most public occasions, they speak with distinction and thereby distinguish themselves from all those who are less well endowed with linguistic capital. By contrast, individuals from petits-bourgeois backgrounds must generally make an effort to adapt their linguistic expressions to the demands of formal markets. The result is that their speech is often accompanied by tension and anxiety, and by a tendency to rectify or correct expressions so that they concur with dominant norms. This hyper-correction of petit-bourgeois speech is the sign of a class divided against itself, whose members are seeking, at the cost of constant anxiety, to produce linguistic expressions which bear the mark of a habitus other than their own. For members of the lower classes, whose conditions of existence are least conducive to the acquisition of a habitus which concurs with formal markets, there are many occasions in which their linguistic products are assigned, by themselves as well as others, a limited value. Hence the tendency of working-class children to eliminate themselves from the educational system, or to resign themselves to vocational courses of training. Hence also the unease, the hesitation leading to silence, which, as we noted earlier, may overcome individuals from lower-class backgrounds on occasions defined as official.

There are other circumstances, of course, in which individuals from lower-class backgrounds are able to speak fluently and confidently, and one of the merits of Bourdieu's approach is that he is able to analyse these so-called 'popular' forms of speech in a way that avoids the kind of intellectual romanticism characteristic of some studies of working-class or peasant culture. Bourdieu prefers to avoid blanket terms like 'popular culture' and 'popular speech', which have themselves become part of a struggle carried out among researchers and commentators in the intellectual field. He prefers, instead, to examine concretely the ways in which those who are most deprived in terms of economic and cultural capital are able to express themselves in the diverse settings of everyday life. These settings – gatherings of friends or peers, conversations among workers in an office or on the shop floor, etc. – can be viewed as markets with their own properties and forms of censorship, so that individuals who wish to speak effectively in these settings must concur to some extent with the demands of the market. Hence forms of speech like slang and 'cant' should not be seen simply as a rejection of dominant modes of speech: they are, at the same time, highly euphemized forms of speech which are adeptly tailored to the markets for which they are produced. In Bourdieu's terms, slang is the product of the pursuit of distinction in a dominated market. It is one of the ways in which those individuals – especially men – who are poorly endowed with economic and cultural capital are able to distinguish themselves from what they regard as weak and effeminate. Their pursuit of distinction therefore goes hand-in-hand with a deep-seated conformity with regard to established hierarchies, such as the hierarchy between the sexes. It also leads them to take for granted, and indeed positively to assert, the very characteristics (e.g. physical strength, lack of education) by virtue of which they occupy a subordinate position in the social space.[28]

In taking for granted certain aspects of established hierarchies even when overtly rejecting dominant modes of speech, individuals from lower-class backgrounds betray the fact that they share, to some extent, a system of evaluation which works against them. This is an example of a general phenomenon with which Bourdieu is concerned throughout his writings, and which he describes as 'symbolic power' (or, in some cases, as 'symbolic violence'). Bourdieu uses the term 'symbolic power' to refer not so much to a specific type of power, but rather to an aspect of most forms of power as they are routinely deployed in social life. For in the routine flow of day-to-day life, power is seldom exercised as overt physical force: instead, it is transmuted into a symbolic form, and thereby endowed with a kind of *legitimacy* that it would not otherwise have. Bourdieu expresses this point by saying that symbolic power is an 'invisible' power which is 'misrecognized' as such and thereby 'recognized' as legitimate. The terms 'recognition' (*reconnaissance*) and 'misrecognition' (*méconnaissance*) play an important role here: they underscore the fact that the exercise of power through symbolic exchange always rests on a foundation of shared belief. That is, the efficacy of symbolic power presupposes certain forms of cognition or belief, in such a way that even those who benefit least from the exercise of power participate, to some extent, in their own subjection. They recognize or tacitly acknowledge the legitimacy of power, or of the hierarchical relations of power in which they are embedded; and hence they fail to see that the hierarchy is, after all, an arbitrary social construction which serves the interests of some groups more than others. To understand the nature of symbolic power, it is therefore crucial to see that it presupposes a kind of *active complicity* on the part of those subjected to it. Dominated individuals are not passive bodies to which symbolic power is applied, as it were, like a scalpel to a corpse. Rather, symbolic power requires, as a condition of its success, that those subjected to it believe in the legitimacy of power and the legitimacy of those who wield it.

Like many of Bourdieu's ideas, the notions of symbolic power and symbolic violence are rather flexible notions which were worked out in specific research contexts, and hence they are best explained by reference to his more concrete anthropological and sociological studies. Bourdieu originally developed the notion of symbolic violence in the context of analysing the nature of the gift exchange in Kabyle society.[29] Instead of analysing the exchange of gifts in terms of a formal structure of reciprocity, in the manner of Lévi-Strauss, Bourdieu views it as a mechanism through which power is exercised and simultaneously disguised. In a society like Kabylia, where there are relatively few institutions in which relations of domination can be given a stable and objective form, individuals must resort to more personalized means of exercising power over others. One such means is debt: an individual can bring another under his or her sway by enforcing the obligations deriving from usury. But there are other, 'softer' and more subtle means of exercising power, like the giving of gifts. By giving a gift – especially a generous one that cannot be met by a counter-gift of comparable quality – the giver creates a lasting obligation and binds the recipient in a relation of personal indebtedness. Giving is also a way of possessing: it is a way of binding another while obscuring the bond in a gesture of generosity. This is what Bourdieu describes as 'symbolic violence', in contrast to the overt violence of the usurer or the ruthless master; it is 'gentle, invisible violence, unrecognized as such, chosen as much as undergone, that of trust, obligation, personal loyalty, hospitality, gifts, debts, piety, in a word, of all the virtues honoured by the ethic of honour'.[30] In a society like this, where symbolic domination has to be sustained primarily through interpersonal relations rather than institutions, symbolic violence is a necessary and effective means of exercising power. For it enables relations of domination to be established and maintained through strategies which are softened and disguised, and which conceal domination beneath the veil of an enchanted relation.

In those societies (including all modern industrial societies like Britain or the United States) which have witnessed the development of objectified institutions, the importance of symbolic mechanisms for sustaining domination through interpersonal relations has declined. The development of institutions enables different kinds of capital to be accumulated and differentially appropriated, while dispensing with the need for individuals to pursue strategies aimed directly at the domination of others: violence is, so to speak, built into the institution itself. Hence, if one wishes to understand the ways in which symbolic power is exercised and reproduced in our societies, one must look more carefully at how, in different markets and fields, institutionalized mechanisms have emerged which tend to fix the value accorded to different products, to allocate these products differentially and to inculcate a belief in their value. The educational system provides a good example of this process: the development of this system involves a certain kind of objectification in which formally defined credentials or qualifications become a mechanism for creating and sustaining inequalities, in such a way that the recourse to overt force is unnecessary.[31] Moreover, by concealing the link between the qualifications obtained by individuals and the cultural capital inherited by virtue of their social background, this mechanism provides a practical justification of the established order. It enables those who benefit most from the system to convince themselves of their own intrinsic worthiness, while preventing those who benefit least from grasping the basis of their own deprivation.

III

The development of Western European societies since the Middle Ages can be characterized very broadly, from Bourdieu's perspective, in terms of the differentiation of distinct spheres or fields of practice, each involving specific forms and combinations of capital and value as well as specific institutions and institutional mechanisms. Through this process of differentiation, a market economy based on capitalist principles was separated out and constituted as a relatively distinct sphere of production and exchange; a centralized state administration and legal system were established and progressively dissociated from religious authority; fields of intellectual and artistic production emerged and acquired a certain autonomy, with their own institutions (universities, museums, publishing houses, etc.) their own professionals (intellectuals, artists, writers, etc.) and their own principles of production, evaluation and exchange. While these and other spheres or fields of practice have emerged historically and acquired a certain autonomy, they are not completely disconnected from one another. They are interlocked in complex ways, and part of the task of a sociological study of these fields, as proposed by Bourdieu, is to bring out the ways in which they are structured and linked while rigorously avoiding the tendency to reduce one field to another, or to treat everything as if it were a mere epiphenomenon of the economy.

This broad perspective on the development of modern societies is a view strongly influenced by the work of Max Weber, to whom Bourdieu owes a significant intellectual debt. Like Weber, Bourdieu is particularly interested in the ways in which groups emerge in different fields and struggle for power and influence. Much of Bourdieu's work on the sociology of fields has been concerned with artistic and intellectual production, but he has also written extensively on other fields, such as religion and politics.[32] In the essays which make up part III of this volume, Bourdieu examines various aspects of the social organization of political fields. The analysis of the field of politics – understood here in the narrow sense of 'politics', i.e. the sphere of political parties, electoral politics and institutionalized political power – is closely related to the theme of language and symbolic power. For the political field is, among other things, the site *par excellence* in which agents seek to form and transform their visions of the world and thereby the world itself: it is the site *par excellence* in which words are actions and the symbolic character of power is at stake. Through the production of slogans, programmes and commentaries of various kinds, agents in the political field are continuously engaged in a labour of representation by which they seek to construct and impose a particular vision of the social world, while at the same time seeking to mobilize the support of those upon whom their power ultimately depends.

To understand the ways in which the political field works in modern societies, it is essential to see, Bourdieu argues, that the development of this field has involved a process of professionalization in which the political means of production (i.e. the means to produce political products like programmes, policies, etc.) have become increasingly concentrated in the hands of professional politicians. The most obvious manifestation of this process is the formation of political parties with their own bureaucratic structures, full-time officials and so on. But the professionalization of political activity, together with the increasing autonomy of the political field, has a paradoxical consequence: individuals cannot constitute themselves as a group with a voice, capable of making itself heard in the political field, unless they *dispossess themselves* in favour of a spokesperson in whom they vest the right to speak on their behalf. And the more that individuals are deprived of the specific competencies and graces that are necessary for participation in a professionalized political field, the more likely they are to hand politics over to the professionals. Hence the risks associated with political dispossession are all the greater in the case of left-wing parties: in seeking to represent those who are most deprived in terms of economic and cultural capital, these parties run the greatest risk of cutting themselves off completely from the people in whose name they claim to speak. The collapse of the communist parties in Eastern Europe, in the wake of the revolutions of 1989, would seem, at least to some extent, to bear out this hypothesis.

Bourdieu analyses the phenomenon of political dispossession as a two-step process of 'delegation'. The first step is that a group creates itself by establishing an institutional framework – a permanent office, a bureaucracy, paid officials, etc. The second step is that the organization then 'mandates' an individual or individuals to speak on behalf of the group. This delegate (Bourdieu uses the French term *mandataire*, i.e. the holder of a mandate) is thus at two removes, as it were, from the individuals whom he or she represents (from the *mandant*, i.e. the 'mandator' or the one who gives a mandate). This distance enables delegates to convince themselves and others that they are politically self-sufficient, the source of their own power and appeal: this is what Bourdieu describes as 'political fetishism', alluding to Marx's notion of the fetishism of commodities, according to which products of human labour appear to be endowed with a life and a value of their own. Once delegates have established their own appearance of self-sufficiency, they can engage in the verbal battles which characterize the political field with a certain degree of autonomy, concealing from themselves and others the social bases upon which their power, and the power of their words, depends.

As political parties and bureaucracies expand, the field of production of political discourses – what Bourdieu sometimes describes as 'ideologies' – becomes more and more autonomous, like a game with its own rules and conditions of entry. The bureaucracies take over responsibility for training the professionals who will enter the game, endowing them with the specialist skills and competencies which they will require in order to succeed. Above all, these professionals must acquire a practical sense or 'feel' for the game, that is, a habitus attuned to the specific conditions of the political field. The discourses produced by political professionals are therefore determined by two broad sets of constraints. One set of constraints derives from the logic of the political field itself, in which professionals are competing with one another, taking stances *vis-à-vis* one another, etc. In this respect, their utterances acquire a *relational* status: that is, they make sense only in relation to other utterances issued from other positions in the same field. It is for this reason that the political field appears to many people as a kind of esoteric culture with which they have little sympathy or empathy: they feel distanced from it, not so much because they fail to understand the words, but because they fail to understand why a distinction between words could matter so much, since they are not themselves involved in the constant attempt to define a distinctive position in the field. (It would be illuminating to examine, from this point of view, the public weariness that accompanied the repeated and ill-fated attempts of the once-proclaimed 'new force' in British politics, formed through the merger of the SDP and the Liberal Party, to find a suitable name for itself.)

The second set of constraints which operates in the production of political discourse derives, not from the field itself, but from the relation between this field and a broader range of social positions, groups and processes. While the political field has a considerable degree of autonomy, it is not completely independent of other fields and forces. Indeed, one of the distinctive characteristics of the political field is that, in order for professionals to succeed within it, they must appeal to groups or forces which lie *outside* the field. This is quite different from, for instance, the fields of science and art, where an appeal to non-professionals is not only unnecessary, but would in all likelihood be counter-productive. In the political field, politicians must constantly appeal to non-professionals in order to secure the support – the 'credit' or 'political capital' – which will enable them to wage a successful battle against other professionals. Hence a significant part of the discursive output of politicians consists of slogans, promises and pledges of support for causes of various kinds, the purpose of such expressions being primarily to build up credit by providing non-professionals with forms of representation and self-representation, in exchange for which they give material and symbolic support (in the form of subscriptions, votes, etc.) to those who claim to represent them in the political field. It is because politicians are dependent on the credit accorded to them by non-professionals that they are especially vulnerable to suspicion and scandal, that is, to anything which threatens the bond of belief and trust which, precisely because their power is symbolic, they must constantly nourish and sustain.

Bourdieu's essays on the field of politics and political discourse should be seen as a contribution to a research project which, in order to be followed through properly, would require more detailed empirical or historical inquiry.[33] None the less, it is clear that Bourdieu has outlined a distinctive approach to political phenomena, an approach which has definite methodological implications. One such implication is that it would be superficial (at best) to try to analyse political discourses or ideologies by focusing on the utterances as such, without reference to the constitution of the political field and the relation between this field and the broader space of social positions and processes. This kind of 'internal analysis' is commonplace in the academic literature, as exemplified by the numerous and varied attempts to apply some form of semiotics or 'discourse analysis' to political speeches. The difficulty with all such attempts is similar to the difficulty that vitiates all 'formalist' approaches to language (or, indeed, all purely 'literary' approaches to literature): they take for granted but fail to take account of the social–historical conditions within which the object of analysis is produced, constructed and received. Bourdieu's approach implies – and in this respect it seems to me that he is entirely justified – that an adequate analysis of political discourse must be based on a systematic reconstruction of the field within which such discourse is produced and received (with its distinctive organizations, schemes of production and perception, etc.) and its relation to the broader social space.

Another implication of Bourdieu's approach is that political phenomena cannot be analysed as if they were no more than a manifestation of socioeconomic processes, or of relations and oppositions between classes. This traditional type of Marxist analysis would involve a methodological short-circuiting which is quite antithetical to Bourdieu's approach. The problem with most forms of Marxist analysis, in Bourdieu's view, is that they tend to treat the social world as a one-dimensional space, in which phenomena or developments are explained, either directly or indirectly, in terms of the unfolding of the economic mode of production and the class oppositions stemming from it. While Bourdieu does not underesti-mate the importance of economic relations, his approach is rather different. He views the social world as a multi-dimensional space, differentiated into relatively autonomous fields; and within each of these fields, individuals occupy positions determined by the quanti-ties of different types of capital they possess. Hence we cannot simply assume that those who occupy dominant positions in the political field will be identical with, or in some way directly linked to, those who occupy dominant positions in the field of economic production. There are likely to be important connections here; it is likely that the fields will correspond in certain ways, so that, for instance, the relations between positions in one field will reflect the relations between positions in another – that is, the fields will display certain 'homologies', as Bourdieu puts it. But if we want to understand these connections properly, there is no alternative to a careful, rigorous reconstruction of the fields and of the links between the positions and agents within them.

There is a further difficulty, in Bourdieu's view, with most forms of Marxist analysis: they tend to confuse theoretical classes with real social groups, and hence they misconstrue a whole series of ques-tions concerning the ways in which agents mobilize themselves through representation. The notion of class plays a fundamental explanatory role in Bourdieu's work, and some readers may feel (with some justification, I think) that Bourdieu is trying to get too much theoretical mileage from this concept. Readers may also feel that he gives insufficient attention to other bases of social division, inequality and conflict in modern societies, such as those connected with gender, ethnicity or the relations between nation-states.[34] These reservations may have some grounds; but it is important to appreciate that Bourdieu's use of the notion of class is quite distinctive, and that it differs in crucial respects from the way this notion is used in the traditional Marxist literature. Bourdieu does not define classes in terms of the ownership or non-ownership of means of production (his use of traditional Marxist terms like 'bourgeois' and 'petit-bourgeois' may be somewhat misleading in this regard, and is best seen as a kind of conceptual shorthand). For Bourdieu, classes are sets of agents who occupy similar positions in the social space, and hence possess similar kinds and similar quantities of capital, similar life chances, similar dispositions, etc.[35] These 'classes on paper' are *theoretical constructs* which the analyst produces in order to explain or make sense of observable social phenomena. Theoretical classes are not identical with real social groups, though they may help to explain why, in certain circumstances, a set of agents constitutes itself as a group. That is, it may be that agents are more likely to constitute themselves as a group if they occupy similar positions in the social space – as happens, for instance, when workers organize themselves into trade unions, or consumers form a pressure group. But a set of agents can organize themselves into a group, with their own organization, spokesperson and so on, only by producing or appropriating a certain *vision* of the social world and of themselves as an identifiable group within this world. It is this process of representation, and the complex symbolic struggles associated with it, that traditional Marxist analysis ignores or fails fully to understand. By tending to elide the distinction between theoretical classes and real social groups, Marxism has contributed to the production of a series of representations which have had real social and historical effects, but Marxist analysis lacks the means of grasping the symbolic mechanisms by which these effects are produced.

While Bourdieu is sharply critical of much traditional Marxist analysis, there can be no doubt that his work is deeply influenced by Marx's approach. The very fact that Bourdieu gives a certain theoretical priority to social classes, and to the role of economic capital in the social space, is ample testimony to his debt. But the way in which Bourdieu uses ideas drawn from Marx is the same as the way he uses notions drawn from Weber or Lévi-Strauss (or, in other respects, Durkheim): he adapts them and re-works them for the purposes of concrete social analysis. Hence it would be quite misleading to view Bourdieu as a contemporary exponent of Marxism, even if a 'disguised' or heavily qualified Marxism, as some commentators are inclined to do.[36] This kind of characterization is based on a rather superficial understanding of the distinctive trajectory and concerns of Bourdieu's work. Moreover, Bourdieu is not a thinker who moves with the fashion, espousing 'structuralism' one day, 'post-structuralism' (or 'post-modernism') the next. He fiercely resists labels of this kind, and he has no sympathy for what he sees as a sort of intellectual faddism.

Bourdieu's work is an exceptionally sophisticated attempt to develop a coherent theoretical framework for the analysis of the social world, a framework of comparable interest and scope to the very different approaches elaborated by such contemporary thinkers as Habermas and Foucault. Throughout his writings Bourdieu displays a firm commitment to the value of empirical investigation, and he makes no apologies for his use (at times extensive) of statistical and quantitative methods. But his work also has a sharp critical edge. As a social scientist first and foremost, Bourdieu rarely engages in normative political theory, nor does he seek to formulate political programmes or policies for particular social groups. But his relentless disclosure of power and privilege in its most varied and subtlest forms, and the respect accorded by his theoretical framework to the agents who make up the social world which he so acutely dissects, give his work an implicit critical potential. For the first step in creating new social relations, alternative ways of organizing social and political life, is to understand the socially instituted limits of the ways of speaking, thinking and acting which are characteristic of our societies today. That Bourdieu has made a major contribution to our understanding of these limits is a judgement that would be difficult to dispute.

General Introduction

In the *Essay on the Introduction of the Concept of Negative Grandeur in Philosophy*, Kant imagines a man who is miserly by ten degrees and who strives towards brotherly love by twelve degrees, in contrast with another man who is miserly by three degrees and capable of a generous intention by seven degrees, and who produces an act marked by four degrees of generosity. He concludes that the first man is morally superior to the second man even though if one measures their actions – two degrees against four – he is unarguably inferior. We should perhaps use a similar arithmetical assessment of merit to judge scientific works . . . The social sciences are evidently in the camp of the ten-degree miser, and we would undoubtedly attain a more accurate assessment of their merits if we knew how to take into account, in a Kantian manner, the social forces they must overcome. This could not be more true when what is at issue is the specific object of the discipline whose influence extends to all social sciences – namely language, one and indivisible, constituted, in the work of Saussure, by the exclusion of all inherent social variation, or, as with Chomsky, by the privilege granted to the formal properties of grammar to the detriment of functional constraints.

Having undertaken, before it became fashionable, an academic study (fortunately never published) which rested on a methodical 'reading' of the *Course in General Linguistics* in order to establish a 'general theory of culture', I was perhaps more sensitive than others to the most visible effects of the domination exercised by the sovereign discipline, whether it concerned literal transcriptions of theoretical writings or the mechanical transfer of concepts taken at face value, and of all the thoughtless borrowing which, by dissociating the *opus operatum* from the *modus operandi*, leads to unexpected and sometimes preposterous re-interpretations. But resistance to fashionable tastes is in no respect a rejection destined to authorize ignorance: initially the work of Saussure, and then, at the point when I became aware of the inadequacy of the model of speech (and practice) as execution, the work of Chomsky, which recognized the importance of generative dispositions, seemed to me to present sociology with some fundamental questions.

It remains the case that these questions cannot have their full impact unless one transcends the limits which are inscribed in the very intention of structural linguistics as pure theory. The entire destiny of modern linguistics is in fact determined by Saussure's inaugural act through which he separates the 'external' elements of linguistics from the 'internal' elements, and, by reserving the title of linguistics for the latter, excludes from it all the investigations which establish a relationship between language and anthropology, the political history of those who speak it, or even the geography of the domain where it is spoken, because all of these things add nothing to a knowledge of language taken in itself. Given that it sprang from the autonomy attributed to language in relation to its social conditions of production, reproduction and use, structural linguistics could not become the dominant social science without exercising an ideological effect, by bestowing the appearance of scientificity on the naturalization of the products of history, that is, on symbolic objects. Transferring the phonological model outside the linguistic field has the effect of generalizing, to the set of symbolic products, taxonomies of kinship, mythical systems or works of art, the inaugural process which makes linguistics *the most natural of the social sciences* by separating the linguistic instrument from its social conditions of production and utilization.

It goes without saying that the different social sciences were unequally predisposed to accommodate this Trojan horse. The particular relationship which binds the anthropologist to his subject, and the neutrality of the 'impartial spectator' conferred by the status of the external observer, made anthropology the prime victim. Together, of course, with the tradition of the history of art or literature: in this case, importing a method of analysis which assumes the neutralization of functions could only consecrate the mode of perceiving the work of art which was always demanded of the connoisseur, namely, a 'pure' and purely 'internal' disposition, which excludes any 'reductive' reference to 'external' elements. Thus, rather like the prayer wheel of another domain, literary semiology has taken the cult of the work of art to a higher degree of rationality without modifying its functions. In any case, bracketing out the social, which allows language or any other symbolic object to be treated like an end in itself, contributed considerably to the success of structuralist linguistics, for it endowed the 'pure' exercises that characterize a purely internal and formal analysis with the charm of a game devoid of consequences.

It was therefore necessary to draw out all the consequences of the fact, so powerfully repressed by linguists and their imitators, that the 'social nature of language is one of its internal characteristics', as the *Course in General Linguistics* asserted, and that social heterogeneity is inherent in language. This must be done while at the same time being aware of the risks involved in the enterprise, not the least of which is the apparent crudeness which can accompany the most rigorous analyses capable – and culpable – of contributing to the return of the repressed; in short, one must choose to pay a higher price for truth while accepting a lower profit of distinction.

Part I

The Economy of Linguistic Exchanges

Sociology can free itself from all the forms of domination which linguistics and its concepts still exercise today over the social sciences only by bringing to light the operations of object construction through which this science was established, and the social conditions of the production and circulation of its fundamental concepts. The linguistic model was transposed with such ease into the domain of anthropology and sociology because one accepted the core intention of linguistics, namely, the *intellectualist philosophy* which treats language as an object of contemplation rather than as an instrument of action and power. To accept the Saussurian model and its presuppositions is to treat the social world as a universe of symbolic exchanges and to reduce action to an act of communication which, like Saussure's *parole*, is destined to be deciphered by means of a cipher or a code, language or culture.[1]

In order to break with this social philosophy one must show that, although it is legitimate to treat social relations – even relations of domination – as symbolic interactions, that is, as relations of communication implying cognition and recognition, one must not forget that the relations of communication *par excellence* – linguistic exchanges – are also relations of symbolic power in which the power relations between speakers or their respective groups are actualized. In short, one must move beyond the usual opposition between economism and culturalism, in order to develop an economy of symbolic exchanges.

Every speech act and, more generally, every action, is a conjuncture, an encounter between independent causal series. On the one hand, there are the socially constructed dispositions of the linguistic habitus, which imply a certain propensity to speak and to say determinate things (the expressive interest) and a certain capacity to speak, which involves both the linguistic capacity to generate an infinite number of grammatically correct discourses, and the social capacity to use this competence adequately in a determinate situation. On the other hand, there are the structures of the linguistic market, which impose themselves as a system of specific sanctions and censorships.

This simple model of linguistic production and circulation, as the relation between linguistic habitus and the markets on which they offer their products, does not seek either to challenge or to replace a strictly linguistic analysis of the code. But it does enable us to understand the errors and failures to which linguistics succumbs when, relying on only one of the factors involved – a strictly linguistic competence, abstractly defined, ignoring everything that it owes to the social conditions of its production – it tries to give an adequate account of discourse in all its conjunctural singularity. In fact, as long as they are unaware of the limits that constitute their science, linguists have no choice but to search desperately in language for something that is actually inscribed in the social relations within which it functions, or to engage in a sociology without knowing it, that is, with the risk of discovering, in grammar itself, something that their spontaneous sociology has unwittingly imported into it.

Grammar defines meaning only very partially: it is in relation to a market that the complete determination of the signification of discourse occurs. Part (and not the least) of the determinations that constitute the practical definition of sense comes to discourse automatically and from outside. The objective meaning engendered in linguistic circulation is based, first of all, on the distinctive value which results from the relationship that the speakers establish, consciously or unconsciously, between the linguistic product offered by a socially characterized speaker, and the other products offered simultaneously in a determinate social space. It is also based on the fact that the linguistic product is only completely realized as a message if it is treated as such, that is to say, if it is decoded, and the associated fact that the schemes of interpretation used by those receiving the message in their creative appropriation of the product offered may diverge, to a greater or lesser extent, from those which guided its production. Through these unavoidable effects, the market plays a part in shaping not only the symbolic value but also the meaning of discourse.

One could re-examine from this standpoint the question of style: this 'individual deviation from the linguistic norm', this particular elaboration which tends to give discourse its distinctive properties, is a being-perceived which exists only in relation to perceiving subjects, endowed with the diacritical dispositions which enable them to make *distinctions* between different *ways of saying*, distinctive manners of speaking. It follows that style, whether it be a matter of poetry as compared with prose or of the diction of a particular (social, sexual or generational) class compared with that of another class, exists only in relation to agents endowed with schemes of perception and appreciation that enable them to constitute it as a set of systematic differences, apprehended syncretically. What circulates on the linguistic market is not 'language' as such, but rather discourses that are stylistically marked both in their production, in so far as each speaker fashions an idiolect from the common language, and in their reception, in so far as each recipient helps to *produce* the message which he perceives and appreciates by bringing to it everything that makes up his singular and collective experience.

One can extend to all discourse what has been said of poetic discourse alone, because it manifests to the highest degree, when it is successful, the effect which consists in awakening experiences which vary from one individual to another. If, in contrast to denotation, which represents 'the stable part, common to all speakers',[2] connotation refers to the singularity of individual experiences, this is because it is constituted in a socially characterized relation to which the recipients bring the diversity of their instruments of symbolic appropriation. The paradox of communication is that it presupposes a common medium, but one which works – as is clearly seen in the limiting case in which, as often in poetry, the aim is to transmit emotions – only by eliciting and reviving singular, and therefore socially marked, experiences. The all-purpose word in the dictionary, a product of the neutralization of the practical relations within which it functions, has no social existence: in practice, it is always immersed in situations, to such an extent that the core meaning which remains relatively invariant through the diversity of markets may pass unnoticed.[3] As Vendryès pointed out, if words always assumed all their meanings at once, discourse would be an endless play on words; but if, as in the case of the French verb *louer* (to rent, from *locare*) and *louer* (to praise, from *laudare*), all the meanings it can take on were totally independent, all plays on words (especially of the ideological sort) would become impossible.[4] The different meanings of a word are defined in the relation between the invariant core and the specific logic of the different markets, themselves objectively situated with respect to the market in which the most common meaning is defined. They exist simultaneously only for the academic mind which elucidates them by breaking the organic solidarity between competence and market.

Religion and politics achieve their most successful ideological effects by exploiting the possibilities contained in the polysemy inherent in the social ubiquity of the legitimate language. In a differentiated society, what are called 'common' nouns – work, family, mother, love, etc. – assume in reality different and even antagonistic meanings, because the members of the same 'linguistic community' use more or less the same language and not several different languages. The unification of the linguistic market means that there are no doubt more and more meanings for each sign.[5] Mikhail Bakhtin reminds us that, in revolutionary situations, common words take on opposite meanings. In fact, there are no neutral words: surveys show, for example, that the words most commonly used to express tastes often receive different, sometimes opposite, meanings from one social class to another. The word *soigné* (neat, clean, conscientious), for example, used approvingly by the petits bourgeois, is rejected by intellectuals for whom, precisely, it evokes everything that is petit-bourgeois, petty and mean-spirited. The polysemy of religious language, and the ideological effect of the *unification of opposites* or denial of divisions which it produces, derive from the fact that, at the cost of the *re-interpretations* implied in the production and reception of the common language by speakers occupying different positions in the social space, and therefore endowed with different intentions and interests, it manages to speak to all groups and all groups speak it – unlike, for example, mathematical language, which can secure the univocal meaning of the word 'group' only by strictly controlling the homogeneity of the group of mathematicians. Religions which are called *universal* are not universal in the same sense and on the same conditions as science.

Recourse to a neutralized language is obligatory whenever it is a matter of establishing a practical consensus between agents or groups of agents having partially or totally different interests. This is the case, of course, first and foremost in the field of legitimate political struggle, but also in the transactions and interactions of everyday life. Communication between classes (or, in colonial or semi-colonial societies, between ethnic groups) always represents a critical situation for the language that is used, whichever it may be. It tends to provoke a return to the sense that is most overtly charged with social connotations: 'When you use the word *paysan* (peasant) in the presence of someone who has just left the countryside, you never know how he is going to take it.' Hence there are no longer any innocent words. This objective effect of unveiling destroys the apparent unity of ordinary language. Each word, each expression, threatens to take on two antagonistic senses, reflecting the way in which it is understood by the sender and the receiver. The logic of the verbal automatisms which insidiously lead back to ordinary usage, with all its associated values and prejudices, harbours the permanent danger of the 'gaff' which can instantly destroy a consensus carefully maintained by means of strategies of mutual accommodation.

But one cannot fully understand the symbolic efficacy of political and religious languages if one reduces it to the effect of the misunderstandings which lead individuals who are opposed in all respects to recognize themselves in the same message. Specialized discourses can derive their efficacy from the hidden correspondence between the structure of the social space within which they are produced – the political field, the religious field, the artistic field, the philosophical field, etc. – and the structure of the field of social classes within which the recipients are situated and in relation to which they interpret the message. The homology between the oppositions constitutive of the specialized fields and the field of social classes is the source of an essential ambiguity which is particularly apparent when esoteric discourses are diffused outside the restricted field and undergo a kind of automatic universalization, ceasing to be merely the utterances of dominant or dominated agents within a specific field and becoming statements valid for all dominant or all dominated individuals.

The fact remains that social science has to take account of the autonomy of language, its specific logic, and its particular rules of operation. In particular, one cannot understand the symbolic effects of language without making allowance for the fact, frequently attested, that language is the exemplary formal mechanism whose generative capacities are without limits. There is nothing that cannot be said and it is possible to say nothing. One can say everything in language, that is, within the limits of grammaticality. We have known since Frege that words can have meaning without referring to anything. In other words, formal rigour can mask *semantic free-wheeling*. All religious theologies and all political theodicies have taken advantage of the fact that the generative capacities of language can surpass the limits of intuition or empirical verification and produce statements that are *formally* impeccable but semantically empty. Rituals are the limiting case of situations of *imposition* in which, through the exercise of a technical competence which may be very imperfect, a social competence is exercised – namely, that of the legitimate speaker, authorized to speak and to speak with authority. Benveniste pointed out that in Indo-European languages the words which are used to utter the law are related to the verb 'to speak'. The right utterance, the one which is formally correct, thereby claims, and with a good chance of success, to utter what is right, i.e. what ought to be. Those who, like Max Weber, have set the magical or charismatic law of the collective oath or the ordeal in opposition to a rational law based on calculability and predictability, forget that the most rigorously rationalized law is never anything more than an act of social magic which works.

Legal discourse is a creative speech which brings into existence that which it utters. It is the limit aimed at by all performative utterances – blessings, curses, orders, wishes or insults. In other words, it is the divine word, the word of divine right, which, like the *intuitus originarius* which Kant ascribed to God, creates what it states, in contrast to all derived, observational statements, which simply record a pre-existent given. One should never forget that language, by virtue of the infinite generative but also *originative* capacity – in the Kantian sense – which it derives from its power to produce existence by producing the collectively recognized, and thus realized, representation of existence, is no doubt the principal support of the dream of absolute power.

1

The Production and Reproduction of Legitimate Language

'As you say, my good knight! There ought to be laws to protect the body of acquired knowledge.

Take one of our good pupils, for example: modest and diligent, from his earliest grammar classes he's kept a little notebook full of phrases.

After hanging on the lips of his teachers for twenty years, he's managed to build up an intellectual stock in trade; doesn't it belong to him as if it were a house, or money?'

P. *Claudel,* Le Soulier de Satin

'Language forms a kind of wealth, which all can make use of at once without causing any diminution of the store, and which thus admits a complete community of enjoyment; for all, freely participating in the general treasure, unconsciously aid in its preservation'.[1] In describing symbolic appropriation as a sort of mystical participation, universally and uniformly accessible and therefore excluding any form of dispossession, Auguste Comte offers an exemplary expression of the illusion of linguistic communism which haunts all linguistic theory. Thus, Saussure resolves the question of the social and economic conditions of the appropriation of language without ever needing to raise it. He does this by resorting, like Comte, to the metaphor of treasure, which he applies indiscriminately to the 'community' and the individual: he speaks of 'inner treasure', of a 'treasure deposited by the practice of speech in subjects belonging to the same community', of 'the sum of individual treasures of language', and of the 'sum of imprints deposited in each brain'.

Chomsky has the merit of explicitly crediting the speaking subject in his universality with the perfect competence which the Saussurian tradition granted him tacitly: 'Linguistic theory is concerned primarily with an *ideal speaker–listener, in a completely homogeneous speech-community, who knows its language perfectly* and is unaffected by such *grammatically irrelevant* conditions as memory limitations, distractions, shifts of attention or interest, and errors (random or characteristic) in applying his knowledge of the language in actual performance. This seems to me to have been the position of the founders of modern general linguistics, and no cogent reason for modifying it has been offered.'[2] In short, from this standpoint, Chomskyan 'competence' is simply another name for Saussure's *langue*.[3] Corresponding to language as a 'universal treasure', as the collective property of the whole group, there is linguistic competence as the 'deposit' of this 'treasure' in each individual or as the participation of each member of the 'linguistic community' in this public good. The shift in vocabulary conceals the *fictio juris* through which Chomsky, converting the immanent laws of legitimate discourse into universal norms of correct linguistic practice, sidesteps the question of the economic and social conditions of the acquisition of the legitimate competence and of the constitution of the market in which this definition of the legitimate and the illegitimate is established and imposed.[4]

OFFICIAL LANGUAGE AND POLITICAL UNITY

As a demonstration of how linguists merely incorporate into their theory a pre-constructed object, ignoring its *social laws of construction* and masking its social genesis, there is no better example than the passage in his *Course in General Linguistics* in which Saussure discusses the relation between language and space.[5] Seeking to prove that it is not space which defines language but language which defines its space, Saussure observes that neither dialects nor languages have natural limits, a phonetic innovation (substitution of 's' for Latin 'c', for example) determining its own area of diffusion by the intrinsic force of its autonomous logic, through the set of speaking subjects who are willing to make themselves its bearers. This philosophy of history, which makes the internal dynamics of a language the sole principle of the limits of its diffusion, conceals the properly political process of unification whereby a determinate set of 'speaking subjects' is led in practice to accept the official language.

Saussure's *langue*, a code both legislative and communicative which exists and subsists independently of its users ('speaking subjects') and its uses (*parole*), has in fact all the properties commonly attributed to official language. As opposed to dialect, it has benefited from the institutional conditions necessary for its generalized codification and imposition. Thus known and recognized (more or less completely) throughout the whole jurisdiction of a certain political authority, it helps in turn to reinforce the authority which is the source of its dominance. It does this by ensuring among all members of the 'linguistic community', traditionally defined, since Bloomfield, as a 'group of people who use the same system of linguistic signs',[6] the minimum of communication which is the precondition for economic production and even for symbolic domination.

To speak of *the* language, without further specification, as linguists do, is tacitly to accept the *official* definition of the *official* language of a political unit. This language is the one which, within the territorial limits of that unit, imposes itself on the whole population as the only legitimate language, especially in situations that are characterized in French as more *officielle* (a very exact translation of the word 'formal' used by English-speaking linguists).[7] Produced by authors who have the authority to write, fixed and codified by grammarians and teachers who are also charged with the task of inculcating its mastery, the language is a *code*, in the sense of a cipher enabling equivalences to be established between sounds and meanings, but also in the sense of a system of norms regulating linguistic practices.

The official language is bound up with the state, both in its genesis and in its social uses. It is in the process of state formation that the conditions are created for the constitution of a unified linguistic market, dominated by the official language. Obligatory on official occasions and in official places (schools, public administrations, political institutions, etc.), this state language becomes the theoretical norm against which all linguistic practices are objectively measured. Ignorance is no excuse; this linguistic law has its body of jurists – the grammarians – and its agents of regulation and imposition – the teachers – who are empowered *universally* to subject the linguistic performance of speaking subjects to examination and to the legal sanction of academic qualification.

In order for one mode of expression among others (a particular language in the case of bilingualism, a particular use of language in the case of a society divided into classes) to impose itself as the only legitimate one, the linguistic market has to be unified and the different dialects (of class, region or ethnic group) have to be measured practically against the legitimate language or usage.

Integration into a single 'linguistic community', which is a product of
the political domination that is endlessly reproduced by institutions
capable of imposing universal recognition of the dominant language,
is the condition for the establishment of relations of linguistic
domination.

THE 'STANDARD' LANGUAGE: A 'NORMALIZED' PRODUCT

Like the different crafts and trades which, before the advent of
large-scale industry, constituted, in Marx's phrase, so many separate
'enclosures', local variants of the *langue d'oïl* differed from one
parish to another until the eighteenth century. This is still true today
of the regional dialects and, as the dialecticians' maps show, the
phonological, morphological and lexicological features are distributed in patterns which are never entirely superimposable and which
only ever correspond to religious or administrative boundaries
through rare coincidence.[8] In fact, in the absence of *objectification* in
writing and especially of the quasi-legal *codification* which is inseparable from the constitution of an official language, 'languages' exist
only in the practical state, i.e. in the form of so many linguistic
habitus which are at least partially orchestrated, and of the oral
productions of these habitus.[9] So long as a language is only expected
to ensure a minimum of mutual understanding in the (very rare)
encounters between people from neighbouring villages or different
regions, there is no question of making one usage the norm for
another (despite the fact that the differences perceived may well
serve as pretexts for declaring one superior to the other).

Until the French Revolution, the process of linguistic unification went
hand in hand with the process of constructing the monarchical state. The
'dialects', which often possessed some of the properties attributed to
'languages' (since most of them were used in written form to record
contracts, the minutes of local assemblies, etc.), and literary languages
(such as the poetic language of the *pays d'oc*), like artificial languages
distinct from each of the dialects used over the whole territory in which
they were current, gave way progressively, from the fourteenth century
on, at least in the central provinces of the *pays d'oïl*, to the common
language which was developed in Paris in cultivated circles and which,
having been promoted to the status of official language, was used in the
form given to it by scholarly, i.e. written, uses. Correlatively, the popular
and purely oral uses of all the regional dialects which had thus been
supplanted degenerated into *patois*, as a result of the compartmentaliza-

tion (linked to the abandonment of the written form) and internal disintegration (through lexical and syntactic borrowing) produced by the social devaluation which they suffered. Having been abandoned to the peasants, they were negatively and pejoratively defined in opposition to distinguished or literate usages. One indication of this, among many others, is the shift in the meaning assigned to the word *patois*, which ceased to mean 'incomprehensible speech' and began to refer to 'corrupted and coarse speech, such as that of the common people' (Furetière's Dictionary, 1690).

The linguistic situation was very different in the *langue d'oc* regions. Not until the sixteenth century, with the progressive constitution of an administrative organization linked to royal power (involving the appearance of a multitude of subordinate administrative agents, lieutenants, provosts, magistrates, etc.), did the Parisian dialect begin to take over from the various *langue d'oc* dialects in legal documents. The imposition of French as the official language did not result in the total abolition of the written use of dialects, whether in administrative, political or even literary texts (dialect literature continued to exist during the *ancien régime*), and their oral uses remained predominant. A situation of bilingualism tended to arise. Whereas the lower classes, particularly the peasantry, were limited to the local dialect, the aristocracy, the commercial and business bourgeoisie and particularly the literate petite bourgeoisie (precisely those who responded to Abbé Grégoire's survey and who had, to varying degrees, attended the Jesuit colleges, which were institutions of linguistic unification) had access much more frequently to the use of the official language, written or spoken, while at the same time possessing the dialect (which was still used in most private and even public situations), a situation in which they were destined to fulfil the function of intermediaries.

The members of these local bourgeoisies of priests, doctors or teachers, who owed their position to their mastery of the instruments of expression, had everything to gain from the Revolutionary policy of linguistic unification. Promotion of the official language to the status of national language gave them that *de facto* monopoly of politics, and more generally of communication with the central government and its representatives, that has defined local notables under all the French republics.

The imposition of the legitimate language in opposition to the dialects and *patois* was an integral part of the political strategies aimed at perpetuating the gains of the Revolution through the production and the reproduction of the 'new man'. Condillac's theory, which saw language as a *method*, made it possible to identify revolutionary language with revolutionary thought. To reform language, to purge it of the usages linked to the old society and impose it in its purified form, was to impose a thought that would itself be purged and purified. It would be naïve to attribute the policy of linguistic unification solely to the technical needs of communication between the different parts of the territory, particularly between Paris and the provinces, or to see it as the direct product of a state centralism determined to crush 'local characteristics'. The conflict between the French of the revolutionary intelligentsia and the dialects or *patois* was a struggle for symbolic power in which what was at stake was the *formation* and *re-formation* of mental structures. In short, it was not only a question of communicating but of gaining recognition for a new language of authority, with its new political vocabulary, its terms of address and reference, its metaphors, its euphemisms and the representation of the social world which it conveys, and which, because it is linked to the new interests of new groups, is inexpressible in the local idioms shaped by usages linked to the specific interests of peasant groups.

Thus, only when the making of the 'nation', an entirely abstract group based on law, creates new usages and functions does it become indispensable to forge a *standard* language, impersonal and anonymous like the official uses it has to serve, and by the same token to undertake the work of normalizing the products of the linguistic habitus. The dictionary is the exemplary result of this labour of codification and normalization. It assembles, by scholarly recording, the totality of the *linguistic resources* accumulated in the course of time and, in particular, all the possible uses of the same word (or all the possible expressions of the same sense), juxtaposing uses that are socially at odds, and even mutually exclusive (to the point of marking those which exceed the bounds of acceptability with a sign of exclusion such as *Obs.*, *Coll.* or *Sl.*). It thereby gives a fairly exact image of language as Saussure understands it, 'the sum of individual treasuries of language', which is predisposed to fulfil the functions of a 'universal' code. The *normalized* language is capable of functioning outside the constraints and without the assistance of the situation, and is suitable for transmitting and decoding by any sender and receiver, who may know nothing of one another. Hence it concurs with the demands of bureaucratic predictability and calculability, which presuppose universal functionaries and clients, having no other qualities than those assigned to them by the administrative definition of their condition.

In the process which leads to the construction, legitimation and imposition of an official language, the educational system plays a decisive role: 'fashioning the similarities from which that community of consciousness which is the cement of the nation stems.' And Georges Davy goes on to state the function of the schoolmaster, a *maître à parler* (teacher of speaking) who is thereby also a *maître à penser* (teacher of thinking): 'He [the primary school teacher], by virtue of his function, works daily on the faculty of expression of every idea and every emotion: on language. In teaching the same clear, fixed language to children who know it only very vaguely or who even speak various dialects or *patois*, he is already inclining them quite naturally to see and feel things in the same way; and he works to build the common consciousness of the nation'.[10] The Whorfian – or, if you like, Humboldtian[11] – theory of language which underlies this view of education as an instrument of 'intellectual and moral integration', in Durkheim's sense, has an affinity with the Durkheimian theory of consensus, an affinity which is also indicated by the shift of the word 'code' from law to linguistics. The code, in the sense of cipher, that governs written language, which is identified with correct language, as opposed to the implicitly inferior conversational language, acquires the force of law in and through the educational system.[12]

The educational system, whose scale of operations grew in extent and intensity throughout the nineteenth century,[13] no doubt directly helped to devalue popular modes of expression, dismissing them as 'slang' and 'gibberish' (as can be seen from teachers' marginal comments on essays) and to impose recognition of the legitimate language. But it was doubtless the dialectical relation between the school system and the labour market – or, more precisely, between the unification of the educational (and linguistic) market, linked to the introduction of educational qualifications valid nation-wide, independent (at least officially) of the social or regional characteristics of their bearers, and the unification of the labour market (including the development of the state administration and the civil service) – which played the most decisive role in devaluing dialects and establishing the new hierarchy of linguistic practices.[14] To induce the holders of dominated linguistic competences to collaborate in the destruction of their instruments of expression, by endeavouring for example to speak 'French' to their children or requiring them to speak 'French' at home, with the more or less explicit intention of increasing their value on the educational market, it was necessary for the school system to be perceived as the principal (indeed, the only) means of access to administrative positions which were all the more attractive in areas where industrialization was least developed. This conjunction of circumstances was found in the regions of 'dialect' (except the east of France) rather than in the *patois* regions of northern France.

UNIFICATION OF THE MARKET AND SYMBOLIC DOMINATION

In fact, while one must not forget the contribution which the political will to unification (also evident in other areas, such as law) makes to the *construction* of the language which linguists accept as a natural datum, one should not regard it as the sole factor responsible for the generalization of the use of the dominant language. This generalization is a dimension of the unification of the market in symbolic goods which accompanies the unification of the economy and also of cultural production and circulation. This is seen clearly in the case of the market in matrimonial exchanges, in which 'products' which would previously have circulated in the protected enclosure of local markets, with their own laws of price formation, are suddenly devalued by the generalization of the dominant criteria of evaluation and the discrediting of 'peasant values', which leads to the collapse of the value of the peasants, who are often condemned to celibacy. Visible in all areas of practice (sport, song, clothing, housing, etc.), the process of unification of both the production and the circulation of economic and cultural goods entails the progressive obsolescence of the earlier mode of production of the habitus and its products. And it is clear why, as sociolinguists have often observed, women are more disposed to adopt the legitimate language (or the legitimate pronunciation): since they are inclined towards docility with regard to the dominant usages both by the sexual division of labour, which makes them specialize in the sphere of consumption, and by the logic of marriage, which is their main if not their only avenue of social advancement and through which they circulate upwards, women are predisposed to accept, from school onwards, the new demands of the market in symbolic goods.

Thus the effects of domination which accompany the unification of the market are always exerted through a whole set of specific institutions and mechanisms, of which the specifically linguistic policy of the state and even the overt interventions of pressure groups form only the most superficial aspect. The fact that these mechanisms presuppose the political or economic unification which they help in turn to reinforce in no way implies that the progress of the official language is to be attributed to the direct effectiveness of legal or quasi-legal constraints. (These can at best impose the acquisition, but not the generalized use and therefore the autonomous reproduction, of the legitimate language.) All symbolic domination presupposes, on the part of those who submit to it, a form of complicity which is neither passive submission to external constraint nor a free adherence to values. The recognition of the legitimacy of the official language has nothing in common with an explicitly professed, deliberate and revocable belief, or with an intentional act of accepting a 'norm'. It is inscribed, in a practical state, in dispositions which are impalpably inculcated, through a long and slow process of acquisition, by the sanctions of the linguistic market, and which are therefore adjusted, without any cynical calculation or consciously experienced constraint, to the chances of material and symbolic profit which the laws of price formation characteristic of a given market objectively offer to the holders of a given linguistic capital.[15]

The distinctiveness of symbolic domination lies precisely in the fact that it assumes, of those who submit to it, an attitude which challenges the usual dichotomy of freedom and constraint. The 'choices' of the habitus (for example, using the 'received' uvular 'r' instead of the rolled 'r' in the presence of legitimate speakers) are accomplished without consciousness or constraint, by virtue of the dispositions which, although they are unquestionably the product of social determinisms, are also constituted outside the spheres of consciousness and constraint. The propensity to reduce the search for causes to a search for responsibilities makes it impossible to see that *intimidation*, a symbolic violence which is not aware of what it is (to the extent that it implies no *act of intimidation*) can only be exerted on a person predisposed (in his habitus) to feel it, whereas others will ignore it. It is already partly true to say that the cause of the timidity lies in the relation between the situation or the intimidating person (who may deny any intimidating intention) and the person intimidated, or rather, between the social conditions of production of each of them. And little by little, one has to take account thereby of the whole social structure.

There is every reason to think that the factors which are most influential in the formation of the habitus are transmitted without passing through language and consciousness, but through suggestions inscribed in the most apparently insignificant aspects of the things, situations and practices of everyday life. Thus the modalities of practices, the ways of looking, sitting, standing, keeping silent, or even of speaking ('reproachful looks' or 'tones', 'disapproving glances' and so on) are full of injunctions that are powerful and hard to resist precisely because they are silent and insidious, insistent and insinuating. (It is this *secret code* which is explicitly denounced in the crises characteristic of the domestic unit, such as marital or teenage crises: the apparent disproportion between the violence of the revolt and the causes which provoke it stems from the fact that the most anodyne actions or words are now seen for what they are – as injunctions, intimidations, warnings, threats – and denounced as such, all the more violently because they continue to act below the level of consciousness and beneath the very revolt which they provoke.) The power of suggestion which is exerted through things and persons and which, instead of telling the child what he must do, tells him what he is, and thus leads him to become durably what he has to be, is the condition for the effectiveness of all kinds of symbolic power that will subsequently be able to operate on a habitus predisposed to respond to them. The relation between two people may be such that one of them has only to appear in order to impose on the other, without even having to want to, let alone formulate any command, a definition of the situation and of himself (as intimidated, for example), which is all the more absolute and undisputed for not having to be stated.

The recognition extorted by this invisible, silent violence is expressed in explicit statements, such as those which enable Labov to establish that one finds the same *evaluation* of the phoneme 'r' among speakers who come from different classes and who therefore differ in their actual *production* of 'r'. But it is never more manifest than in all the corrections, whether *ad hoc* or permanent, to which dominated speakers, as they strive desperately for correctness, consciously or unconsciously subject the stigmatized aspects of their pronunciation, their diction (involving various forms of euphemism) and their syntax, or in the disarray which leaves them 'speechless', 'tongue-tied', 'at a loss for words', as if they were suddenly dispossessed of their own language.[16]

DISTINCTIVE DEVIATIONS AND SOCIAL VALUE

Thus, if one fails to perceive both the special value objectively accorded to the legitimate use of language and the social foundations of this privilege, one inevitably falls into one or other of two opposing errors. Either one unconsciously absolutizes that which is objectively relative and in that sense arbitrary, namely the dominant usage, failing to look beyond the properties of language itself, such as the complexity of its syntactic structure, in order to identify the basis of the value that is accorded to it, particularly in the educational market; or one escapes this form of fetishism only to fall into the naïvety *par excellence* of the scholarly relativism which forgets that the naïve gaze is not relativist, and ignores the fact of legitimacy, through an arbitrary relativization of the dominant usage, which is socially recognized as legitimate, and not only by those who are dominant.

> To reproduce in scholarly discourse the fetishizing of the legitimate language which actually takes place in society, one only has to follow the example of Basil Bernstein, who describes the properties of the 'elaborated code' without relating this social product to the social conditions of its production and reproduction, or even, as one might expect from the sociology of education, to its academic conditions. The 'elaborated code' is thus constituted as the absolute norm of all linguistic practices which then can only be conceived in terms of the logic of *deprivation*. Conversely, ignorance of what popular and educated usage owe to their objective relations and to the structure of the relation of domination between classes, which they reproduce in their own logic, leads to the *canonization* as such of the 'language' of the dominated classes. Labov leans in this direction when his concern to rehabilitate 'popular speech' against the theorists of deprivation leads him to contrast the verbosity and pompous verbiage of middle-class adolescents with the precision and conciseness of black children from the ghettos. This overlooks the fact that, as he himself has shown (with the example of recent immigrants who judge deviant accents, including their own, with particular severity), the linguistic 'norm' is imposed on all members of the same 'linguistic community', most especially in the educational market and in all formal situations in which verbosity is often *de rigueur*.

Political unification and the accompanying imposition of an official language establish relations between *the different uses of the same language* which differ fundamentally from the theoretical relations (such as that between *mouton* and 'sheep' which Saussure cites as the basis for the arbitrariness of the sign) between different languages, spoken by politically and economically independent groups. All linguistic practices are measured against the legitimate practices, i.e. the practices of those who are dominant. The probable value objectively assigned to the linguistic productions of different speakers and therefore the relation which each of them can have to the language, and hence to his own production, is defined within the system of practically competing variants which is actually established whenever the extra-linguistic conditions for the constitution of a linguistic market are fulfilled.

Thus, for example, the linguistic differences between people from different regions cease to be incommensurable particularisms. Measured *de facto* against the single standard of the 'common' language, they are found wanting and cast into the outer darkness of *regionalisms*, the 'corrupt expressions and mispronunciations' which schoolmasters decry.[17] Reduced to the status of quaint or vulgar jargons, in either case unsuitable for formal occasions, popular uses of the official language undergo a systematic devaluation. A system of *sociologically pertinent* linguistic oppositions tends to be constituted, which has nothing in common with the system of *linguistically pertinent* linguistic oppositions. In other words, the differences which emerge from the confrontation of speech varieties are not reducible to those the linguist constructs in terms of his own criterion of pertinence. However great the proportion of the functioning of a language that is not subject to variation, there exists, in the area of pronunciation, diction and even grammar, a whole set of differences significantly associated with social differences which, though negligible in the eyes of the linguist, are pertinent from the sociologist's standpoint because they belong to a system of linguistic oppositions which is the *re-translation* of a system of social differences. A structural sociology of language, inspired by Saussure but constructed in opposition to the abstraction he imposes, must take as its object *the relationship between the structured systems of sociologically pertinent linguistic differences and the equally structured systems of social differences*.

The social uses of language owe their specifically social value to the fact that they tend to be organized in systems of differences (between prosodic and articulatory or lexical and syntactic variants) which reproduce, in the symbolic order of differential deviations, the system of social differences. To speak is to appropriate one or other of the expressive styles already constituted in and through usage and objectively marked by their position in a hierarchy of styles which expresses the hierarchy of corresponding social groups. These styles, systems of differences which are both classified and classifying, ranked and ranking, mark those who appropriate them. And a spontaneous stylistics, armed with a practical sense of the equivalences between the two orders of differences, apprehends social classes through classes of stylistic indices.

In emphasizing the linguistically pertinent constants at the expense of the sociologically significant variations in order to construct that artefact which is the 'common' language, the linguist proceeds as if the *capacity to speak*, which is virtually universal, could be identified with *the socially conditioned way of realizing this natural capacity*, which presents as many variants as there are social conditions of acquisition. The competence adequate to produce sentences that are likely to be understood may be quite inadequate to produce sentences that are likely to be *listened to*, likely to be recognized as *acceptable* in all the situations in which there is occasion to speak. Here again, social acceptability is not reducible to mere grammaticality. Speakers lacking the legitimate competence are *de facto* excluded from the social domains in which this competence is required, or are condemned to silence. What is rare, then, is not the capacity to speak, which, being part of our biological heritage, is universal and therefore essentially non-distinctive,[18] but rather the competence necessary in order to speak the legitimate language which, depending on social inheritance, re-translates social distinctions into the specifically symbolic logic of differential deviations, or, in short, distinction.[19]

The constitution of a linguistic market creates the conditions for an objective competition in and through which the legitimate competence can function as linguistic capital, producing a *profit of distinction* on the occasion of each social exchange. Because it derives in part from the scarcity of the products (and of the corresponding competences), this profit does not correspond solely to the cost of training.

The cost of training is not a simple, socially neutral notion. To an extent which varies depending on national traditions in education, the historical period and the academic discipline in question, it includes expenditure which may far exceed the minimum 'technically' required in order to ensure the transmission of the strictly defined competence (if indeed it is possible to give a purely technical definition of the training necessary and sufficient to fulfil a function and of the function itself, bearing in mind that 'role distance' – distance from the function – enters increasingly into the definition of the function as one moves up the hierarchy of functions). In some cases, for example, the duration of study (which provides a good measure of the economic cost of training) tends to be valued for its own sake, independently of the result it produces (encouraging, among the 'elite schools', a kind of competition in the sheer length of courses). In other cases – not that the two options are mutually exclusive – the social quality of the competence acquired, which is reflected in the symbolic modality of practices, i.e. in the *manner* of performing technical acts and implementing the competence, appears as inseparable from the *slowness* of the acquisition, short or 'crash' courses always being suspected of leaving on their products the marks of 'cramming' or the stigmata of 'catching up'. This conspicuous consumption of training (i.e.

of time), an apparent technical wastage which fulfils social functions of legitimation, enters into the value socially attributed to a socially guaranteed competence (which means, nowadays, one 'certified' by the educational system).

Since the profit of distinction results from the fact that the supply of products (or speakers) corresponding to a given level of linguistic (or, more generally, cultural) qualification is lower than it would be if all speakers had benefited from the conditions of acquisition of the legitimate competence to the same extent as the holders of the rarest competence,[20] it is logically distributed as a function of the chances of access to these conditions, that is, as a function of the position occupied in the social structure.

> Despite certain appearances, we could not be further from the Saussurian model of *homo linguisticus* who, like the economic subject in the Walrasian tradition, is formally free to do as he likes in his verbal productions (free, for example, to say 'tat' for 'hat', as children do) but can be understood, can exchange and communicate only on condition that he conforms to the rules of the common code. This market, which knows only pure, perfect competition among agents who are as interchangeable as the products they exchange and the 'situations' in which they exchange, and who are all identically subject to the principle of the maximization of informative efficiency (analogous to the principle of the maximization of utilities), is, as will shortly become clearer, as remote from the real linguistic market as the 'pure' market of the economists is from the real economic market, with its monopolies and oligopolies.

Added to the specific effect of distinctive rarity is the fact that, by virtue of the relationship between the system of linguistic differences and the system of economic and social differences, one is dealing not with a relativistic universe of differences capable of relativizing one another, but with a hierarchical universe of deviations with respect to a form of speech that is (virtually) universally recognized as legitimate, i.e. as the standard measure of the value of linguistic products. The dominant competence functions as linguistic capital, securing a profit of distinction in its relation to other competences only in so far as certain conditions (the unification of the market and the unequal distribution of the chances of access to the means of production of the legitimate competence, and to the legitimate places of expression) are continuously fulfilled, so that the groups which possess that competence are able to impose it as the only legitimate one in the formal markets (the fashionable, educational, political and administrative markets) and in most of the linguistic interactions in which they are involved.[21]

It is for this reason that those who seek to defend a threatened linguistic capital, such as knowledge of the classical languages in present-day France, are obliged to wage a total struggle. One cannot save the *value* of a competence unless one saves the market, in other words, the whole set of political and social conditions of production of the producers/consumers. The defenders of Latin or, in other contexts, of French or Arabic, often talk as if the language they favour could have some value outside the market, by intrinsic virtues such as its 'logical' qualities; but, in practice, they are defending the market. The position which the educational system gives to the different languages (or the different cultural contents) is such an important issue only because this institution has the monopoly in the large-scale production of producers/consumers, and therefore in the reproduction of the market without which the social value of the linguistic competence, its capacity to function as linguistic capital, would cease to exist.

THE LITERARY FIELD AND THE STRUGGLE FOR LINGUISTIC AUTHORITY

Thus, through the medium of the structure of the linguistic field, conceived as a system of specifically linguistic relations of power based on the unequal distribution of linguistic capital (or, to put it another way, of the chances of assimilating the objectified linguistic resources), the structure of the space of expressive styles reproduces in its own terms the structure of the differences which objectively separate conditions of existence. In order fully to understand the structure of this field and, in particular, the existence, within the field of linguistic production, of a sub-field of restricted production which derives its fundamental properties from the fact that the producers within it produce first and foremost for other producers, it is necessary to distinguish between the capital necessary for the simple production of more or less legitimate ordinary speech, on the one hand, and the capital of instruments of expression (presupposing appropriation of the resources deposited in objectified form in libraries – books, and in particular in the 'classics', grammars and dictionaries) which is needed to produce a written discourse worthy of being published, that is to say, made official, on the other. This production of instruments of production, such as rhetorical devices, genres, legitimate styles and manners and, more generally, all the formulations destined to be 'authoritative' and to be cited as examples of 'good usage', confers on those who engage in it a power over language and thereby over the ordinary users of language, as well as over their capital.

The legitimate language no more contains within itself the power to ensure its own perpetuation in time than it has the power to define its extension in space. Only the process of continuous creation, which occurs through the unceasing struggles between the different authorities who compete within the field of specialized production for the monopolistic power to impose the legitimate mode of expression, can ensure the permanence of the legitimate language and of its value, that is, of the recognition accorded to it. It is one of the generic properties of fields that the struggle for specific stakes masks the objective collusion concerning the principles underlying the game. More precisely, the struggle tends constantly to produce and reproduce the game and its stakes by reproducing, primarily in those who are directly involved, but not in them alone, the practical commitment to the value of the game and its stakes which defines the recognition of legitimacy. What would become of the literary world if one began to argue, not about the value of this or that author's style, but about the value of arguments about style? The game is over when people start wondering if the cake is worth the candle. The struggles among writers over the legitimate art of writing contribute, through their very existence, to producing both the legitimate language, defined by its distance from the 'common' language, and belief in its legitimacy.

> It is not a question of the symbolic power which writers, grammarians or teachers may exert over the language in their personal capacity, and which is no doubt much more limited than the power they can exert over culture (for example, by imposing a new definition of legitimate litera-ture which may transform the 'market situation'). Rather, it is a question of the contribution they make, independently of any intentional pursuit of distinction, to the production, consecration and imposition of a distinct and distinctive language. In the collective labour which is pursued through the struggles for what Horace called *arbitrium et jus et norma loquendi*, writers – more or less authorized authors – have to reckon with the grammarians, who hold the monopoly of the consecra-tion and canonization of legitimate writers and writing. They play their part in constructing the legitimate language by selecting, from among the products on offer, those which seem to them worthy of being consecrated and incorporated into the legitimate competence through educational

inculcation, subjecting them, for this purpose, to a process of normalization and codification intended to render them consciously assimilable and therefore easily reproducible. The grammarians, who, for their part, may find allies among establishment writers and in the academies, and who take upon themselves the power to set up and impose norms, tend to consecrate and codify a particular use of language by rationalizing it and 'giving reason' to it. In so doing they help to determine the value which the linguistic products of the different users of the language will receive in the different markets – particularly those most directly subject to their control, such as the educational market – by delimiting the universe of acceptable pronunciations, words or expressions, and fixing a language censored and purged of all popular usages, particularly the most recent ones.

The variations corresponding to the different configurations of the relation of power between the authorities, who constantly clash in the field of literary production by appealing to very different principles of legitimation, cannot disguise the structural invariants which, in the most diverse historical situations, impel the protagonists to resort to the same strategies and the same arguments in order to assert and legitimate their right to legislate on language and in order to denounce the claims of their rivals. Thus, against the 'fine style' of high society and the writers' claim to possess an instinctive art of good usage, the grammarians always invoke 'reasoned usage', the 'feel for the language' which comes from knowledge of the principles of 'reason' and 'taste' which constitute grammar. Conversely, the writers, whose pretensions were most confidently expressed during the Romantic period, invoke genius against the rule, flouting the injunctions of those whom Hugo disdainfully called 'grammatists'.[22]

The objective dispossession of the dominated classes may never be intended as such by any of the actors engaged in literary struggles (and there have, of course, always been writers who, like Hugo, claimed to 'revolutionize dictionaries' or who sought to mimic popular speech). The fact remains that this dispossession is inseparable from the existence of a body of professionals, objectively invested with the monopoly of the legitimate use of the legitimate language, who produce for their own use a special language predisposed to fulfil, *as a by-product*, a social function of distinction in the relations between classes and in the struggles they wage on the terrain of language. It is not unconnected, moreover, with the existence of the educational system which, charged with the task of sanctioning heretical products in the name of grammar and inculcating the specific norms which block the effects of the laws of evolution, contributes significantly to constituting the dominated uses of language as such by consecrating the dominant use as the only legitimate one, by the mere fact of inculcating it. But one would obviously be missing the essential point if one related the activity of artists or teachers directly to the effect to which it objectively contributes, namely, the devaluation of the common language which results from the very existence of a literary language. Those who operate in the literary field contribute to symbolic domination only because the effects that their position in the field and its associated interests lead them to pursue always conceal from themselves and from others the external effects which are a by-product of this very misrecognition.

The properties which characterize linguistic excellence may be summed up in two words: distinction and correctness. The work performed in the literary field produces the appearances of an original language by resorting to a set of derivations whose common principle is that of a deviation from the most frequent, i.e. 'common', 'ordinary', 'vulgar', usages. Value always arises from deviation, *deliberate or not*, with respect to the most widespread usage, 'commonplaces', 'ordinary sentiments', 'trivial' phrases, 'vulgar' expressions, 'facile' style.[23] In the uses of language as in life-styles, all definition is relational. Language that is 'recherché', 'well chosen', 'elevated', 'lofty', 'dignified' or 'distinguished' contains a negative reference (the very words used to name it show this) to 'common' 'everyday', 'ordinary', 'spoken', 'colloquial', 'familiar' language and, beyond this, to 'popular', 'crude', 'coarse', 'vulgar', 'sloppy', 'loose', 'trivial', 'uncouth' language (not to mention the unspeakable, 'gibberish', 'pidgin' or 'slang'). The oppositions from which this series is generated, and which, being derived from the legitimate language, is organized from the standpoint of the dominant users, can be reduced to two: the opposition between 'distinguished' and 'vulgar' (or 'rare' and 'common') and the opposition between 'tense' (or 'sustained') and 'relaxed' (or 'loose'), which no doubt represents the specifically linguistic version of the first, very general, opposition. It is as if the principle behind the ranking of class languages were nothing other than the degree of *control* they manifested and the intensity of the *correctness* they presupposed.

It follows that the legitimate language is a semi-artificial language which has to be sustained by a permanent effort of correction, a task which falls both to institutions specially designed for this purpose and to individual speakers. Through its grammarians, who fix and codify legitimate usage, and its teachers who impose and inculcate it through innumerable acts of correction, the educational system tends, in this area as elsewhere, to produce the need for its own services and its own products, i.e. the labour and instruments of correction.[24] The legitimate language owes its (relative) constancy in time (as in space) to the fact that it is continuously protected by a prolonged labour of inculcation against the inclination towards the economy of effort and tension which leads, for example, to analogical simplification (e.g. of irregular verbs in French – *vous faisez* and *vous disez* for *vous faites* and *vous dites*). Moreover, the correct, i.e. corrected, expression owes the essential part of its social properties to the fact that it can be produced only by speakers possessing practical mastery of scholarly rules, explicitly constituted by a process of codification and expressly inculcated through pedagogic work. Indeed, the paradox of all institutionalized pedagogy is that it aims to implant, as schemes that function in a practical state, rules which grammarians have laboured to extract from the practice of the professionals of written expression (from the past), by a process of retrospective formulation and codification. 'Correct usage' is the product of a competence which is an *incorporated grammar*, the word grammar being used explicitly (and not tacitly, as it is by the linguists) in its true sense of a system of scholarly rules, derived *ex post facto* from expressed discourse and set up as imperative norms for discourse yet to be expressed. It follows that one cannot fully account for the properties and social effects of the legitimate language unless one takes account, not only of the social conditions of the production of literary language and its grammar, but also of the social conditions in which this scholarly code is imposed and inculcated as the principle of the production and evaluation of speech.[25]

THE DYNAMICS OF THE LINGUISTIC FIELD

The laws of the transmission of linguistic capital are a particular case of the laws of the legitimate transmission of cultural capital between the generations, and it may therefore be posited that the linguistic competence measured by academic criteria depends, like the other dimensions of cultural capital, on the level of education (measured in terms of qualifications obtained) and on the social trajectory. Since mastery of the legitimate language may be acquired through familiarization, that is, by more or less prolonged exposure to the legitimate language, or through the deliberate inculcation of explicit rules, the major classes of modes of expression correspond to classes of modes of acquisition, that is, to different forms of the combination between the two principal factors of production of the legitimate competence, namely, the family and the educational system.

In this sense, like the sociology of culture, the sociology of language is logically inseparable from a sociology of education. As a linguistic market strictly subject to the verdicts of the guardians of legitimate culture, the educational market is strictly dominated by the linguistic products of the dominant class and tends to sanction the pre-existing differences in capital. The combined effect of low cultural capital and the associated low propensity to increase it through educational investment condemns the least favoured classes to the negative sanctions of the scholastic market, i.e. exclusion or early self-exclusion induced by lack of success. The initial disparities therefore tend to be reproduced since the length of inculcation tends to vary with its efficiency: those least inclined and least able to accept and adopt the language of the school are also those exposed for the shortest time to this language and to educational monitoring, correction and sanction.

Given that the educational system possesses the delegated authority necessary to engage in a universal process of durable inculcation in matters of language, and given that it tends to vary the duration and intensity of this inculcation in proportion to inherited cultural capital, it follows that the social mechanisms of cultural transmission tend to reproduce the structural disparity between the very unequal *knowledge* of the legitimate language and the much more uniform *recognition* of this language. This disparity is one of the determinant factors in the dynamics of the linguistic field and therefore in changes in the language. For the linguistic struggles which are the ultimate source of these changes presuppose that speakers have virtually the same recognition of authorized usage, but very unequal knowledge of this usage. Thus, if the linguistic strategies of the petite bourgeoisie, and in particular its tendency to hypercorrection – a very typical expression of 'cultural goodwill' which is manifested in all areas of practice – have sometimes been seen as the main factor in linguistic change, this is because the disparity between knowledge and recognition, between aspirations and the means of satisfying them – a disparity that generates tension and pretension – is greatest in the intermediate regions of the social space. This pretension, a recognition of distinction which is revealed in the very effort to deny it by appropriating it, introduces a permanent pressure into the field of competition which inevitably induces new strategies of distinction on the part of the holders of distinctive marks that are socially recognized as distinguished.

The petit-bourgeois hypercorrection which seeks its models and instruments of correction from the most consecrated arbiters of legitimate usage – Academicians, grammarians, teachers – is defined in the subjective and objective relationship to popular 'vulgarity' and bourgeois 'distinction'. Consequently, the contribution which this striving for assimilation (to the bourgeois classes) and, at the same time, dissimilation (with respect to the lower classes) makes to linguistic change is simply more visible than the dissimilation strategies which, in turn, it provokes from the holders of a rarer competence. Conscious or unconscious avoidance of the most visible marks of the linguistic tension and exertion of petit-bourgeois speakers (for example, in French, spoken use of the past historic, associated with old-fashioned schoolmasters) can lead the bourgeois and the intellectuals towards the controlled hypocorrection which combines confident relaxation and lofty ignorance of pedantic rules with the exhibition of ease on the most dangerous ground.[26] Showing tension where the ordinary speaker succumbs to relaxation, facility where he betrays effort, and the ease in tension which differs utterly from petit-bourgeois or popular tension and ease: these are all strategies of distinction (for the most part unconscious) giving rise to endless refinements, with constant reversals of value which tend to discourage the search for non-relational properties of linguistic styles.

> Thus, in order to account for the new style of speaking adopted by intellectuals, which can be observed in America as well as in France – a somewhat hesitant, even faltering, interrogative manner (*'non?'*, 'right?', 'OK?' etc.) – one would have to take into account the whole *structure of usages* in relation to which it is differentially defined. On the one hand, there is the old academic manner (with – in French – its long periods, imperfect subjunctives, etc.), associated with a devalued image of the professorial role; on the other, the new petit-bourgeois usages resulting from wider diffusion of scholarly usage and ranging from 'liberated' usage, a blend of tension and relaxation which tends to characterize the new petite bourgeoisie, to the hypercorrection of an over-refined speech, immediately devalued by an all-too-visible ambition, which is the mark of the upwardly mobile petite bourgeoisie.

The fact that these distinctive practices can be understood only in relation to the universe of possible practices does not mean that they have to be traced back to a conscious concern to distinguish oneself from them. There is every reason to believe that they are rooted in a practical sense of the rarity of distinctive marks (linguistic or otherwise) and of its evolution over time. Words which become popularized lose their *discriminatory power* and thereby tend to be perceived as intrinsically banal, common, *facile* – or (since diffusion is linked to time) as *worn out*. It is no doubt the weariness deriving from repeated exposure which, combined with the sense of rarity, gives rise to the unconscious drift towards more 'distinguished' stylistic features or towards rarer usages of common features.

Thus distinctive deviations are the driving force of the unceasing movement which, though intended to annul them, tends in fact to reproduce them (a paradox which is in no way surprising once one realizes that constancy may presuppose change). Not only do the strategies of assimilation and dissimilation which underlie the changes in the different uses of language not affect the structure of the distribution of different uses of language, and consequently the system of the systems of distinctive deviations (expressive styles) in which those uses are manifested, but they tend to reproduce it (albeit in a superficially different form). Since the very motor of change is nothing less than the whole linguistic field or, more precisely, the whole set of actions and reactions which are continuously generated in the universe of competitive relations constituting the field, the centre of this perpetual movement is everywhere and nowhere. Those who remain trapped in a philosophy of cultural diffusion based on a hydraulic imagery of 'two-step flow' or 'trickle-down', and who persist in locating the principle of change in a determinate site in the linguistic field, will always be greatly disappointed. What is described as a phenomenon of diffusion is nothing other than the process resulting from the *competitive struggle* which leads each agent, through countless strategies of assimilation and dissimilation (*vis-à-vis* those who are ahead of and behind him in the social space and in time) constantly to change his substantial properties (here, pronunciation, diction, syntactic devices, etc.), while maintaining, precisely by running in the race, the disparity which underlies the race. This structural constancy of the social values of the uses of the legitimate language becomes intelligible when one knows that the logic and the aims of the strategies seeking to modify it are governed by the structure itself, through the position occupied in the structure by the agent who performs them. The 'interactionist' approach, which fails to go beyond the actions and reactions apprehended in their directly visible immediacy, is unable to discover that the different agents' linguistic strategies are strictly dependent on their positions in the structure of the distribution of linguistic capital, which can in turn be shown to depend, via the structure of chances of access to the educational system, on the structure of class relations.

Hence, interactionism can know nothing of the deep mechanisms which, through surface changes, tend to reproduce the structure of distinctive deviations and to maintain the profits accruing to those who possess a rare and therefore distinctive competence.

2

Price Formation and the
Anticipation of Profits

*Perhaps from force of occupational habit, perhaps by virtue of
the calm that is acquired by every important man who is
consulted for his advice and who, knowing that he will keep
control over the situation, sits back and lets his interlocutor flap
and fluster, perhaps also in order to show to advantage the
character of his head (which he believed to be Grecian, in spite
of his whiskers), while something was being explained to him,
M. de Norpois maintained an immobility of expression as
absolute as if you had been speaking in front of some classical –
and deaf – bust in a museum.*
      Marcel Proust, A la recherche du temps perdu

Linguistic exchange – a relation of communication between a sender
and a receiver, based on enciphering and deciphering, and therefore
on the implementation of a code or a generative competence – is also
an economic exchange which is established within a particular
symbolic relation of power between a producer, endowed with a
certain linguistic capital, and a consumer (or a market), and which is
capable of procuring a certain material or symbolic profit. In other
words, utterances are not only (save in exceptional circumstances)
signs to be understood and deciphered; they are also *signs of wealth*,
intended to be evaluated and appreciated, and *signs of authority*,
intended to be believed and obeyed. Quite apart from the literary
(and especially poetic) uses of language, it is rare in everyday life for
language to function as a pure instrument of communication. The
pursuit of maximum informative efficiency is only exceptionally the

exclusive goal of linguistic production and the distinctly instrumental use of language which it implies generally clashes with the often unconscious pursuit of symbolic profit. For in addition to the information expressly declared, linguistic practice inevitably communicates information about the (differential) manner of communicating, i.e. about the *expressive style*, which, being perceived and appreciated with reference to the universe of theoretically or practically competing styles, takes on a social value and a symbolic efficacy.

CAPITAL, MARKET AND PRICE

Utterances receive their value (and their sense) only in their relation to a market, characterized by a particular law of price formation. The value of the utterance depends on the relation of power that is concretely established between the speakers' linguistic competences, understood both as their capacity for production and as their capacity for appropriation and appreciation; it depends, in other words, on the capacity of the various agents involved in the exchange to impose the criteria of appreciation most favourable to their own products. This capacity is not determined in linguistic terms alone. It is certain that the relation between linguistic competences – which, as socially classified productive capacities, characterize socially classified linguistic units of production and, as capacities of appropriation and appreciation, define markets that are themselves socially classified – helps to determine the law of price formation that obtains in a particular exchange. But the linguistic relation of power is not completely determined by the prevailing linguistic forces alone: by virtue of the languages spoken, the speakers who use them and the groups defined by possession of the corresponding competence, the whole social structure is present in each interaction (and thereby in the discourse uttered). That is what is ignored by the interactionist perspective, which treats interaction as a closed world, forgetting that what happens between two persons – between an employer and an employee or, in a colonial situation, between a French speaker and an Arabic speaker or, in the post-colonial situation, between two members of the formerly colonized nation, one Arabic-speaking, one French-speaking – derives its particular form from the objective relation between the corresponding languages or usages, that is, between the groups who speak those languages.

The concern to return to the things themselves and to get a firmer grip on 'reality', a concern which often inspires the projects of 'micro-sociology', can lead one purely and simply to miss a 'reality' that does not yield to immediate intuition because it lies in structures transcending the interaction which they inform. There is no better example of this than that provided by *strategies of condescension*. Thus a French-language newspaper published in Béarn (a province of south-west France) wrote of the mayor of Pau who, in the course of a ceremony in honour of a Béarnais poet, had addressed the assembled company in Béarnais: 'The audience was greatly moved by this thoughtful gesture'.[1] In order for an audience of people whose mother tongue is Béarnais to perceive as a 'thoughtful gesture' the fact that a Béarnais mayor should speak to them in Béarnais, they must tacitly recognize the unwritten law which prescribes French as the only acceptable language for formal speeches in formal situations. The strategy of condescension consists in deriving *profit* from the objective relation of power between the languages that confront one another in practice (even and especially when French is absent) in the very act of symbolically negating that relation, namely, the hierarchy of the languages and of those who speak them. Such a strategy is possible whenever the objective disparity between the persons present (that is, between their social properties) is sufficiently known and recognized by everyone (particularly those involved in the interaction, as agents or spectators) so that the symbolic negation of the hierarchy (by using the 'common touch', for instance) enables the speaker to combine the profits linked to the undiminished hierarchy with those derived from the distinctly symbolic negation of the hierarchy – not the least of which is the strengthening of the hierarchy implied by the recognition accorded to the way of using the hierarchical relation. In reality, the Béarnais mayor can create this condescension effect only because, as mayor of a large town, attesting to his urbanity, he also possesses all the titles (he is a qualified professor) which guarantee his rightful participation in the 'superiority' of the 'superior' language (no one, and especially not a provincial journalist, would think of praising the mayor's French in the same way as his Béarnais, since he is a qualified, licensed speaker who speaks 'good quality' French by definition, *ex officio*). What is praised as 'good quality Béarnais', coming from the mouth of the legitimate speaker of the legitimate language, would be totally devoid of value – and furthermore would be sociologically impossible in a formal situation – coming from the mouth of a peasant, such as the man who, in order to explain why he did not dream of becoming mayor of his village even though he had obtained the biggest share of the vote, said (in French) that he 'didn't know how to speak' (meaning French), implying a definition of linguistic competence that is entirely sociological. One can see in passing that strategies for the subversion of objective hierarchies in the sphere of language, as in the sphere of culture, are *also* likely to be strategies of condescension, reserved for those who are sufficiently confident of their position in the objective hierarchies to be able to deny them without appearing to be ignorant or incapable of satisfying their demands. If Béarnais (or, elsewhere, Creole) is one day spoken on formal occasions, this will be by virtue of its takeover by speakers of the dominant language, who have enough claims to linguistic legitimacy (at least in the eyes of their interlocutors) to avoid being suspected of resorting to the stigmatized language *faute de mieux*.

The relations of power that obtain in the linguistic market, and whose variations determine the variations in the price that the same discourse may receive on different markets, are manifested and realized in the fact that certain agents are incapable of applying to the linguistic products offered, either by themselves or others, the criteria that are most favourable to their own products. This effect of the imposition of legitimacy is greater – and the laws of the market are more favourable to the products offered by the holders of the greatest linguistic competence – when the use of the legitimate language is more imperative, that is, when the situation is more formal (and when it is more favourable, therefore, to those who are more or less formally delegated to speak), and when consumers grant more complete recognition to the legitimate language and legitimate competence (but a recognition which is relatively independent of their knowledge of that language). In other words, the more formal the market is, the more practically congruent with the norms of the legitimate language, the more it is dominated by the dominant, i.e. by the holders of the legitimate competence, authorized to speak with authority. Linguistic competence is not a simple technical capacity but a statutory capacity with which the technical capacity is generally paired, if only because it imposes the acquisition of the latter through the effect of statutory attribution (*noblesse oblige*), as opposed to the commonly held belief that regards technical capacity as the basis for statutory capacity. Legitimate competence is the statutorily recognized capacity of an authorized person – an 'authority' – to use, on formal occasions, the legitimate (i.e. formal) language, the authorized, authoritative language, speech that is accredited, worthy of being believed, or, in a word, *performative*, claiming (with the greatest chances of success) to be effective. Given that legitimate competence, thus defined, implies the effectiveness of the performative, one can understand how certain experiments in social psychology have been able to establish that the efficacy of an utterance, the power of conviction which is granted to it, depends on the *pronunciation* (and secondarily the vocabulary) of the person who utters it; that is, through this particularly reliable measure of statutory competence, it depends on the authority of the speaker. The practical evaluation of the symbolic relation of power that determines the criteria of evaluation prevailing in the market concerned takes into account the specifically linguistic properties of discourse only in so far as they express the social authority and social competence of those who utter them. They do so in the same way as other non-linguistic properties such as the character of the voice (nasalization or pharynxization), a durable disposition of the vocal apparatus that is one of the most powerful of social markers, and all of the more overtly social qualities such as aristocratic and academic titles: clothing, especially uniforms and formal dress; institutional attributes like the priest's pulpit, the professor's platform, the orator's rostrum and microphone, all of which place the legitimate speaker in a pre-eminent position and structure the interaction through the spatial structure which they impose on it; and, finally, the very composition of the group in which the exchange occurs.

Thus the more formal a situation is, the more likely it is that the dominant linguistic competence will function in a particular market as linguistic capital capable of imposing the law of price formation which is the most favourable to its products and of procuring the corresponding symbolic profit. For the more formal the situation is, the more it is able to impose by itself alone the recognition of the legitimacy of the dominant mode of expression, converting the optional variants (at least on the level of pronunciation) which characterize it into imperative rules, *'de rigueur'* (like black ties at formal dinners), making the recipients of these linguistic products more inclined to know and recognize the legitimacy of this mode of expression, even outside the constraints of the formal situation. In other words, the more these different conditions converge and the higher the degree to which this occurs on a market, the narrower the gap between the values accorded in practice to the linguistic products which confront each other on that market and the theoretical value which would be attributed to them, in a hypothetical unified market, in relation to their position in a complete system of linguistic styles.

Conversely, as the degree of formality in an exchange situation and the degree to which the exchange is dominated by highly authorized speakers diminish, so the law of price formation tends to become less unfavourable to the products of dominated linguistic habitus.

It is true that the definition of the symbolic relation of power which is constitutive of the market can be the subject of *negotiation* and that the market can be manipulated, within certain limits, by a metadiscourse concerning the conditions of use of discourse. This includes, for example, the expressions which are used to introduce or excuse speech which is too free or shocking ('with your permission', 'if I may say so', 'if you'll pardon the expression', 'with all due respect', etc.) or those which reinforce, through explicit articulation, the candour enjoyed on a particular market ('off the record', 'strictly between ourselves', etc.). But it goes without saying that the capacity to manipulate is greater the more capital one possesses, as is shown by the strategies of condescension. It is also true that the unification of the market is never so complete as to prevent dominated individuals from finding, in the space provided by private life, among friends, markets where the laws of price formation which apply to more formal markets are suspended.[2] In these private exchanges between homogeneous partners, the 'illegitimate' linguistic products are judged according to criteria which, since they are adjusted to their principles of production, free them from the necessarily comparative logic of distinction and of value. Despite this, the formal law, which is thus provisionally suspended rather than truly transgressed,[3] remains valid, and it re-imposes itself on dominated individuals once they leave the unregulated areas where they can be outspoken (and where they can spend all their lives), as is shown by the fact that it governs the production of their spokespersons as soon as they are placed in a formal situation. It would be quite mistaken, therefore, to see a 'true' popular language in the use of language which obtains in this oasis of freedom, where one has licence (a typical 'dictionary word') because one is among friends and not forced to 'watch oneself'. It is also true that popular competence, when confronted with a formal market, like the one constituted by a linguistic survey or investigation (unless specific precautions are taken), is, as it were, annihilated. The reality of linguistic legitimacy consists precisely in the fact that dominated individuals are always under the *potential jurisdiction* of formal law, even when they spend all their lives, like the thief described by Weber, beyond its reach, so that when placed in a formal situation they are doomed to silence or to the broken discourse which linguistic investigation also often records.

This means that the productions of the same linguistic habitus vary according to the market and that any linguistic observation records a discourse which is the product of the relationship between a linguistic competence and the particular market constituted by the linguistic investigation. This market has a high degree of tension since the laws of price formation which govern it are related to those of the academic market. All attempts to pin down the variables that could explain the variations thus recorded run the risk of overlooking the effect of the investigative situation itself, *a hidden variable which is doubtless the source of the differential weight of different variables.* Those who, wishing to break with linguistic abstractions, try to establish statistically the social factors of linguistic competence (measured by this or that phonological, lexical or syntactic index) are only going half-way: they are in fact forgetting that the different factors measured in a particular market situation – that created by the inquiry – could, in a different situation, have very different relative weights, and that what is important therefore is to determine how the explanatory weights of the different factors which determine competence vary according to the market situation (which would require the development of a proper experimental project).

SYMBOLIC CAPITAL: A RECOGNIZED POWER

The question of performative utterances becomes clearer if one sees it as a particular case of the effects of symbolic domination, which occurs in all linguistic exchanges. The linguistic relation of power is never defined solely by the relation between the linguistic competences present. And the weight of different agents depends on their symbolic capital, i.e. on the *recognition*, institutionalized or not, that they receive from a group. Symbolic imposition – that kind of magical efficacy which not only the command and the password, but also ritual discourse or a simple injunction, or even threats or insults, purport to exercise – can function only if there is a convergence of social conditions which are altogether distinct from the strictly linguistic logic of discourse. For the philosopher's language to be granted the importance it claims, there has to be a convergence of the social conditions which enable it to secure from others a recognition of the importance which it attributes to itself.[4] Equally, the setting up of a ritual exchange, such as a mass, presupposes, among other things, that all the social conditions are in place to ensure the production of appropriate senders and receivers, who are therefore agreed among themselves. It is certainly the case that the symbolic efficacy of religious language is threatened when the set of mechanisms capable of ensuring the reproduction of the relationship of recognition, which is the basis of its authority, ceases to function. This is also true of any relation of symbolic imposition, even of the one implied by the use of the legitimate language which, as such, involves the claim to be heard, believed and obeyed, and which can exercise its specific efficacy only as long as it can count on the effectiveness of all the mechanisms, analysed above, which secure the reproduction of the dominant language and the recognition of its legitimacy. One may note, in passing, that the source of the profit of distinction, procured by any use of the legitimate language, derives from the totality of the social universe and the relations of domination that give structure to it, although one of the most important constituents of this profit lies in the fact that it appears to be based on the qualities of the person alone.

Austin's account of performative utterances cannot be restricted to the sphere of linguistics. The magical efficacy of these *acts of institution* is inseparable from the existence of an institution defining the conditions (regarding the agent, the time or place, etc.) which have to be fulfilled for the magic of words to operate. As is indicated in the examples analysed by Austin, these 'conditions of felicity' are social conditions, and the person who wishes to proceed *felicitously* with the christening of a ship or of a person must be *entitled* to do so, in the same way that, to be able to give an order, one must have a recognized authority over the recipient of that order. It is true that linguists have often rushed to find, in Austin's inconsistent definition of the performative, an excuse for dismissing the problem which Austin had set them, in order to return to a narrowly linguistic definition that ignores the market effect. They did this by distinguishing between explicit performatives, which are necessarily self-verifying since they represent in themselves the accomplishment of the act, and performatives conceived more broadly to mean statements that are used to accomplish an act other than the simple fact of saying something, or, to put it more simply, the difference between a properly linguistic act (e.g. declaring the meeting open) and the extra-linguistic act (opening the meeting by the fact of declaring it open). In this way, they justified to themselves the rejection of any analysis of the social conditions in which performative utterances function. The conditions of felicity discussed by Austin concern only the extra-linguistic act; only to open the meeting effectively does one need to be entitled to do so, as anyone can declare it open, even if his declaration remains totally ineffective.[5]

Was it necessary to employ so much ingenuity to discover that when my doing consists in my saying, what I do is necessarily what I say? But by pushing to the limit the consequences of the distinction between the linguistic and the extra-linguistic, on which it purports to base its autonomy (notably with regard to sociology), pragmatics demonstrates by *reductio ad absurdum* that illocutionary acts as described by Austin are acts of institution that cannot be sanctioned unless they have, in some way, the whole social order behind them. 'Whereas one clearly must be "entitled" to open the meeting, it is not necessary to be in a position of superiority to give an order; a soldier can give an order to his commanding officer, even though his order has little chance of being obeyed'.[6] Or, again: 'To claim legitimately to open the meeting, one needs to be authorized by the institution and not everyone is; but everyone has the authority to accomplish a speech act like an order, so that everyone can claim to accomplish such an act'.[7] The construction of these 'pure' performatives, represented by explicit performatives, has the virtue of bringing out *a contrario* the presuppositions of ordinary performatives, which imply a reference to the social conditions for their success. From a strictly linguistic point of view, anyone can say anything and the private can order his captain to 'clean the latrines'; but from a sociological point of view (the one adopted in fact by Austin when he reflects on the conditions of felicity), it is clear that not anyone can assert anything, or else does so at his peril, as with an insult. 'Anybody can shout in the public square, "I decree a general mobilization," and as it cannot be an *act* because the requisite authority is lacking, such an utterance is no more than *words*; it reduces itself to futile clamour, childishness, or lunacy.'[8] The logical exercise of separating the act of speech from its conditions of execution shows, through the absurdities that this abstraction engenders, that the performative utterance, as an act of institution, cannot socio-logically exist independently of the institution which gives it its *raison d'être*, and if it were to be produced in spite of everything, it would be socially deprived of sense.[9] Since an order, or even a password, can work only if it is backed up by the order of things and its accomplishment depends on all the relations of order which define the social order, one would have to be crazy, as they say, to dream up and give an order for which the conditions of felicity are not fulfilled. The anticipated conditions of felicity help to determine the utterance by allowing it to be thought of and experienced as reasonable and realistic. Only a hopeless soldier (or a 'pure' linguist) could imagine that it was possible to give his captain an order. The performative utterance implies 'an overt claim to possess such or such power',[10] a claim that is more or less recognized and therefore more or less sanctioned socially. This claim to act on the social world through words, i.e. magically, is more or less crazy or reasonable depending on whether it is more or less based on the objectivity of the social world.[11] Thus we can counterpose two acts of magical naming that are, socially, very unequally guaranteed: the insult ('you're only a professor') which, lacking authorization, risks rebounding against its author, and the official naming or 'nomination' ('I appoint you professor'), powerfully invested with all the authority of the group and capable of instituting a legitimate, that is, universally recognized, identity.

The limiting case of the performative utterance is the legal act which, when it is pronounced, as it should be, by someone who has the right to do so,[12] i.e. by an agent acting on behalf of a whole group, can replace action with speech, which will, as they say, have an effect: the judge need say no more than 'I find you guilty' because there is a set of agents and institutions which guarantee that the sentence will be executed. The inquiry into the specifically linguistic principle behind the 'illocutionary power' of discourse thus gives way to the distinctly sociological inquiry into the conditions in which an individual agent can find himself and his speech invested with such power. The real source of the magic of performative utterances lies in the mystery of ministry, i.e. the delegation by virtue of which an individual – king, priest or spokesperson – is mandated to speak and act on behalf of a group, thus constituted in him and by him.[13] More precisely, it lies in the social conditions of the *institution* of the ministry, which constitutes the legitimate representative as an agent capable of acting on the social world through words, by instituting him as a medium between the group and the social world; and it does that, among other things, by equipping him with the signs and the insignia aimed at underlining the fact that he is not acting in his own name and under his own authority.

There is no symbolic power without the symbolism of power. Symbolic attributes – as is well illustrated in the paradigmatic case of the *skeptron* and the sanctions against the improper wearing of uniforms – are a public display and thereby an officialization of the contract of delegation: the ermine and the robe declare that the judge or the doctor is recognized as having just cause (in the collective recognition) for declaring himself judge or doctor, that his imposture – in the sense of the pretension expressed by his appearance – is legitimate. The competence that is specifically linguistic – the Latin once spoken by doctors or the eloquence of the spokesperson – is also one of the manifestations of competence in the sense of the right to speech and to power through speech. There is a whole dimension of authorized language, its rhetoric, syntax, vocabulary and even pronunciation, which exists purely to underline the authority of its author and the trust he demands. In this respect, style is an element of the *mechanism*, in the Pascalian sense, through which language aims to produce and impose the representation of its own importance and thereby help to ensure its own credibility.[14] The symbolic efficacy of the discourse of authority always depends, in part, on the linguistic competence of the person who utters it. This is more true, of course, when the authority of the speaker is less clearly institutionalized. It follows that the exercise of symbolic power is accompanied by work on the *form* of discourse which, as is clearly demonstrated in the case of poets in archaic societies, has the purpose of demonstrating the orator's mastery and gaining him the recognition of the group. (This logic is also found in the popular rhetoric of insults which seeks, by flagrant overstatement and the regulated deformation of ritual formulas, to produce the expressive accomplishment which allows one to 'get those laughing on one's side'.)

Thus, just as the relation to the market defines, in the case of constatives, the conditions of acceptability and thereby the very form of the discourse, so too the relation to the possibilities offered by a particular market determines, in the case of performative utterances, the conditions of felicity. One must therefore assert, against all the forms of autonomization of a distinctly linguistic order, that all speech is produced for and through the market to which it owes its existence and its most specific properties.

THE ANTICIPATION OF PROFITS

Since a discourse can only exist, in the form in which it exists, so long as it is not simply grammatically correct but also, and above all, socially acceptable, i.e. heard, believed, and therefore effective within a given state of relations of production and circulation, it follows that the scientific analysis of discourse must take into account the laws of price formation which characterize the market concerned or, in other words, the laws defining the social conditions of acceptability (which include the specifically linguistic laws of grammaticality). In reality, the conditions of reception envisaged are part of the conditions of production, and anticipation of the sanctions of the market helps to determine the production of the discourse. This anticipation, which bears no resemblance to a conscious calculation, is an aspect of the linguistic habitus which, being the product of a prolonged and primordial relation to the laws of a certain market, tends to function as a practical sense of the acceptability and the probable value of one's own linguistic productions and those of others on different markets.[15] It is this sense of acceptability, and not some form of rational calculation oriented towards the maximization of symbolic profits, which, by encouraging one to take account of the probable value of discourse during the process of production, determines corrections and all forms of self-censorship – the concessions one makes to a social world by accepting to make oneself acceptable in it.

Since linguistic signs are also goods destined to be given a price by powers capable of providing credit (varying according to the laws of the market on which they are placed), linguistic production is inevitably affected by the anticipation of market sanctions: all verbal expressions – whether words exchanged between friends, the bureaucratic discourse of an authorized spokesperson or the academic discourse of a scientific paper – are marked by their conditions of reception and owe some of their properties (even at a grammatical level) to the fact that, on the basis of a practical anticipation of the laws of the market concerned, their authors, most often unwittingly, and without expressly seeking to do so, try to maximize the symbolic profit they can obtain from practices which are, inseparably, oriented towards communication and exposed to evaluation.[16] This means that the market fixes the price for a linguistic product, the nature, and therefore the objective value, of which the practical anticipation of this price helped to determine; and it means that the practical relation to the market (ease, timidity, tension, embarrassment, silence, etc.), which helps to establish the market sanction, thus provides an apparent justification for the sanction by which it is partly produced.

In the case of symbolic production, the constraint exercised by the market via the anticipation of possible profit naturally takes the form of an anticipated *censorship*, of a self-censorship which determines not only the manner of saying, that is, the choice of language – 'code switching' in situations of bilingualism – or the 'level' of language, but also what it will be possible or not possible to say.[17]

> Everything happens as if, in each particular situation, the linguistic norm
> (the law of price formation) is imposed by the holder of the competence

which is closest to the legitimate competence, i.e. by the dominant speaker in the interaction, and in a way that is all the more rigorous when the exchange has a higher degree of formality (in public, in a formal setting, etc.). It is as if the effect of censorship which is exercised over the dominated speaker and the necessity for him to adopt the legitimate mode of expression (French in the case of a *patois* speaker), or to come close to it, is more powerfully experienced, all other things being equal, when the disparity between the different kinds of capital is greater – whereas this constraint disappears between holders of an equivalent symbolic and linguistic capital, for example between peasants. Situations of bilingualism enable one to observe quasi-experimentally how the language used varies according to the relation between the speakers (and their instruments of expression), analysed in terms of the structure of the distribution of specifically linguistic capital and of other kinds of capital. Thus, in a series of interactions observed in 1963 in a small Béarnais town, the same person (an elderly woman living in one of the neighbouring villages) first used a '*patois*-French' to a young woman shopkeeper in the town, who was originally from another, larger town in the Béarn (and who, being more of a 'city-dweller', might not understand Béarnais or could feign ignorance). The next moment, she spoke in Béarnais to a woman who lived in that town but who was originally from the villages and more or less of her own age; then she used a French that was strongly 'corrected' to a minor town official; and, finally, she spoke in Béarnais to a roadworker in the town, originally from the villages and about her age. It is clear that the interviewer, as an 'educated' city-dweller, will only encounter strongly corrected French or silence; and if he uses Béarnais himself, this may well ease the tension of the exchange, but, whatever his intentions, it cannot fail to function as a strategy of condescension likely to create a situation no less artificial than the initial relationship.

The practical cognition and recognition of the immanent laws of a market and the sanctions through which they are manifested determine the strategic modifications of discourse, whether they concern the effort to 'correct' a devalued pronunciation in the presence of representatives of the legitimate pronunciation and, more generally, all the corrections which tend to valorize the linguistic product by a more intense mobilization of the available resources, or, conversely, the tendency to resort to a less complex syntax, to the short phrases which social psychologists have observed in adults when they address children. Discourses are always to some extent *euphemisms* inspired by the concern to 'speak well', to 'speak properly', to produce the products that respond to the demands of a certain market; they are *compromise formations* resulting from a transaction between the expressive interest (what is to be said) and the censorship inherent in particular relations of linguistic production (whether it is the struc-ture of linguistic interaction or the structure of a specialized field), a censorship which is imposed on a speaker or writer endowed with a certain social competence, that is, a more or less significant symbolic power over these relations of symbolic power.[18]

Variations in the *form* of discourse, and more precisely the degree to which it is controlled, monitored and refined in form (*formal*), thus depend, on the one hand, on the *objective tension* of the market, that is, on the degree of formality of the situation and, in the case of an interaction, on the extent of the social distance (in the structure of the distribution of linguistic and other kinds of capital) between the sender and the receiver, or the respective groups to which they belong; and, on the other hand, on the 'sensitivity' of the speaker to this tension and the censorship it implies, as well as the closely related aptitude to respond to a high degree of tension with an expression which is highly controlled, and therefore strongly euphemized. In other words, the form and the content of a discourse depend on the relation between a habitus (which is itself the product of sanctions on a market with a given level of tension), and a market defined by a level of tension which is more or less heightened, hence by the severity of the sanctions it inflicts on those who pay insuf-ficient attention to 'correctness' and to 'the imposition of form' which formal usage presupposes.

It is, therefore, not clear how one could understand, other than in terms of variations in the tension of the market, the *stylistic variations* of which Bally gives a good example,[19] with a series of expressions (represented here by approximate English equivalents) which are seemingly interchangeable, since they are all oriented towards the same practical result: 'Come!', 'Do come!', 'Wouldn't you like to come?', 'You will come, won't you?', 'Do say you'll come', 'Suppose you came?', 'You ought to come', 'Come here', 'Here!' – to which could be added 'Will you come?', 'You will come', 'Kindly come', 'Would you be so good as to come', 'Be a sport, do come', 'Come please!', 'Come, I beg you', 'I hope you will come', 'I'm counting on you . . .' and so on *ad infinitum*. Although such expressions are theoretically equivalent, they are not so in practice. Each of them, when used appropriately, achieves the optimum form of the compromise between the expressive intention – in this case, insistence, which runs the risk of appearing as unreasonable intru-sion or unacceptable pressure – and the censorship inherent in a more or less asymmetrical social relationship, by making maximum use of the available resources, whether they are already objectified and codified, like expressions of politeness, or remain in a virtual state. This is as much insistence as one can 'allow oneself' to exert, so long as the 'forms' are observed. Where 'If you would do me the honour of coming' is appropriate, 'You ought to come' would be out of place, because too off-hand, and 'Will you come?' would be distinctly 'crude'. In social formalism, as in magical formalism, there is only one formula in each case which 'works'. And the whole labour of politeness strives to get as close as possible to the perfect formula that would be immediately self-evident if one had a perfect mastery of the market situation.

Form and the information it imparts condense and symbolize the entire structure of the social relation from which they derive their existence and their efficacy (the celebrated 'illocutionary force'). What is called tact or adroitness consists in the art of taking account of the relative positions of the sender and the receiver in the hierarchy of different kinds of capital, and also of sex and age, and of the limits inscribed in this relation, ritually transgressing them, if need be, by means of euphemization. The attenuation of the injunction, reduced to zero in 'Here', 'Come', or 'Come here', is more marked in 'If you would be so good as to come this way'. The form used to neutralize 'impoliteness' may be a simple interrogative ('Will you come?'), or a doubly delicate negative question ('Won't you come?'), which acknowledges the possibility of refusal. It may be a formula of insistence which pretends not to insist by declaring both the possibility of refusal and the value set on compliance, in which case it may take a colloquial form, appropriate between peers ('Do me a favour and come'), a 'stilted' form ('Would you be so kind as to come'), even an obsequious form ('If you would do me the honour of coming'); or it may be a metalinguistic inquiry into the very legitimacy of the question ('May I ask you to come?').

What our social sense detects in a form which is a kind of symbolic expression of all the sociologically pertinent features of the market situation is precisely that which oriented the production of the discourse, namely, the entire set of characteristics of the social relation obtaining between the interlocutors and the expressive capacities which the speaker was able to invest in the process of euphemization. The interdependence between linguistic forms and the structure of the social relation within and for which it is produced can be seen clearly, in French, in the oscillations between the forms of address, *vous* and *tu*, which sometimes occur when the objective structure of the relation between two speakers (e.g. disparity in age or social status) conflicts with the length and continuity of their acquaintance, and therefore with the intimacy and familiarity of their interaction. It then seems as if they are feeling their way towards a readjustment of the mode of expression and of the social relation through spontaneous or calculated slips of the tongue and progressive lapses, which often culminate in a sort of linguistic contract designed to establish the new expressive order on an official basis: 'Let's use *tu*.' But the subordination of the form of discourse to the form of the social relationship in which it is used is most strikingly apparent in situations of *stylistic collision*, when the speaker is confronted with a socially heterogeneous audience or simply with two interlocutors socially and culturally so far apart that the sociologically exclusive modes of expression called for, which are normally produced through more or less conscious adjustment in separate social spaces, cannot be produced simultaneously.

What guides linguistic production is not the degree of tension of the market or, more precisely, its degree of formality, defined in the abstract, for any speaker, but rather the relation between a degree of 'average' objective tension and a linguistic habitus itself characterized by a particular degree of sensitivity to the tension of the market; or, in other words, it is the anticipation of profits, which can scarcely be called a subjective anticipation since it is the product of the encounter between an objective circumstance, that is, the average probability of success, and an incorporated objectivity, that is, the disposition towards a more or less rigorous evaluation of that probability.[20] The practical anticipation of the potential rewards or penalties is a practical quasi-corporeal sense of the reality of the objective relation between a certain linguistic and social competence and a certain market, through which this relation is accomplished. It can range from the certainty of a positive sanction, which is the basis of *certitudo sui*, of *self-assurance*, to the certainty of a negative sanction, which induces surrender and silence, through all the intermediate forms of insecurity and timidity.

THE LINGUISTIC HABITUS AND BODILY HEXIS

The definition of acceptability is found not in the situation but in the relationship between a market and a habitus, which itself is the product of the whole history of its relations with markets. The habitus is, indeed, linked to the market no less through its conditions of acquisition than through its conditions of use. We have not learned to speak simply by hearing a certain kind of speech spoken but also by speaking, thus by offering a determinate form of speech on a determinate market. This occurs through exchanges within a family occupying a particular position in the social space and thus presenting the child's imitative propensity with models and sanctions that diverge more or less from legitimate usage.[21] And we have learned the value that the products offered on this primary market, together with the authority which it provides, receive on other markets (like that of the school). The system of successive reinforcements or refutations has thus constituted in each one of us a certain sense of the social value of linguistic usages and of the relation between the different usages and the different markets, which organizes all subsequent perceptions of linguistic products, tending to endow it with considerable stability. (We know, in general terms, that the effects that a new experience can have on the habitus depend on the relation of practical 'compatibility' between this experience and the experiences that have already been assimilated by the habitus, in the form of schemes of production and evaluation, and that, in the process of selective re-interpretation which results from this dialectic, the informative efficacy of all new experiences tends to diminish continuously.) This linguistic 'sense of place' governs the degree of constraint which a given field will bring to bear on the production of discourse, imposing silence or a hyper-controlled language on some people while allowing others the liberties of a language that is securely established. This means that competence, which is acquired in a social context and through practice, is inseparable from the practical mastery of a usage of language and the practical mastery of situations in which this usage of language is *socially acceptable*. The sense of the value of one's own linguistic products is a fundamental dimension of the sense of knowing the place which one occupies in the social space. One's original relation with different markets and the experience of the sanctions applied to one's own productions, together with the experience of the price attributed to one's own body, are doubtless some of the mediations which help to constitute that *sense of one's own social worth* which governs the practical relation to different markets (shyness, confidence, etc.) and, more generally, one's whole physical posture in the social world.

While every speaker is both a producer and a consumer of his own linguistic productions, not all speakers, as we have seen, are able to apply to their own products the schemes according to which they were produced. The unhappy relation which the petits bourgeois have to their own productions (and especially with regard to their pronunciation, which, as Labov shows, they judge with particular severity); their especially keen sensitivity to the tension of the market and, by the same token, to linguistic correction in themselves and in others,[22] which pushes them to hyper-correction; their insecurity, which reaches a state of paroxysm on formal occasions, creating 'incorrectness' through hyper-correction or the embarrassingly rash utterances prompted by an artificial confidence – are all things that result from a divorce between the schemes of production and the schemes of evaluation. Divided against themselves, so to speak, the petits bourgeois are those who are both the most 'conscious' of the objective truth of their products (the one defined in the academic hypothesis of the perfectly unified market) and the most determined to reject it, deny it, and contradict it by their efforts. As is very evident in this case, what expresses itself through the linguistic habitus is the whole class habitus of which it is one dimension, which means in fact, the position that is occupied, synchronically and diachronically, in the social structure.

As we have seen, hyper-correction is inscribed in the logic of pretension which leads the petits bourgeois to attempt to appropriate prematurely, at the cost of constant tension, the properties of those who are dominant. The particular intensity of the insecurity and anxiety felt by women of the petite bourgeoisie with regard to language (and equally with regard to cosmetics or personal appearance) can be understood in the framework of the same logic: destined, by the division of labour between the sexes, to seek social mobility through their capacity for symbolic production and consumption, they are even more inclined to invest in the acquisition of legitimate competences. The linguistic practices of the petite bourgeoisie could not fail to strike those who, like Labov, observed them on the particularly tense markets created by linguistic investigation. Situated at the maximum point of subjective tension through their particular sensitivity to objective tension (which is the effect of an especially marked disparity between recognition and cognition), the petits bourgeois are distinct from members of the lower classes who, lacking the means to exercise the liberties of plain speaking, which they reserve for private usage, have no choice but to opt for the broken forms of a borrowed and clumsy language or to escape into abstention and silence. But the petits bourgeois are no less distinct from the members of the dominant class, whose linguistic habitus (especially if they were born in that class) is the *realization of the norm* and who can express all the self-confidence that is associated with a situation where the principles of evaluation and the principles of production coincide perfectly.[23]

In this case, as, at the other extreme, in the case of popular outspokenness on the popular market, the demands of the market and the dispositions of the habitus are perfectly attuned; the law of the market does not need to be imposed by means of constraint or external censorship since it is accomplished through the relation to the market which is its incorporated form. When the objective structures which it confronts coincide with those which have produced it, the habitus anticipates the objective demands of the field. Such is the basis of the most frequent and best concealed form of censorship, the kind which is applied by placing, in positions which imply the right to speak, those agents who are endowed with expressive dispositions that are 'censored' in advance, since they coincide with the exigencies inscribed in those positions. As the principle underlying all the distinctive features of the dominant mode of expression, *relaxation in tension* is the expression of a relation to the market which can only be acquired through prolonged and precocious familiarity with markets that are characterized, even under ordinary circumstances, by a high level of control and by that constantly sustained attention to forms and formalities which defines the 'stylization of life'.

It is certainly true that, as one rises in the social order, the degree of censorship and the correlative prominence given to the imposition of form and euphemization increase steadily, not only on public or official occasions (as is the case among the lower classes and especially among the petite bourgeoisie, who establish a marked opposition between the ordinary and the extra-ordinary), but also in the routines of everyday life. This can be seen in styles of dressing or eating, but also in styles of speaking, which tend to exclude the casualness, the laxness or the licence which we allow ourselves in other circumstances, when we are 'among our own kind'. That is what Lakoff notes indirectly when he observes that the kind of behaviour among friends, where someone asks openly about the price of an object ('Hey, that's a nice rug. What did it cost?'), which would be acceptable among the lower classes (where it might even seem like a compliment), would be 'misplaced' in the bourgeoisie, where it would have to be given an attenuated form ('May I ask you what the rug cost?').[24]

Linked to this higher degree of censorship, which demands a consistently higher degree of euphemization and a more systematic effort to *observe formalities*, is the fact that the practical mastery of the instruments of euphemization which are objectively demanded on the markets with the greatest tension, like the academic market or the high-society market, increases as one rises in the social order, i.e. with the increased frequency of the social occasions (from childhood on) when one finds oneself subject to these demands, and therefore able to acquire practically the means to satisfy them. Thus bourgeois usage is characterized, according to Lakoff, by the use of what he calls *hedges*, e.g. 'sort of', 'pretty much', 'rather', 'strictly speaking', 'loosely speaking', 'technically', 'regular', *'par excellence'*, etc., and, according to Labov, by intensive use of what he calls *filler phrases*, e.g. 'such a thing as', 'some things like that', 'particularly'.[25] It is not enough to say, as Labov does (with a view to rehabilitating popular speech, which leads him simply to invert the system of values), that these expressions are responsible for the *verbosity* and verbal inflation of bourgeois speech. Though superfluous in terms of a strict economy of communication, they fulfil an important function in determining the value of a way of communicating. Not only does their very redundancy bear witness to the extent of the available resources and the disinterested relation to those resources which is therefore possible, but they are also elements of a *practical metalanguage* and, as such, they function as marks of the *neutralizing distance* which is one of the characteristics of the bourgeois relation to language and to the social world. Having the effect, as Lakoff puts it, of 'heightening intermediate values and toning down extreme values', or, as Labov says, of 'avoiding all error and exaggeration', these expressions are an affirmation of the speaker's capacity to keep his distance from his own utterances, and therefore his own interests – and, by the same token, from those who cannot keep such a distance but let themselves be carried away by their own words, surrendering without restraint or censorship to their expressive impulse. Such a mode of expression, which is produced by and for markets requiring 'axiological neutrality' (and not only in language use), is also adjusted in advance to markets which require that other form of neutralization and distancing of reality (and distancing of the other classes which are immersed in it) which compromises the stylization of life: that forming of practices which gives priority in all things to manner, style and form, to the detriment of function. It is also suited to all formal markets and to social rituals where the need to impose form and to observe formalities, which defines the appropriate form of language – i.e. *formal language* – is absolutely imperative and prevails to the detriment of the communicative function, which can disappear as long as the performative logic of symbolic domination operates.

It is no coincidence that bourgeois distinction invests the same intention in its relation to language as it invests in its relation to the body. The sense of acceptability which orients linguistic practices is inscribed in the most deep-rooted of bodily dispositions: it is the whole body which responds by its posture, but also by its inner reactions or, more specifically, the articulatory ones, to the tension of the market. Language is a body technique, and specifically linguistic, especially phonetic, competence is a dimension of bodily hexis in which one's whole relation to the social world, and one's whole socially informed relation to the world, are expressed. There is every reason to think that, through the mediation of what Pierre Guiraud calls 'articulatory style', the bodily hexis characteristic of a social class determines the system of phonological features which characterizes a class pronunciation. The most frequent articulatory position is an element in an *overall way of using the mouth* (in talking but also in eating, drinking, laughing, etc.) and therefore a component of the bodily hexis, which implies a *systematic informing* of the whole phonological aspect of speech. This 'articulatory style', a life-style 'made flesh', like the whole bodily hexis, welds phonological features – which are often studied in isolation, each one (the phoneme 'r', for example) being compared with its equivalent in other class pronunciations – into an indivisible totality which must be treated as such.

Thus, in the case of the lower classes, articulatory style is quite clearly part of a relation to the body that is dominated by the refusal of 'airs and graces' (i.e., the refusal of stylization and the imposition of form) and by the valorization of virility – one aspect of a more general disposition to appreciate what is 'natural'. Labov is no doubt right when he ascribes the resistance of male speakers in New York to the imposition of the legitimate language to the fact that they associate the idea of virility with their way of speaking or, more precisely, their way of using the mouth and throat when speaking. In France, it is surely no accident that popular usage condenses the opposition between the bourgeois relation and the popular relation to language in the sexually over-determined opposition between two words for the mouth: *la bouche*, which is more closed, pinched, i.e. tense and censored, and therefore feminine, and *la gueule*, unashamedly wide open, as in 'split' (*fendue, se fendre la gueule*, 'split oneself laughing'), i.e. relaxed and free, and therefore masculine.[26] Bourgeois dispositions, as they are envisaged in the popular mind, and in their most caricatured, petit-bourgeois form, convey in their physical postures of tension and exertion (*bouche fine, pincée, lèvres pincées, serrées, du bout des lèvres, bouche en cul-de-poule* – to be fastidious, supercilious, 'tight-lipped') the bodily indices of quite general dispositions towards the world and other people (and particularly, in the case of the mouth, towards food), such as haughtiness and disdain (*faire la fine bouche, la petite bouche* – to be fussy about food, difficult to please), and the conspicuous distance from the things of the body and those who are unable to mark that distance. *La gueule*, by contrast, is associated with the manly dispositions which, according to the popular ideal, are rooted in the calm certainty of strength which rules out censorships – prudence and deviousness as well as 'airs and graces' – and which make it possible to be 'natural' (*la gueule* is on the side of nature), to be 'open' and 'outspoken' (*jouer franc-jeu, avoir son franc-parler*) or simply to sulk (*faire la gueule*). It designates a capacity for verbal violence, identified with the sheer strength of the voice (*fort en gueule, coup de gueule, grande gueule, engueuler, s'engueuler, gueuler, aller gueuler* – 'loud-mouthed', a 'dressing-down', 'bawl', 'have a slanging match', 'mouth-off'). It also designates a capacity for the physical violence to which it alludes, especially in insults (*casser la gueule, mon poing sur la gueule, ferme ta gueule* – 'smash your face in', 'a punch in the mouth', 'shut your face'), which, through the *gueule*, regarded both as the 'seat' of personal identity (*bonne gueule, sale gueule* – 'nice guy', 'ugly mug') and as its main means of expression (consider the meaning of *ouvrir sa gueule*, or *l'ouvrir*, as opposed to *la fermer, la boucler, taire sa gueule, s'écraser* – 'say one's piece', as opposed to 'shut it', 'belt up', 'shut your mouth', 'pipe down'), aims at the very essence of the interlocutor's social identity and self-image. Applying the same 'intention' to the site of food intake and the site of speech output, the popular vision, which has a clear grasp of the unity of habitus and bodily hexis, also associates *la gueule* with the frank acceptance (*s'en foutre plein la gueule, se rincer la gueule* – stuffing oneself with food and drink) and frank manifestation (*se fendre la gueule*) of elementary pleasure.[27]

On the one hand, domesticated language, censorship made natural, which proscribes 'gross' remarks, 'coarse' jokes and 'thick' accents, goes hand in hand with the domestication of the body which excludes all excessive manifestations of appetites or feelings (exclamations as much as tears or sweeping gestures), and which subjects the body to all kinds of discipline and censorship aimed at denaturalizing it. On the other hand, the 'relaxation of articulatory tension', which leads, as Bernard Laks has pointed out, to the dropping of the final 'r' and 'l' (and which is probably not so much an effect of *laisser-aller*[28] as the expression of a refusal to 'overdo it', to conform too strictly on the points most strictly demanded by the dominant code, even if the effort is made in other areas), is associated with rejection of the censorship which propriety imposes, particularly on the tabooed body, and with the outspokenness whose daring is less innocent than it seems since, in reducing humanity to its common nature – belly, bum, bollocks, grub, guts and shit – it tends to turn the social world upside down, arse over head. Popular festivity as described by Bakhtin and especially revolutionary crisis highlight, through the verbal explosion which they facilitate, the pressure and repression which the everyday order imposes, particularly on the dominated class, through the seemingly insignificant constraints and controls of politeness which, by means of the stylistic variations in ways of talking (the formulae of politeness) or of bodily deportment in relation to the degree of objective tension of the market, exacts recognition of the hierarchical differences between the classes, the sexes and the generations.

It is not surprising that, from the standpoint of the dominated classes, the adoption of the dominant style is seen as a denial of social and sexual identity, a repudiation of the virile values which constitute class membership. That is why women can identify with the dominant culture without cutting themselves off from their class as radically as men. 'Opening one's big mouth' (*ouvrir sa grande gueule*) means refusing to submit, refusing to 'shut it' (*la fermer*) and to manifest the signs of docility that are the precondition of mobility. To adopt the dominant style, especially a feature as marked as the legitimate pronunciation, is in a sense doubly to negate one's virility because the very fact of acquiring it requires docility, a disposition imposed on women by the traditional sexual division of labour (and the traditional division of sexual labour), and because this docility leads one towards dispositions that are themselves perceived as effeminate.

In drawing attention to the articulatory features which, like the degree of 'aperture', sonority or rhythm, best express, in their own logic, the deep-rooted dispositions of the habitus and, more precisely, of the bodily hexis, spontaneous sociolinguistics demonstrates that a differential phonology should never fail to select and interpret the articulatory features characteristic of a class or class fraction in relation not only to the other systems with reference to which they take on their distinctive value, and therefore their social value, but also in relation to the synthetic unity of the bodily hexis from which they spring, and by virtue of which they represent the ethical or aesthetic expression of the necessity inscribed in a social condition.

The linguist, who has developed an abnormally acute perception (particularly at the phonological level), may notice differences where ordinary speakers hear none. Moreover, because he has to concentrate on discrete criteria (such as the dropping of the final 'r' or 'l') for the purposes of statistical measurement, he is inclined towards an analytical perception very different in its logic from the ordinary perception which underlies the classificatory judgements and the delimitation of homogeneous groups in everyday life. Not only are linguistic features never clearly separated from the speaker's whole set of social properties (bodily hexis, physiognomy, cosmetics, clothing), but phonological (or lexical, or any other) features are never clearly separated from other levels of language; and the judgement which classifies a speech form as 'popular' or a person as 'vulgar' is based, like all practical predication, on sets of indices which never impinge on consciousness in that form, even if those which are designated by stereotypes (such as the 'peasant' 'r' or the southern *ceusse*) have greater weight.

The close correspondence between the uses of the body, of language and no doubt also of time is due to the fact that it is essentially through bodily and linguistic disciplines and censorships, which often imply a temporal rule, that groups inculcate the virtues which are the transfigured form of their necessity, and to the fact that the 'choices' constitutive of a relationship with the economic and social world are incorporated in the form of durable frames that are partly beyond the grasp of consciousness and will.[29]

Appendix

Did You Say 'Popular'?

Sayings containing the magical epithet 'popular' are shielded from scrutiny by the fact that any critical analysis of a notion which bears closely or remotely on 'the people' is apt to be identified immediately as a symbolic aggression against the reality designated – and thus immediately castigated by all those who feel duty bound to defend 'the people', thereby enjoying the profits that the defence of 'good causes' can bring.[1] Equally, the notion of 'popular speech', like all the sayings from the same family ('popular culture', 'popular art', 'popular religion', etc.), is defined only in relational terms, as the set of things which are excluded from the legitimate language by, among other things, the durable effect of inculcation and imposition together with the sanctions implemented by the educational system.

As the dictionaries of slang and 'unconventional language' clearly show, what is called 'popular' or 'colloquial' vocabulary is nothing other than the set of words which are excluded from dictionaries of the legitimate language or which only appear in them with negative 'labels of use': *fam.*, familiar, 'i.e. common in ordinary spoken language and in rather free written language', *pop.*, popular, 'i.e. common in urban working-class areas, but disapproved of or avoided by the cultivated bourgeoisie as a whole'.[2] To define thoroughly this 'unconventional' or 'popular' language – which would be more fruitfully described as *pop.*, to remind us of its social conditions of production – one would have to specify what comes under the heading 'working-class areas' (*milieux populaires*) and what one understands by 'common' usage.

Like elastic concepts such as 'the working classes', 'the people' or 'the workers', which owe their political virtues to the fact that one can extend the referent at will to include (during election time, for

instance) peasants, managers and small businessmen, or, conversely,
limit it to industrial workers only, or even just steelworkers (and
their appointed representatives), the indeterminately extensive notion of 'working-class areas' owes its mystifying virtues, in the sphere
of scholarly production, to the fact that, as in a psychological
projection, everyone can unconsciously manipulate its extension in
order to adjust it to their interests, prejudices or social fantasies.
Thus, when it comes to designating the speakers of 'popular speech',
there is a general tendency to think of the 'underworld', in keeping
with the idea that 'tough guys' play a determinant role in the
production and circulation of slang. Also certain to be included are
the workers who live in the old urban centres, and who are brought
almost automatically to mind by the word 'popular', while peasants
are likely to be rejected without further consideration (no doubt
because they are doomed to what the dictionaries classify as *region.*,
i.e. regional speech). But there is no question – and that is one of the
most precious functions of these catch-all notions – of whether small
shopkeepers should be excluded, and notably the *bistrot* owners,
who are undoubtedly excluded by the populist imagination even
though, in culture and in speech, they are unquestionably closer to
manual workers than to salaried employees. And it is in any case
certain that the fantasy, nourished more by the films of Carné than
by careful observation, which generally turns the folk memories of
nostalgic class fugitives towards the 'purest' and most 'authentic'
representatives of the 'people', excludes without a second thought all
immigrants, whether Spanish or Portuguese, Algerian or Moroccan,
Malian or Senegalese, who we know occupy a larger place in the
population of industrial workers than they do in the proletarian
imagination.[3]

A parallel examination of the populations which are supposed to
produce or consume what is called 'popular culture' would serve to
highlight once again the confusion in the partial coherence which
almost always underlies *implicit definitions*. In this case, the 'underworld', which was supposed to play a central role in shaping 'popular
speech', would be excluded, as would the *Lumpenproletariat*, whereas the exclusion of peasants would not be automatic, although
difficulties do arise when attempting to put peasants and workers in
the same category. In the case of 'popular art' – as an examination of
that other objectification of the 'popular', the 'Museums of Art and
Popular Culture', would show – it seems that, until recently, 'the
people' meant only peasants and rural craftsmen. And what is one to
make of 'popular medicine' and 'popular religion'? In such cases,

peasants are as indispensable as 'tough guys' are in the case of popular speech.

> In their concern to treat it like a 'language' – i.e. with all the rigour that one reserves ordinarily for the legitimate language – all those who have tried to describe or write the *pop.*, whether linguists or authors, have condemned themselves to producing artefacts which bear more or less no relation to the ordinary speech which speakers least familiar with the legitimate language employ in their internal exchanges.[4] Thus, in order to conform to the dominant dictionary model which must only record words seen to have 'a significant frequency and duration', authors of dictionaries of unconventional language rely exclusively on texts[5] and, making a selection within a selection, subject the speech forms concerned to an essential alteration, by meddling with the frequencies which make all the difference between speech forms and markets which are more or less tense.[6] Among other things, these authors forget that to write a speech form which, like that of the working classes, excludes any *literary* intention (and not transcribe or record it), one must remove oneself from the situations and even the social condition in which it is spoken, and that the interest in these 'discoveries', or even the fact of selective recollection alone, excluding everything one comes across *also* in the standard language, totally undermines the structure of frequencies.

If, notwithstanding their incoherences and uncertainties (and partly due to them), notions belonging to the family of the 'popular' are frequently used, even in scholarly discourse, it is because they are deeply embedded in the network of confused and quasi-mythical representations which social subjects create to meet the needs of an everyday knowledge of the social world. The vision of the social world, and most especially *the perception of others*, of their bodily hexis, the shape and size of their bodies, particularly the face, and also the voice, pronunciation and vocabulary, is in fact organized according to interconnected and partially independent oppositions which one can begin to grasp by examining the expressive resources deposited and preserved in language, especially in the *system of paired adjectives* employed by the users of the legitimate language to classify others and to judge their *quality*, and in which the term designating the properties ascribed to the dominant always receives a positive value.[7]

> If social science must give a privileged place to the science which examines the everyday knowledge of the social world, it is not only with a critical purpose and with a view to freeing the understanding of the social world of all the presuppositions it tends to absorb through ordinary

words and the objects they construct ('popular language', 'slang', *patois*, etc.). It is also because this practical knowledge, in opposition to which science must establish itself – and first by trying to objectify it – is an integral part of the very world which science is supposed to discover: it helps to create this world by helping to create the vision which agents may have of it and, in so doing, orienting their actions, particularly those aimed at preserving or transforming this world. Thus a rigorous science of the spontaneous sociolinguistics which agents employ to anticipate the reactions of others, and to impose the representation which they wish to give of themselves, would enable one to understand, among other things, a good part of what, in linguistic practice, is the object or the product of a conscious intervention, whether individual or collective, spontaneous or institutionalized. One example of this is all the *corrections* that speakers subject themselves to or are subjected to – in the family or at school – on the basis of a practical knowledge, partially recorded in the language itself (a 'sharp accent', a 'suburban working-class accent', etc.), and the correspondences between linguistic differences and social differences based on the more or less conscious observation of the linguistic features which are marked or remarked upon as imperfect or faulty (notably in all the books on form, on what should and should not be said), or, conversely, as valorizing and distinguished.[8]

The notion of 'popular speech' is one of the products of the application of dualistic taxonomies which structure the social world according to the categories of high and low (a 'low' form of speech), refined and coarse (coarse language) or rude (rude jokes), distinguished and vulgar, rare and common, well mannered and sloppy: in short, categories of culture and nature. (Do we not talk of *langue verte*, 'slang' or 'fruity language', and *mots crus*, language that is 'raw', as in 'raw humour'?) These are the mythical categories which introduce a decisive break in the continuum of speech forms, ignoring, for example, all the overlapping that occurs between the relaxed speech of dominant speakers (the *fam.*) and the tense speech of dominated speakers (which observers like Bauche or Frei class with *pop.*), and above all the extreme diversity of speech forms which are universally relegated to the negative category of 'popular speech'.[9]

But by a kind of paradoxical repetition, which is one of the standard effects of symbolic domination, the dominated speakers themselves, or at least certain groups among them, may apply to their own social universe principles of division (such as strong/weak, submissive; intelligent/sensitive, sensual; hard/soft, supple; straight, frank/bent, cunning, false, etc.) which reproduce within their order the fundamental structure of the system of dominant oppositions

pertaining to language.[10] This representation of the social world
retains the essence of the dominant vision by affirming the opposition between virility and docility, strength and weakness, real men,
'tough guys', 'lads', and others, like the females or effeminates who
are doomed to submission and contempt.[11] Slang, which has been
turned into the form *par excellence* of 'popular speech', is the
product of the kind of repetition which leads to the application, to
'popular speech' itself, of the principles of division which produce it.
The vague feeling that linguistic conformity implies a form of
recognition and submission which raises doubts about the virility of
men who abide by it,[12] together with the active pursuit of the
distinctive deviation which creates style, lead to a refusal to 'try too
hard'; and this in turn leads to a rejection of the most strongly
marked aspects of the dominant speech form, and especially the
most tense pronunciations or syntactic forms, as well as leading to
the pursuit of expressiveness based on the transgression of dominant
censorships – notably in matters of sexuality – and on the will to
distinguish oneself *vis-à-vis* ordinary forms of expression.[13] The
transgression of official norms, linguistic or otherwise, is, at the very
least, directed as much against the 'ordinary' dominated individuals
who submit to them, as against dominant individuals or, *a fortiori*,
against domination as such. Linguistic licence is part of the *labour of
representation* and of theatrical production which 'tough guys',
especially adolescents, must pursue in order to impose on others and
assume for themselves the image of the 'lad' who can take anything
and is ready for anything, and who refuses to give in to feelings and
to sacrifice anything to feminine sensitivity. And even if it may suit
the propensity of all dominated speakers to vulgarize distinction (i.e.
specific difference) by reducing it to the universality of the biological
sphere through irony, sarcasm or parody, nevertheless the systematic denigration of affective, moral or aesthetic values, in which
analysts have identified the deep-seated 'intention' of slang vocabulary, is above all the assertion of an aristocratic inclination.

   Regarded, even by certain dominant speakers, as the distinguished
form of 'vulgar' language, slang is the product of the pursuit of
distinction, but is consequently dominated and condemned to produce paradoxical effects which cannot be understood if one tries to
force them into the dichotomy of resistance or submission, which
governs ordinary ways of thinking about 'popular speech' (or
culture). One can perceive the effects of counter-finality inherent in
any dominated position by simply stepping outside the logic of the
mythic vision. When the dominated pursuit of distinction leads

dominated speakers to assert what distinguishes them – that is, the very thing in the name of which they are dominated and constituted as vulgar – according to a logic analogous to the kind which leads stigmatized groups to claim the stigma as the basis for their identity, should one talk of resistance? And when, conversely, they strive to shed that which marks them as vulgar, and to appropriate what would allow them to become assimilated, should one talk of submission?

To avoid the effect of the dualist mode of thought which leads to the opposition of a 'standard' language, as measure of any language, and a 'popular' language, one must return to the model of all linguistic production and rediscover in it the source of the extreme diversity of speech forms which result from the diversity of possible combinations between the different classes of linguistic habitus and markets. Among the factors which exercise a determining influence on the habitus and which appear relevant, on the one hand, in terms of the propensity to recognize and acknowledge the *censorships* which constitute dominant markets or to profit from the *obligatory freedoms* offered by certain free markets, and, on the other hand, in terms of the ability to satisfy the demands of both kinds of market, one can therefore cite the following: *sex*, a source of very different relations to different possible markets, and particularly the dominant market; *generation*, i.e. the mode of generation, through the family and especially through the school, of linguistic competence; *social position*, characterized especially in terms of the social composition of the workplace, and the socially homogeneous exchanges (with dominated individuals) or heterogeneous ones (with dominant individuals, e.g. as in the case of service staff) that it favours; *social origin*, whether rural or urban, and in the latter case, whether old or recent; and finally, *ethnic origin*.

It is clearly among men, and especially among the youngest and those who are currently and above all potentially the least integrated in the economic and social order, such as adolescents from immigrant families, that one finds the most marked rejection of the submissiveness and docility implied by the adoption of legitimate ways of speaking. The ethic of brute force which is pursued in the cult of violence and quasi-suicidal games, of bikes, alcohol or hard drugs, in which those who can expect nothing from the future assert their relation to the future, is undoubtedly just one of the ways of making a virtue of necessity. The manifestation of an unreasoning commitment to realism and cynicism, the rejection of the feeling and sensitivity identified with feminine sentimentality and effeminacy, the obligation to be tough with oneself and others which leads to the desperate daredevil acts born of the outcast's aristocratism, are a way of resigning oneself to a world with no way out, dominated by poverty and the law of the jungle, discrimination and violence, where morality and sensitivity bring no benefit whatsoever.[14] The morality which converts transgression into duty imposes a manifest resistance to official norms, linguistic or otherwise, which can only be permanently sustained at the cost of extraordinary tension and, especially for adolescents, with the constant support of the group. Like popular realism, which presupposes and matches expectations to opportunities, it constitutes a defence and survival mechanism. Those who are forced to stand outside the law to obtain the satisfactions that others obtain within it know only too well the cost of revolt. As rightly observed by Paul Willis, the poses and postures of bravado (e.g. *vis-à-vis* authority and especially the police) can co-exist with a deep-seated conformism regarding everything concerning hierarchies, and not only between the sexes; and the ostentatious toughness which human self-respect imposes in no way excludes a nostalgic yearning for the solidarity, indeed the affection, which, simultaneously gratified and repressed by the highly censored exchanges of the gang, expresses or betrays itself in moments of unself-conscious reflection.[15] Slang (and this, together with the effect of symbolic imposition, is one of the reasons why it has spread well beyond the fringes of society) constitutes *one* of the exemplary, and one might say, ideal, expressions – with which more diplomatic expressions must reckon and even compromise – of the vision, developed essentially to combat feminine (or effeminate) 'weakness' and 'submissiveness', through which the men most deprived of economic and cultural capital grasp their virile identity and perceive a social world conceived of purely in terms of toughness.[16]

One must be careful, however, not to overlook the profound transformations which borrowed words and sayings undergo, in their function and significance, when they enter into the ordinary speech of everyday exchanges: thus some of the most typical products of the aristocratic cynicism of 'tough guys' can, in their common use, function as kinds of neutralized and neutralizing conventions which allow men to speak (within the limits of a strict sense of decency) of affection, love or friendship, or, quite simply, to name loved ones, parents, son, wife (the more or less ironic use of terms of reference like 'the boss', 'the queen mother', or 'her ladyship', for example, provide a way of avoiding terms like 'my wife' or simply a first name, which are felt to be too familiar).[17]

At the other extreme in the hierarchy of dispositions towards the legitimate language, one would doubtless find the youngest and the most educated women who, though linked professionally or through marriage to the world of agents poorly endowed with economic or cultural capital, are undoubtedly sensitive to the demands of the dominant market and have the ability to respond to it which gives them something in common with the petite bourgeoisie. The effect of generation is in essence confused with the effect of changes in the mode of generation, that is, with the effect of access to the educational system, which certainly represents the most important of the differentiating factors between age groups. However, it is not certain that schooling has the homogenizing effect on linguistic competences that it endeavours to have and that one might be tempted to ascribe to it: first, because the academic norms of expression, when they are accepted, may remain limited in their application to oral and especially written academic productions; second, because the school system tends to distribute pupils in classes that are as homogeneous as possible with regard to academic criteria, and, correlatively, with regard to social criteria, so that the peer group tends to have an influence which, as one moves down the social hierarchy of institutions and sections and therefore of social origins, contradicts with increasing force the effects that may be produced by the educational process; and finally because, paradoxically, in creating durable and homogeneous groups of adolescents who have broken with the school system and, through it, with the social order, and who are placed in a situation of virtual inactivity and prolonged irresponsibility,[18] the sections to which the children from the most deprived classes are doomed – and notably the sons of immigrants, especially North African ones – have undoubtedly helped to provide the most favourable conditions for the elaboration of a kind of 'delinquent culture' which, among other manifestations, expresses itself in a speech form which has broken with the norms of the legitimate language.

No one can completely ignore the linguistic or cultural law. Every time they enter into an exchange with the holders of the legitimate competence, and especially when they find themselves in a formal situation, dominated individuals are condemned to a practical, corporeal recognition of the laws of price formation which are the least favourable to their linguistic productions and which condemns them to a more or less desperate attempt to be correct, or to *silence*. One may classify the markets by which they are confronted according to their degree of autonomy, from those most completely subjected to the dominant norms (like those which obtain in dealings with the law, medicine or the school) to those most uninhibited by these laws (like those constituted in prisons or juvenile gangs). The assertion of linguistic counter-legitimacy, and, by the same token, the production of discourse based on a more or less deliberate disregard of the conventions and proprieties of dominant markets, are only possible within the limits of *free markets*, governed by their own laws of price formation, that is, in spaces that belong to the dominated classes, haunts or refuges for excluded individuals from which dominant individuals are in fact excluded, at least symbolically, and for the accredited holders of the social and linguistic competence which is recognized on these markets. The slang of the 'underworld', as a real transgression of the fundamental principles of cultural legitimacy, constitutes an important assertion of social and cultural identity which is not only different from but opposed to it, and the vision of the world which it expresses represents the *limit* towards which (male) members of the dominated classes tend in linguistic exchanges *within the class* and, more particularly, in the most controlled and sustained of these exchanges, like those in cafés, which are completely dominated by the values of force and virility, comprising one of the rare principles of effective resistance, together with politics, against the dominant manners of speech and action.

Internal markets differ from each other according to the tension which characterizes them and, by the same token, according to the degree of censorship which they impose, and we may put forward the hypothesis that the frequency of the most affected or stylized forms (of slang) decreases in proportion to the decrease of tension in markets and the linguistic competence of speakers. This is minimal in private and familiar exchanges (first of all in exchanges within the family), where independence with regard to the norms of legitimate speech is marked above all by a more or less complete freedom to ignore the conventions and properties of the dominant speech form. And it no doubt reaches a maximum in the (more or less exclusively masculine) public exchanges which call for a veritable stylistic quest, like the verbal sparring and ostentatious attempts to outdo one another that occur in some café conversations.

In spite of the enormous simplification which it presupposes, this model brings out the extreme diversity of discourses that are created practically in the relation between the different linguistic competences which correspond to the different combinations of characteristics belonging to producers and the different classes of markets. But furthermore, it allows one to draw up a programme of methodical observation and to highlight the most significant cases which illustrate the whole range of linguistic productions of the speakers most deprived of linguistic capital: whether they are, first, the forms of discourse offered by the virtuosi on the free markets which are the most tense (i.e. public), and notably slang; second, the expressions produced for the dominant markets, i.e. for the private exchanges between dominant and dominated speakers, or for *formal* situations, and which can take either the form of speech which is embarrassed or broken through the effect of intimidation, or the form of silence, very often the only form of expression left to dominated speakers; and finally, the discourses produced for familiar and private exchanges, for example between women. These last two categories of discourse are always excluded by those who, in characterizing linguistic productions solely by the characteristics of the speakers, ought logically to include them in 'popular speech'.

The censorship effect exercised by any relatively tense market is seen in the fact that the utterances that are exchanged in the public places reserved in practice (at least at certain times) for the adult males of the lower classes, like certain cafés, are highly ritualized and subject to strict rules: one does not go to the pub only to drink, but also to participate actively in a collective pastime capable of giving the participants a feeling of freedom from daily necessities, and of producing an atmosphere of social euphoria and economic freedom which, obviously, the consumption of alcohol can only enhance. One goes there to laugh and to make others laugh, and everyone must do his best to contribute to the exchange of comments and jokes, or, at the very least, make his contribution to the fun by underlining the success of others in adding his laughter, and his shouts of approval ('Oh, What a lad!'). The possession of a talent for being 'the life and soul of the party', capable of incarnating, at the cost of a conscious and constant labour of research and accumulation, the ideal of the 'funny guy' which crowns an approved form of sociability, is a very precious form of capital. Thus a good pub landlord finds, in the mastery of the expressive conventions suitable for this market (jokes, funny stories, and puns that his central and permanent position allows him to acquire and exhibit), and also in his special knowledge of both the rules of the game and the peculiarities of each of the players (names, nicknames, habits, oddities, specialities and talents from which he can profit), the necessary resources for exciting, sustaining, and also containing, by prodding, reminding and discretely calling them to order, the exchanges capable of producing the effervescent social atmosphere which his clients come

for and to which they must themselves contribute.[19] The quality of
the conversation offered depends on the quality of the participants,
which itself depends on the quality of the conversation, therefore on
the person who is at the centre of it and who must know how to deny
the commercial relation in which he is implicated by asserting his will
and ability to enlist as an ordinary participant in the round of
exchanges – with 'the landlord's round' or games for the regulars –
and in this way contribute to the suspension of the economic
necessities and social constraints which one expects from the collective worship of the good life.[20]

One can understand why the discourse which obtains on this
market gives the appearance of total freedom and absolute natural-
ness only to those who are unaware of its rules or principles. Thus
the eloquence which, viewed from the outside, is apprehended as a
kind of unbridled zest, is in its way neither more nor less free than
the improvisations of academic eloquence; it overlooks neither the
search for effect, nor the attention to the public and its reactions, nor
the rhetorical strategies aimed at currying favour or gaining its
goodwill: it rests on tried and tested schemes of invention and
expression which are also capable, however, of giving those who do
not possess them the feeling that they are witnessing brilliant
manifestations of analytical finesse or of psychological or political
lucidity. Through the enormous redundancy tolerated by its rhetoric,
through the space it allows for the repetition of the forms and ritual
phrases which are the obligatory manifestations of 'good manners',
through the systematic resort to concrete images of a known world,
through the obsessional obstinacy it employs in reasserting – to the
point of explicitly renewing them – the fundamental values of the
group, this discourse expresses and reinforces a profoundly stable
and rigid view of the world. In this system of self-evident truths
which are untiringly reasserted and collectively guaranteed, and
which assigns an essential identity, and therefore a place and rank, to
each class of agents, the representation of the division of labour
between the sexes occupies a central position; perhaps this is
because the cult of virility, i.e. of harshness, of physical strength and
surly coarseness, established as a chosen refusal of effeminate
refinement, is one of the most effective ways of struggling against the
cultural inferiority which unites all those who feel deprived of
cultural capital, whether or not they might be rich in economic
capital, like shopkeepers.[21]

At the opposite extreme in the class of free markets, the market
for exchanges between friends, and especially between women,

stands out in that the very idea of search and effect is more or less absent from it, so that the discourse which obtains on that market differs in form, as we have noted, from that of public exchanges in cafés, etc.: it is in the logic of privation rather than rejection that this discourse is defined in relation to the legitimate discourse. As for the dominant markets, public and formal or private, they pose such difficult problems for those who are the most economically and culturally deprived that, if one limited oneself to that definition of speech forms based on the social characteristics of speakers which is implicitly adopted by the defenders of 'popular speech', one would have to say that the most frequent form of this speech is silence. In fact, the contradiction that arises from the need to confront dominant markets without capitulating to the pursuit of correctness is resolved, once again, according to the logic of the division of labour between the sexes. Since it is accepted (and above all by women, although they may pretend to deplore it) that a man is defined by the right and the duty to be true to himself, which constitutes his identity ('that's the way he is') and that he can rest content with a silence which enables him to preserve his virile dignity, it is often incumbent upon women, socially defined as pliable and submissive by nature, to make the effort necessary to confront dangerous situations, like meeting the doctor, describing symptoms and discussing the treatment with him, sorting things out with the teacher, or the social security people, etc.[22] It therefore follows that the 'mistakes' which spring from an unfortunate pursuit of correctness or a misguided desire for distinction and which, like all deformed words, especially medical ones, are mercilessly highlighted by the petits bourgeois – and the grammar books of 'popular speech' – are mostly made by women (who may be mocked by 'their' men – which is yet another way of suggesting that women 'by nature' create fuss and embarrassment).[23]

In fact, even in this case, manifestations of docility are never stripped of ambivalence and always threaten to become aggressive at the slightest snub, the merest sign of irony or haughtiness, which turns them into obligatory homages to statutory dependence. The person who, in entering into a social relationship which is too unequal, adopts too obviously the appropriate speech and manner, is liable to be constrained to think and to experience the respect which is willingly accorded to the other as obligatory submissiveness or self-interested servility. The image of the servant, who must conspicuously display his conformity to the norms of verbal propriety and proper dress, haunts all relations between those who are dominated and those who are dominant, and notably in the exchanges of services, as is shown by the virtually insoluble problems posed by the matter of 'remuneration'. That is why the ambivalence towards the dominant and their life-style, so common among men who perform service roles – who hover between the inclination to anxious conformity and the temptation to bring the dominant down a peg by using the familiarities that put them on an equal footing – undoubtedly represents the truth and the limit of the relation which the men most deprived of linguistic capital, and doomed to either coarseness or servility, maintain with the dominant mode of expression.[24] Paradoxically, it is only on occasions whose solemnity justifies them, in their eyes, in turning to the most noble register without feeling ridiculous or servile – for example, to express love or show sympathy in bereavement – that they can adopt the most conventional forms of speech, but in their minds the only suitable one for saying serious things: that is, in the very situation when the dominant norms require that one should abandon conventions and ready-made phrases in order to show the force of one's sincerity and feeling.

It thus appears that the linguistic and cultural productions of dominated individuals vary profoundly according to their inclination and their aptitude to benefit from the regulated liberties offered by free markets or to accept the constraints imposed by dominant markets. This explains why, in the polymorphous reality which one discovers by considering all the speech forms produced for all the markets by all the categories of producers, everyone who believes they have a right or a duty to speak of the 'people' can find an objective prop for their interests or fantasies.

Part II

The Social Institution of Symbolic Power

The social sciences deal with pre-named, pre-classified realities which bear proper nouns and common nouns, titles, signs and acronyms. At the risk of unwittingly assuming responsibility for the acts of constitution of whose logic and necessity they are unaware, the social sciences must take as their object of study the social operations of *naming* and the rites of institution through which they are accomplished. But on a deeper level, they must examine the part played by words in the construction of social reality and the contribution which the struggle over classifications, a dimension of all class struggles, makes to the constitution of classes – classes defined in terms of age, sex or social position, but also clans, tribes, ethnic groups or nations.

So far as the social world is concerned, the neo-Kantian theory, which gives language and, more generally, representations a specifically symbolic efficacy in the construction of reality, is perfectly justified. By structuring the perception which social agents have of the social world, the act of naming helps to establish the structure of this world, and does so all the more significantly the more widely it is recognized, i.e. authorized. There is no social agent who does not aspire, as far as his circumstances permit, to have the power to name and to create the world through naming: gossip, slander, lies, insults, commendations, criticisms, arguments and praises are all daily and petty manifestations of the solemn and collective acts of naming, be they celebrations or condemnations, which are performed by generally recognized authorities. In contrast to common nouns which have a common sense, the *consensus* or *homologein* of an entire group, and which, in short, involve the official act of naming or nomination through which a recognized delegate bestows an official title (like an academic qualification), the 'qualifying nouns' ('idiot', 'bastard') which feature in insult have a very limited symbolic efficacy, as *idios logos*, and involve only the person who offers them.[1] But what both have in common is what may be called a performative or magical intention. Insults, like naming, belong to a class of more or less socially based acts of institution and destitution through which an individual, acting in his own name or in the name of a group that is more or less important in terms of its size and social significance, indicates to someone that he possesses such and such property, and indicates to him at the time that he must conduct himself in accordance with the social essence which is thereby assigned to him.

In short, social science must include in its theory of the social world a theory of the theory effect which, by helping to impose a more or less authorized way of seeing the social world, helps to construct the reality of that world. The word or, *a fortiori*, the dictum, the proverb and all the stereotyped or ritual forms of expression are programmes of perception and different, more or less ritualized strategies for the symbolic struggles of everyday life, just like the great collective rituals of naming or nomination – or, more clearly still, the clashes between the visions and previsions of specifically political struggles – imply a certain claim to symbolic authority as the socially recognized power to impose a certain vision of the social world, i.e. of the divisions of the social world. In the struggle to impose the legitimate vision, in which science itself is inevitably caught up, agents possess power in proportion to their symbolic capital, i.e. in proportion to the recognition they receive from a group. The authority that underlies the performative efficacy of discourse is a *percipi*, a being-known, which allows a *percipere* to be imposed, or, more precisely, which allows the consensus concerning the meaning of the social world which grounds common sense to be imposed officially, i.e. in front of everyone and in the name of everyone.

The mystery of performative magic is thus resolved in the mystery of ministry (to use a pun close to the heart of medieval canonists), i.e. in the alchemy of *representation* (in the different senses of the term) through which the representative creates the group which creates him: the spokesperson endowed with the full power to speak and act on behalf of the group, and first of all to act on the group through the magic of the slogan, is the substitute for the group, which exists solely through this *procuration*. Group made man, he personifies a fictitious person, which he lifts out of the state of a simple aggregate of separate individuals, enabling them to act and speak, through him, 'like a single person'. Conversely, he receives the right to speak and act in the name of the group, to 'take himself for' the group he incarnates, to identify with the function to which 'he gives his body and soul', thus giving a biological body to a constituted body. *Status est magistratus*; 'l'Etat, c'est moi'. Or, what amounts to the same thing, the world is my representation.

3

Authorized Language

The Social Conditions for the Effectiveness of Ritual Discourse

Suppose, for example, I see a vessel on the stocks, walk up and smash the bottle hung at the stem, proclaim 'I name this ship the Mr Stalin' *and for good measure kick away the chocks: but the trouble is, I was not the person chosen to name it . . .*
                    J. L. Austin, How to do Things with Words

The naïve question of the power of words is logically implicated in the initial suppression of the question of the uses of language, and therefore of the social conditions in which words are employed. As soon as one treats language as an autonomous object, accepting the radical separation which Saussure made between internal and external linguistics, between the science of language and the science of the social uses of language, one is condemned to looking within words for the power of words, that is, looking for it where it is not to be found. In fact, the illocutionary force of expressions cannot be found in the very words, such as 'performatives', in which that force is *indicated* or, better, *represented* – in both senses of this term. It is only in exceptional cases (in the abstract and artificial situations created by experimentation) that symbolic exchanges are reduced to relations of pure communication, and that the informative content of the message exhausts the content of the communication. The power of words is nothing other than the *delegated power* of the spokesperson, and his speech – that is, the substance of his discourse and, inseparably, his way of speaking – is no more than a testimony, and one among others, of the *guarantee of delegation* which is vested in him.

This is the essence of the error which is expressed in its most accomplished form by Austin (and after him, Habermas) when he

THE NEW LITURGY OR THE MISFORTUNES OF PERFORMATIVE VIRTUE*

'I must admit that we are utterly dismayed by the encouragement being given to desert the churches in favour of celebrating the Eucharist in small communities [1], at home [2], or in chapels [2] where one helps oneself [1] to the communion wafer served on trays by lay people [1], in order to take communion wherever one finds oneself [2], etc.' (p. 47).

'You will always be able to say a prayer for your church. But what would be the meaning of such a prayer in a church deprived of the holy sacrament [2]? One might as well recite it at home' (p. 48).

'We no longer celebrate mass in our little church, we say it in somebody's home [2]' (p. 59).

'We are not lucky in the diocese of B. We are subjected to the extravagant notions of a "quartet of young priests" who last year had the idea – before abolishing it altogether – of holding the solemn first communion in the Sports Centre [2], even though we have two large and beautiful churches which had plenty of room for everyone' (p. 66).

'My mother was horrified by the chaplain at ACI, who wanted to celebrate mass over the dining room table [2]' (p. 90).

---

* All these quotations (indicated by the page numbers in round brackets) refer to the work by R. P. Lelong, *Le dossier noir de la communion solennelle* (Paris: Mame, 1972). The figures in square brackets refer to errors in the liturgy noted by the faithful: [1] error of the person presiding; [2] error in place; [3] error in time; [4] error in tempo; [5] error in behaviour; [6] error in language; [7] error in dress; [8] error in sacraments.

thinks that he has found in discourse itself – in the specifically linguistic substance of speech, as it were – the key to the efficacy of speech. By trying to understand the power of linguistic manifestations linguistically, by looking in language for the principle underlying the logic and effectiveness of the language of institution, one forgets that authority comes to language from outside, a fact concretely exemplified by the *skeptron* that, in Homer, is passed to the orator who is about to speak.[1] Language at most *represents* this authority, manifests and symbolizes it. There is a rhetoric which characterizes all discourses of institution, that is to say, the official speech of the authorized spokesperson expressing himself in a solemn situation, with an authority whose limits are identical with the extent of delegation by the institution. The stylistic features which characterize the language of priests, teachers and, more generally, all institutions, like routinization, stereotyping and neutralization, all stem from the position occupied in a competitive field by these persons entrusted with delegated authority.

It is not enough to say, as people sometimes do, in order to avoid the difficulties inherent in a purely internalist approach to language, that the use made of language in a determinate situation by a determinate speaker, with his style, rhetoric and socially marked identity, provides words with 'connotations' that are tied to a particular context, introducing into discourse that surplus of meaning which gives it its 'illocutionary force'. In fact, the use of language, the manner as much as the substance of discourse, depends on the social position of the speaker, which governs the access he can have to the language of the institution, that is, to the official, orthodox and legitimate speech. It is the access to the legitimate instruments of expression, and therefore the participation in the authority of the institution, which makes *all* the difference – irreducible to discourse as such – between the straightforward imposture of masqueraders, who disguise a performative utterance as a descriptive or constative statement,[2] and the authorized imposture of those who do the same thing with the authorization and the authority of an institution. The spokesperson is an impostor endowed with the *skeptron*.

If, as Austin observes, there are utterances whose role is not only to 'describe a state of affairs or state some fact', but also to 'execute an action', this is because the power of words resides in the fact that they are not pronounced on behalf of the person who is only the 'carrier' of these words: the authorized spokesperson is only able to use words to act on other agents and, through their action, on things

'*Tell me also what you think, Father, of a communion which, like in my parish, is performed in the morning [3] and followed by no other ceremony?' [5] 'We'll spend the day around the table, eating and drinking', a distressed mother told me (p. 72).*

'*In certain parishes near here they no longer do anything. In ours there is the profession of faith in the afternoon [3], which lasts barely an hour [4], without mass or communion [5], and the children go to mass the following day [3]' (p. 87).*

'*What is one to make of the attitude of certain priests (all priests in some parishes – it must be contagious) who make no gesture of respect [5], either by genuflecting or a slight bow, when they are taking or returning the holy sacraments to the tabernacle?' (p. 82).*

'*In the past one used to say: "Let us not fall into temptation", but now one says [6]: "Submit us not" or "Lead us not into temptation". It's monstrous. I've never been able to make myself say it' (p. 50).*

'*It was remarkable to hear, in an ancient Gothic church, the formal version of "Hail Mary" ("Je vous salue Marie") employed with a much more familiar form of address "Hello, Mary" ("J'te salue Marie"). This familiarity [6] does not match the spirit of our French language' (p. 86).*

'*On returning, after two days of "retreat" [6], solemn communion was reduced to a profession of faith at five o'clock [3] one Saturday evening [3], in everyday dress [7] (without mass [5] and without communion). "Private" communion is already nothing more than a piece of bread [8] and ... no confession [5]!' (p. 87).*

'*But I suggest that, with regard to "standing" [5], you must make a particular reference to those who receive the Eucharist as if they are in a hurry [4], which is quite shocking' (p. 49).*

themselves, because his speech concentrates within it the accumulated symbolic capital of the group which has delegated him and of which he is the *authorized representative*. The laws of social physics are only apparently independent of the laws of physics, and the power which certain *slogans* have to secure efforts from others without expending effort themselves – which is the very aim of magical action[3] – is rooted in the capital which the group has accumulated through its effort and whose effective use is subordinated to a whole set of conditions, those which define the *rituals of social magic*. Most of the conditions that have to be fulfilled in order for a performative utterance to succeed come down to the question of the appropriateness of the speaker – or, better still, his social function – and of the discourse he utters. A performative utterance is destined to fail each time that it is not pronounced by a person who has the 'power' to pronounce it, or, more generally, each time that the 'particular persons and circumstances in a given case' are not 'appropriate for the invocation of the particular procedure invoked';[4] in short, each time that the speaker does not have the authority to emit the words that he utters. But perhaps the most important thing to remember is that the success of these operations of social magic – comprised by *acts of authority*, or, what amounts to the same thing, *authorized acts* – is dependent on the combination of a systematic set of interdependent conditions which constitute social rituals.

It is clear that all the efforts to find, in the specifically linguistic logic of different forms of argumentation, rhetoric and style, the source of their symbolic efficacy are destined to fail as long as they do not establish the relationship between the properties of discourses, the properties of the person who pronounces them and the properties of the institution which authorizes him to pronounce them. The limits (and the interest) of Austin's attempt to define performative utterances lie in the fact that he does not exactly do what he thinks he is doing, and this prevents him from following it through to the end. Believing that he was contributing to the philosophy of language, he was in fact working out a theory of a particular class of symbolic expressions, of which the discourse of authority is only the paradigmatic form, and whose specific efficacy stems from the fact that they seem to possess *in themselves* the source of a power which in reality resides in the institutional conditions of their production and reception.

The specificity of the discourse of authority (e.g. a lecture, sermon, etc.) consists in the fact that it is not enough for it to be

'There is no warning, the vicar trots along at any time
[3], everything is done all at once, the wafer comes out of
a pocket [5] and off we go! We count ourselves lucky
when it isn't some lay person [1] who arrives with the
holy sacrament in a powder compact [8] or a cheap gilt
pill box [8]' (p. 120).

'He has deliberately adopted the following method of
communion: the worshippers stand in a semi-circle
behind the altar and the tray containing the holy sacraments is handed around. Then the priest himself offers
the chalice (every Sunday – I thought that the Holy
Father had made an exception for that). Feeling incapable of helping myself to the sacraments [5] ("God bless
those who touch the Saviour's sacred vessels" . . . But
what about the Saviour himself? . . .), I had to negotiate
and argue in order to have the eucharist offered up to my
lips in the traditional way [5]' (pp. 62–3).

'This winter, recovering from illness and having been
deprived of Holy Communion for several weeks, I went
to a chapel to celebrate mass. I found myself being
refused [5] Holy Communion because I wouldn't help
myself to the sacrament [5] and drink from the chalice
[5]' (p. 91).

'The grandfather of the girl being confirmed was
horrified by the size of the wafers [8]; each one "could
have been a complete snack"' (p. 82).

'I found myself in a church where the priest who was
celebrating mass had invited along pop musicians [1]. I
don't understand music, I think they were playing very
well, but in my humble opinion this kind of music wasn't
conducive to prayer' (pp. 58–9).

'This year our confirmation candidates had neither
book nor rosary [8], but a sheet of paper on which some
hymns, which they didn't even know, were written, and
which were sung by a group of amateurs [1]' (p. 79).

understood (in certain cases it may even fail to be understood without losing its power), and that it exercises its specific effect only when it is *recognized* as such. This recognition – whether accompanied by understanding or not – is granted, in the manner of something taken for granted, only under certain conditions, namely, those which define legitimate usage: it must be uttered by the person legitimately licensed to do so, the holder of the *skeptron*, known and recognized as being able and enabled to produce this particular class of discourse: a priest, a teacher, a poet, etc.; it must be uttered in a legitimate situation, that is, in front of legitimate receivers (one cannot read a piece of Dadaist poetry at a Cabinet meeting); finally, it must be enunciated according to the legitimate forms (syntactic, phonetic, etc.). What one might call the *liturgical* conditions, namely, the set of prescriptions which govern the *form* of the public manifestation of authority, like ceremonial etiquette, the code of gestures and officially prescribed rites, are clearly only an *element*, albeit the most visible one, in a system of conditions of which the most important and indispensable are those which produce the disposition towards recognition in the sense of misrecognition and belief, that is, the delegation of authority which confers its authority on authorized discourse. By focusing exclusively on the formal conditions for the effectiveness of ritual, one overlooks the fact that the ritual conditions that must be fulfilled in order for ritual to function and for the sacrament to be both *valid* and *effective* are never sufficient as long as the conditions which produce the recognition of this ritual are not met: the language of authority never governs without the collaboration of those it governs, without the help of the social mechanisms capable of producing this complicity, based on misrecognition, which is the basis of all authority. In order to gauge the magnitude of the error in Austin's and all other strictly formalist analyses of symbolic systems, it suffices to show that the language of authority is only the limiting case of the legitimate language, whose authority does not reside, as the racism of social class would have it, in the set of prosodic and articulatory variations which define distinguished pronunciation, or in the complexity of the syntax or the richness of the vocabulary, in other words in the intrinsic properties of discourse itself, but rather in the social conditions of production and reproduction of the distribution between the classes of the knowledge and recognition of the legitimate language.

These analyses find quasi-experimental verification in the concomitant occurrence of the crisis in institutionalized religion and the

'I would therefore add a plea in favour of the sacraments [8] that we relinquish so cheaply (holy water in the church entrance, consecrated branches of box trees on Palm Sundays, which they are beginning to do away with . . .), devotions to the Sacred Heart (more or less killed off), to the Holy Virgin, the "graves" on Maundy Thursday, difficult – indeed impossible – to reconcile with the evening service; the Gregorian chants, of course, with the many admirable texts of which we are now deprived; even the Rogations of yesteryear, etc.' (p. 60).

'Very recently, in a religious house where young people from all over France with a "priestly ambition" were gathered, the priest used neither ornaments nor sacred vessels [8] to celebrate mass. Dressed in civilian clothes [7], he used an ordinary table [2], ordinary bread and wine [8], and ordinary utensils [8]' (p. 183).

'We have seen such disconcerting masses on television . . . verging on sacrilege (little tables used at Lille, Holy (?) Communion offered by women [1] with baskets [8], jazz [5], etc.) that from now on I will abstain from following these incredible ceremonies!' (p. 158).

'Women [1] read epistles from the pulpit publicly, there are very few or no children in the choir [1], and women even offer communion [1], like at Alençon' (p. 44).

'. . . that is when the sacraments aren't given out like lollipops by laymen [1], in parishes where there is more likely to be a plethora than a penury of vicars' (p. 49).

'When the time came for communion, a woman [1] emerged from the ranks, took the chalice and offered the communion wine [8] to the assistants' (p. 182).

crisis in the ritual discourse which it upheld and which upheld it. Austin's analysis of the conditions of validity and efficacy of performative utterances seems very bland and thin, in its purely formal ingenuity, when one compares it with the real analysis and criticism which, occasioned by the crisis in the Church, separates out the components of religious ritual – agents, instruments, moments, places, etc. – which hitherto had been inseparably united in a system as coherent and as uniform as the institution responsible for its production and its reproduction. What emerges from the indignant enumeration of all the infringements of the traditional liturgy is a picture – a kind of photographic negative – of the set of institutional conditions which must be fulfilled in order for ritual discourse to be *recognized*, i.e. received and accepted as such. For ritual to function and operate it must first of all present itself and be perceived as legitimate, with stereotyped symbols serving precisely to show that the agent does not act in his own name and on his own authority, but in his capacity as a delegate. 'Two years ago an old lady who was a neighbour of mine lay dying, and asked me to fetch the priest. He arrived but without being able to give communion, and, after administering the last rites, kissed her. If, in my last moments on earth, I ask for a priest, it isn't so that he can kiss me, but so that he can bring me what I need to make the journey to eternity. That kiss was an act of paternalism and not of the sacred Ministry.' Ritual symbolism is not effective on its own, but only in so far as it *represents* – in the theatrical sense of the term – the delegation. Rigorous observance of the code of the uniform liturgy, which governs the sacramental gestures and words, constitutes both the manifestation and the counterpart of the contract of delegation, which makes the priest the holder of 'a monopoly in the manipulation of the goods of salvation'. Conversely, the abdication of the symbolic attributes of authority, like the cassock, Latin, and consecrated objects and places, highlights a break with the ancient contract of delegation which united a priest with the faithful through the intermediary of the Church. The indignation of the faithful underlines the fact that the conditions which render ritual effective can be brought together only by an institution which is invested with the power to control its manipulation. What is at stake in the crisis of the liturgy is the whole system of conditions which must be fulfilled in order for the institution to function, i.e. the institution which authorizes and regulates the use of the liturgy and which ensures its uniformity through time and space by ensuring the conformity of those who are delegated to carry it out. The crisis over language thus points to the crisis in the mechanisms which ensured the production of legitimate senders and receivers. The outraged faithful are not wrong when they associate the anarchic diversification of ritual with a crisis in the religious institution: 'Every parish priest has become a little pope or a little bishop, and the faithful are in disarray. Some worshippers, faced with this torrent of changes, no longer believe that the church is solid and that it posseses the truth.'[5] The diversification of the liturgy, which is the most obvious manifestation of the redefinition of the contract of delegation uniting the priest and the Church and, through it, the priest and the faithful, is experienced in such a dramatic way by a large body of worshippers and priests only because they reveal the transformation of the relations of power within the Church (in particular, between the high and the common clergy), which is linked to a transformation of the social conditions for the reproduction of the priesthood (a crisis of priestly 'calling') and of the lay public ('dechristianization').

The crisis over the liturgy points to the crisis in the priesthood (and the whole clerical field), which itself points to a general crisis of religious belief. It reveals, through a kind of quasi-experimental dismantling, the 'conditions of felicity' which allow a set of agents engaged in a rite to accomplish it *felicitously*; it also shows retrospectively that this objective and subjective felicity is based on a total lack of awareness of these conditions, a lack of awareness which, in so far as it defines the doxic relation to social rituals, constitutes the most indispensable condition for their effective accomplishment. The performative magic of ritual functions fully only as long as the religious official who is responsible for carrying it out in the name of the group acts as a kind of *medium* between the group and itself: it is the group which, through its intermediary, exercises on itself the magical efficacy contained in the performative utterance.

The symbolic efficacy of words is exercised only in so far as the person subjected to it recognizes the person who exercises it as authorized to do so, or, what amounts to the same thing, only in so far as he fails to realize that, in submitting to it, he himself has contributed, through his recognition, to its establishment. It rests entirely on the belief which is the foundation of the social fiction called ministry, and which goes much deeper than the beliefs and the mysteries which the ministry preaches and guarantees.[6] That is why the crisis of religious language and its performative efficacy is not limited, as is often believed, to the collapse of a world of representations: it is part of the disintegration of an entire universe of social relations of which it was constitutive.

4

Rites of Institution

With the notion of rites of passage, Arnold Van Gennep *named*, indeed described a social phenomenon of great importance. I do not believe that he did much more and neither did those who, like Victor Turner, have taken up his theory and offered a more explicit and more systematic description of the phases of *ritual*. In fact, it seems to me that in order to develop the theory of rites of passage any further, one has to ask the questions that this theory does not raise, and in particular those regarding the *social* function of ritual and the social significance of the boundaries or limits which the ritual allows one to pass over or transgress in a lawful way. One can ask oneself whether, by stressing the temporal transition – e.g. from childhood to adulthood – this theory does not conceal one of the essential effects of rites, namely that of separating those who have undergone it, not from those who have not yet undergone it, but from those who will not undergo it in any sense, and thereby instituting a lasting difference between those to whom the rite pertains and those to whom it does not pertain. That is why, rather than describing them as rites of passage, I would prefer to call them rites of consecration, or rites of legitimation, or, quite simply, *rites of institution* – giving this word the active sense it has, for example, in expressions like *'institution d'un héritier'* ('appointing an heir'). Why substitute one word for another in this way? I would quote Poincaré, who defined mathematical generalization as 'the art of giving the same name to different things', and who insisted on the decisive importance of the choice of words: as he used to say, when the language has been well chosen, then what has been shown with regard to a known object can be applied to all sorts of new objects. The analyses which I shall put forward are produced by generalizing from the results of an analysis of the ways in which elite schools function.[1] In a somewhat risky exercise, I will endeavour to bring out the invariant properties of social rituals understood as rites of institution.

To speak of rites of institution is to suggest that all rites tend to consecrate or legitimate an *arbitrary boundary*, by fostering a misrecognition of the arbitrary nature of the limit and encouraging a recognition of it as legitimate; or, what amounts to the same thing, they tend to involve a solemn transgression, i.e. one conducted in a lawful and extra-ordinary way, of the limits which constitute the social and mental order which rites are designed to safeguard at all costs – like the division between the sexes with regard to the rituals of marriage. By solemnly marking the passage over a line which establishes a fundamental division in the social order, rites draw the attention of the observer to the passage (whence the expression 'rites of passage'), whereas the important thing is the line. What, in effect, does this line separate? Obviously, it separates a before and an after: the uncircumcised child and the circumcised child; or even the whole set of uncircumcised children and the set of circumcised adults. In fact, the most important division, and one which passes unnoticed, is the division it creates between all those who are subject to circumcision, boys and men, children or adult, and those who are not subject to it, i.e. girls and women. There is thus a hidden set of individuals in relation to which the instituted group is defined. The most important effect of the rite is the one which attracts the least attention: by treating men and women differently, the rite *consecrates* the difference, institutes it, while at the same time instituting man as man, i.e. circumcised, and woman as woman, i.e. not subject to this ritual operation. An analysis of the Kabyle ritual illustrates this clearly: circumcision separates the young boy not so much from his childhood, or from boys still in childhood, but from women and the feminine world, i.e. from the mother and from everything that is associated with her – humidity, greenness, rawness, spring, milk, blandness, etc. One can see in passing that, as the process of institution consists of assigning properties of a *social* nature in a way that makes them seem like properties of natural nature, the rite of institution tends logically, as Pierre Centilivres and Luc de Heusch have observed, to integrate specifically social oppositions, such as masculine/feminine, into series of cosmological oppositions – with relations like: man is to women as the sun is to the moon – which represents a very effective way of naturalizing them. Thus sexually differentiated rites consecrate the difference between the sexes: they constitute a simple difference of fact as a legitimate distinction, as an institution. The separation accomplished in the ritual (which itself effects a separation) exercises an effect of consecration.

But do we really know what it means to consecrate, and particularly to consecrate a difference? How is what I would call the 'magical' consecration of a difference achieved, and what are its technical effects? Does the fact of socially instituting, through an act of *constitution*, a pre-existing difference – like the one separating the sexes – have only symbolic effects, in the sense that we give to this term when we speak of the symbolic gift, in other words, no effects at all? There is a Latin expression that means 'you're teaching fish to swim'. That is exactly what the ritual of institution does. It says: this man is a man – implying that he is a real man, which is not always immediately obvious. It tends to make the smallest, weakest, in short, the most effeminate man into a truly manly man, separated by a difference in nature and essence from the most masculine woman, the tallest, strongest woman, etc. To institute, in this case, is to consecrate, that is, to sanction and sanctify a particular state of things, an established order, in exactly the same way that a *constitution* does in the legal and political sense of the term. An *investiture* (of a knight, Deputy, President of the Republic, etc.) consists of sanctioning and sanctifying a difference (pre-existent or not) by making it *known* and *recognized*; it consists of making it exist as a social difference, known and recognized as such by the agent invested and everyone else.

In short, if it wishes to understand the most fundamental social phenomena, which occur as much in pre-capitalist societies as in our own world (degrees are just as much a part of magic as are amulets), social science must take account of the symbolic efficacy of rites of institution, that is, the power they possess to act on reality by acting on its representation. The process of investiture, for example, exercises a symbolic efficacy that is quite real in that it really transforms the person consecrated: first, because it transforms the representations others have of him and above all the behaviour they adopt towards him (the most visible changes being the fact that he is given titles of respect and the respect actually associated with these enunciations); and second, because it simultaneously transforms the representation that the invested person has of himself, and the behaviour he feels obliged to adopt in order to conform to that representation. By the same logic, one can understand the effect of all social titles of credit and credence – of *credentials* – which, like aristocratic titles and academic qualifications, increase in a durable way the value of their bearer by increasing the extent and the intensity of the belief in their value.

The act of institution is an act of social magic that can create difference *ex nihilo*, or else (as is more often the case) by exploiting as it were pre-existing differences, like the biological differences between the sexes or, as in the case of the institution of an heir on the basis of primogeniture, the difference in age. In this sense, as with religion according to Durkheim, it is a 'well-founded delusion', a symbolic imposition but *cum fundamento in re*. The distinctions that are the most efficacious socially are those which give the appearance of being based on objective differences (I think, for example, of the notion of 'natural boundary' in geography). None the less, as is very clear in the case of social classes, we are always dealing with continua, with continuous distributions, due to the fact that different principles of differentiation produce different divisions that are never completely congruent. However, social magic always manages to produce discontinuity out of continuity. The paradigmatic example of this, and my starting point, is the competitive academic examination (*concours*): between the last person to pass and the first person to fail, the competitive examination creates differences of all or nothing that can last a lifetime. The former will graduate from an elite institution like the *Ecole Polytechnique* and enjoy all the associated advantages and perks, while the latter will become a nobody.

None of the criteria that one can use to justify technically the distinction (understood as legitimate difference) of the nobility fits perfectly. For example, the poorest nobleman-fencer remains noble (even if his image is subsequently tarnished, to a degree that varies according to national traditions and historical periods); conversely, the best commoner-fencer remains common (even if he is able to draw a form of 'nobility' from his excellence at a typically noble practice). And the same holds for every criterion defining the nobility at any given moment in time: bearing, elegance and so on. The institution of an identity, which can be a title of nobility or a stigma ('you're nothing but a . . .'), is the imposition of a name, i.e. of a social essence. To institute, to assign an essence, a competence, is to impose a right to be that is an obligation of being so (or to be so). It is to *signify* to someone what he is and how he should conduct himself as a consequence. In this case, the indicative is an imperative. The code of honour is only a developed form of the expression that says of a man: 'he's a man's man'. To institute, to give a social definition, an identity, is also to impose *boundaries*. Thus *noblesse oblige* might translate Plato's *ta heautou prattein*, acting in keeping with one's essence and nothing else, which, in the case of a nobleman, means acting in keeping with one's rank and refusing to demean oneself. It behoves the noble to behave nobly, and the source of nobility is just as clear in a noble act as the source of noble actions is in nobility itself. I read the following this morning in the newspaper: 'It behoved Mr Kurt Furgler, the President of the Confederation, to express, on Tuesday evening, the condolences of the Federal Council to the Egyptian people after the death of president Anwar Sadat.' The authorized spokesperson is the one whom it behoves and on whom it is incumbent to speak on behalf of the collectivity. It is both his privilege and his duty, his proper function, in a word, his competence (in the legal sense of the term). Social essence is the set of those social attributes and attributions produced by the act of institution as a solemn act of categorization which tends to produce what it designates.

The act of institution is thus an act of communication, but of a particular kind: it *signifies* to someone what his identity is, but in a way that both expresses it to him and imposes it on him by expressing it in front of everyone (*kategorein*, meaning originally, to accuse publicly) and thus informing him in an authoritative manner of what he is and what he must be. This is clearly evident in the insult, a kind of curse (*sacer* also signifies cursed) which attempts to imprison its victim in an accusation which also depicts his destiny. But this is even truer of an investiture or an act of naming, a specifically social judgement of attribution which assigns to the person involved everything that is inscribed in a social definition. It is through the effect of statutory assignation (*noblesse oblige*) that the ritual of institution produces its most 'real' effects: the person instituted feels obliged to comply with his definition, with the status of his function. The designated heir (according to a more or less arbitrary criterion) is recognized and treated as such by the whole group, beginning with his family, and this different and distinctive treatment can only encourage him to fulfil his essence, to live in conformity with his social essence. The sociology of science has shown that the greatest scientific successes are achieved by researchers who come from the most prestigious academic institutions. This is largely explained by the high level of subjective aspirations determined by the collective (i.e. objective) recognition of these aspirations and their assignation to a class of agents (men, students in elite institutions, established writers, etc.) to whom these aspirations are not only accorded and recognized as rights or privileges (in contrast to the pretentious pretensions of pretenders), but assigned, imposed, like duties, through emphasis, encouragement and incessant calls to order. I think of the cartoon by Schulz which shows Snoopy perched on the roof of his kennel saying: 'How can one be modest when one is the best?' One would have to say simply: when it is common knowledge – which is the effect of officialization – that one is the best, *aristos*.

'Become what you are': that is the principle behind the performative magic of all acts of institution. The essence assigned through naming and investiture is, literally, a *fatum* (this is also and especially true of *injunctions*, sometimes tacit and sometimes explicit, which members of the family group address continually to the young child, varying in intention and intensity according to social class and, within the latter, according to sex and rank within the kinship unit). All social destinies, positive or negative, by consecration or stigma, are equally *fatal* – by which I mean mortal – because they enclose those whom they characterize within the limits that are assigned to them and that they are made to recognize. The self-respecting heir will behave like an heir and, according to Marx's expression, will be inherited by the heritage: that is, invested in the things and appropriated by the things which he has himself appropriated. This, of course, is barring accidents. There are exceptions: the unworthy heir, the priest who abandons his calling, the nobleman who demeans himself and the bourgeois who turns common. Nevertheless, the limit, the sacred boundary remains clear. Owen Lattimore used to say that the Great Wall of China was meant not only to stop foreigners entering China but also to stop Chinese leaving it. That is also the function of all magical boundaries (whether the boundary between masculine and feminine, or between those selected and those rejected by the educational system): to stop those who are inside, on the right side of the line, from leaving, demeaning or down-grading themselves. Pareto used to say that elites are destined to 'waste away' when they cease to believe in themselves, when they lose their morale and their morality, and begin to cross the line in the wrong direction. This is also one of the functions of the act of institution: to discourage permanently any attempt to cross the line, to transgress, desert, or *quit*.

All aristocracies must expend considerable energy to convince the elect of the need to accept the sacrifices that are implied by privilege, or by the acquisition of durable dispositions which are a condition for the preservation of privilege. When the party of the dominant is the party of culture, i.e. almost invariably the party of asceticism, of tension and contention, the work of institution must reckon with the temptation presented by nature, or by the counter-culture. (I would like to add in parenthesis that, in speaking of the work of institution and by making the more or less painful inculcation of durable dispositions an essential component of the social action of institution, I have merely tried to attribute to the word 'institution' its full significance. Having stressed, with Poincaré, the importance of the choice of words, it may be useful to suggest that one has only to assemble the different senses of *instituere* and of *institutio* to form an idea of an inaugural act of constitution, of foundation, indeed of the invention which, through education, leads to durable dispositions, habits and usages.) The universally adopted strategy for effectively denouncing the temptation to demean oneself is to naturalize difference, to turn it into a second nature through inculcation and incorporation in the form of the habitus. This explains the role given to ascetic practices, even physical suffering, in all the negative rites which are destined, as Durkheim said, to produce people who are out of the ordinary, in a word, distinguished. It also explains the role of the training which is universally imposed on the future members of the 'elite' (the learning of dead languages, the experience of prolonged isolation, etc.). All groups entrust the body, treated like a kind of memory, with their most precious possessions, and the use made of the suffering inflicted on the body by rites of initiation in all societies is understandable if one realizes, as numerous psychological experiments have shown, that people's adherence to an institution is directly proportional to the severity and painfulness of the rites of initiation. The work of inculcation through which the lasting imposition of the arbitrary limit is achieved can seek to naturalize the decisive breaks that constitute an arbitrary cultural limit – those expressed in fundamental oppositions like masculine/feminine, etc. – in the form of a *sense of limits*, which inclines some people to maintain their rank and distance and others to know their place and be happy with what they are, to be what they have to be, thus depriving them of the very sense of deprivation. It can also tend to inculcate durable dispositions like class tastes which, being the principle behind the 'choice' of outward signs expressing social position, like clothes, but also bodily hexis or language, make all social agents the carriers of distinctive signs, of which the signs of distinction are but a sub-class, capable of uniting and separating people as surely as explicit prohibitions and barriers – I am thinking here of class endogamy. More convincingly than the external signs which adorn the body (like decorations, uniforms, army stripes, insignia, etc.), the incorporated signs (such as manners, ways of speaking – accents –, ways of walking or standing – gait, posture, bearing –, table manners, etc. and taste) which underlie the production of all practices aimed, intentionally or not, both at signifying and at signifying social position through the interplay of distinctive differences, are destined to function as so many calls to order, by virtue of which those who might have forgotten (or forgotten themselves) are reminded of the position assigned to them by the institution.

The power of the categorical judgement of attribution, realized through the institution, is so great that it is capable of resisting all practical refutations. Kantorowicz's analysis of the king's two bodies is a familiar one: the invested king outlives the biological king, who is mortal, prone to illness, imbecility or death. Similarly, if the student at an elite institution like the *Ecole Polytechnique* shows that he is useless at mathematics, it will be assumed that he is doing it on purpose or that he has invested his intellectual energies in other, more important things. But what best illustrates the autonomy of *ascription* in relation to *achievement* (one can, for once, refer to Talcott Parsons), of social being in relation to doing, is undoubtedly the possibility of resorting to the strategies of condescension which allow one to push the denial of social definition to the limit while still being perceived through it. Strategies of condescension are those symbolic transgressions of limits which provide, at one and the same time, the benefits that result from conformity to a social definition and the benefits that result from transgression. An example would be the aristocrat who patted his coachman on the arse and of whom they would have said, 'He's a straightforward chap,' meaning straightforward for an aristocrat, i.e. for a man who is essentially superior, and whose essence did not in principle entail that kind of behaviour.

It is, in fact, not that simple, and one would have to introduce a distinction: in one of his works Schopenhauer spoke of the 'pedantically comical', that is, of the laughter provoked by a character when he produces an action that is not inscribed within the limits of the concept which defines him – in the manner, remarked Schopenhauer, of a stage horse which begins to leave droppings on the stage. And he referred to professors, particularly German professors, like Unrat in *The Blue Angel*, who are conceived within limits that are so powerfully and narrowly defined that their transgression becomes very obvious. Unlike Professor Unrat who, carried away by passion, loses any sense of the ridiculous or – what amounts to the same thing – any sense of dignity, the condescending and consecrated person chooses deliberately to transgress the boundary; he enjoys the privilege of privileges, that which consists of taking liberties with his privilege. That is why, with regard to speech, the bourgeois and especially the intellectual can permit themselves forms of hypo-correction, and of the relaxation of tension, that are forbidden to petits-bourgeois individuals, who are condemned to hyper-correction. In short, one of the privileges of consecration consists in the fact that, by conferring an undeniable and indelible essence on the individuals consecrated, it authorizes transgressions that would otherwise be forbidden. The person who is sure of his cultural identity can play with the rules of the cultural game; he can confess that he likes Tchaikovsky or Gershwin, and even have the 'nerve' to say that he likes Charles Aznavour or 'B' movies.

Acts of social magic as diverse as marriage or circumcision, the attribution of titles or degrees, the conferring of knighthoods, the appointment to offices, posts or honours, the attribution of a quality label, or the corroboration by a signature or initials, are all acts which can only succeed if the institution – meaning to institute in an active way someone or something endowed with this or that status or property – is guaranteed by the whole group or by a recognized institution. Even when the act is accomplished by a sole agent duly empowered to accomplish it and to do so within the recognized forms (that is, according to the conventions regarded as appropriate concerning time, place, means, etc., the whole set of which constitutes correct, i.e. socially valid and therefore efficient ritual), it rests fundamentally on the belief of an entire group (which may be physically present), that is, on the socially fashioned dispositions to know and recognize the institutional conditions of a valid ritual. (And this implies that the symbolic efficacy of the ritual will vary – simultaneously or successively – according to the degree to which the people for whom the ritual is performed are more or less prepared, or more or less disposed, to receive it.)

This is what is forgotten by linguists who, following Austin, look in words themselves for the 'illocutionary force' which they sometimes possess as performative utterances. In contrast to the impostor who is not what he appears to be, who, in other words, usurps the name, title, rights and honours of another person, in contrast also to the mere 'stand-in', the trainee or substitute who plays the part of the teacher or headmaster without having the qualifications, the legitimate representative (e.g. the authorized spokesperson) is an object of guaranteed belief, certified as correct. He lives up in reality to his appearance, he really is what everyone believes him to be because his reality – whether priest, teacher or minister – is based not on his personal conviction or pretension (always liable to be rebuffed and snubbed: What's his game? Who does he think he is? etc.) but rather on the collective belief, guaranteed by the institution and made concrete through qualifications and symbols like stripes, uniforms and other attributes. The marks of respect, such as those which consist in addressing people by their titles (Mr President, Your Excellency, etc.), are so many repetitions of the inaugural act of institution carried out by a universally recognized authority and therefore based on the *consensus omnium*. They are valid as oaths of allegiance, proofs of recognition regarding the particular person to whom they are addressed, but above all regarding the institution which instituted him (that is why the respect for forms and the forms of respect that define politeness are so profoundly political). The belief of everyone, which pre-exists ritual, is the condition for the effectiveness of ritual. One only preaches to the converted. And the miracle of symbolic efficacy disappears if one sees that the magic of words merely releases the 'springs' – the dispositions – which are wound up beforehand.

I would like to conclude by posing a final question which, I fear, may seem somewhat metaphysical: could rites of institution, whichever they may be, exercise their power (I think of the most obvious example, what Napoleon used to call 'baubles', i.e. decorations and other distinctions) if they were not capable of giving at least the appearance of a meaning, a purpose, to those beings without a purpose who constitute humanity, of giving them the feeling of having a role or, quite simply, some importance, and thus tearing them from the clutches of insignificance? The veritable miracle produced by acts of institution lies undoubtedly in the fact that they manage to make consecrated individuals believe that their existence is justified, that their existence serves some purpose. But, through a kind of curse, because of the essentially diacritical, differential and distinctive nature of symbolic power, the rise of the distinguished class to Being has, as an inevitable counterpart, the slide of the complementary class into Nothingness or the lowest Being.

5

Description and Prescription

The Conditions of Possibility and the Limits of Political Effectiveness

Specifically political action is possible because agents, who are part of the social world, have a (more or less adequate) knowledge of this world and because one can act on the social world by acting on their knowledge of this world. This action aims to produce and impose representations (mental, verbal, visual or theatrical) of the social world which may be capable of acting on this world by acting on agents' representation of it. Or, more precisely, it aims to make or unmake groups – and, by the same token, the collective actions they can undertake to transform the social world in accordance with their interests – by producing, reproducing or destroying the representations that make groups visible for themselves and for others.

As an object of knowledge for the agents who inhabit it, the economic and social world exerts a force upon them not in the form of a mechanical determination, but in the form of a knowledge effect. It is clear that, at least in the case of dominated individuals, this effect does not tend to favour political action. We know that the social order owes some measure of its permanence to the fact that it imposes schemes of classification which, being adjusted to objective classifications, produce a form of recognition of this order, the kind implied by the misrecognition of the arbitrariness of its foundations: the correspondence between objective divisions and classificatory schemes, between objective structures and mental structures, under-lies a kind of original adherence to the established order. Politics begins, strictly speaking, with the denunciation of this tacit contract of adherence to the established order which defines the original doxa; in other words, political subversion presupposes cognitive subversion, a conversion of the vision of the world.

But the heretical break with the established order, and with the dispositions and representations engendered by it among the agents moulded according to its structures, itself presupposes a conjuncture of critical discourse and an objective crisis, capable of disrupting the close correspondence between the incorporated structures and the objective structures which produce them, and of instituting a kind of practical *épochè*, a suspension of the initial adherence to the established order.

Heretical subversion exploits the possibility of changing the social world by changing the representation of this world which contributes to its reality or, more precisely, by counterposing a *paradoxical pre-vision*, a utopia, a project or programme, to the ordinary vision which apprehends the social world as a natural world: the *performative* utterance, the political pre-vision, is in itself a pre-diction which aims to bring about what it utters. It contributes practically to the reality of what it announces by the fact of uttering it, of pre-dicting it and making it pre-dicted, of making it conceivable and above all credible and thus creating the collective representation and will which contribute to its production. Every theory, as the word itself suggests, is a programme of perception, but this is all the more true of theories about the social world. And there are, no doubt, relatively few cases in which the structuring power of words, their capacity to prescribe while seeming to describe and to denounce while seeming to enunciate, is so clear. Many 'intellectual debates' are less unrealistic than they seem if one is aware of the degree to which one can modify social reality by modifying the agents' representation of it. One can see the extent to which the social reality of something like alcoholism (and one could say the same of abortion, drug abuse or euthanasia) changes according to whether it is perceived and thought of as a hereditary weakness, a moral failure, a cultural tradition or a way of compensating for something. A word like *paternalism* wreaks havoc by throwing suspicion on everything which, by a permanent denial of self-interest, transforms the relation of domination into an enchanted relation. Like hierarchical relations organized according to the model of enchanted relations, of which the domestic group is the site *par excellence*, all forms of symbolic capital – prestige, charisma, charm – and the relations of exchange through which this capital accumulates – the exchange of services, gifts, attention, care, affection – are particularly vulnerable to the destructive effect of words which expose and disenchant. But the constitutive power of (religious or political) language, and of the schemes of perception and thought which it procures, is never clearer than in situations of crisis: these *paradoxical* and *extra-ordinary* situations call for an extra-ordinary kind of discourse, capable of raising the practical principles of an ethos to the level of explicit principles which generate (quasi-) systematic responses, and of expressing all the unheard-of and ineffable characteristics of the situation created by the crisis.

Heretical discourse must not only help to sever the adherence to the world of common sense by publicly proclaiming a break with the ordinary order, it must also produce a new common sense and integrate within it the previously tacit or repressed practices and experiences of an entire group, investing them with the legitimacy conferred by public expression and collective recognition. Indeed, since every language that makes itself heard by an entire group is an authorized language, invested with the authority of this group, it authorizes what it designates at the same time as it expresses it, drawing its legitimacy from the group over which it exercises its authority and which it helps to produce as such by offering it a unitary expression of its experiences. The efficacy of heretical discourse does not reside in the magic of a force immanent to language, such as Austin's 'illocutionary force', or in the person of its author, such as Weber's 'charisma' (two screen-like concepts which prevent one from examining the reasons for the effects which they merely designate), but rather in the dialectic between the authorizing and authorized language and the dispositions of the group which authorizes it and authorizes itself to use it. This dialectical process is accomplished, in the case of each of the agents concerned and, most of all, in the case of the person producing the heretical discourse, in and through the *labour of enunciation* which is necessary in order to externalize the inwardness, to name the unnamed and to give the beginnings of objectification to pre-verbal and pre-reflexive dispositions and ineffable and unobservable experiences, through words which by their nature make them common and communicable, therefore meaningful and socially sanctioned. It may also be accomplished in the labour of dramatization, particularly visible in exemplary prophecy, which alone is capable of destroying the self-evident truths of the doxa, and in the transgression which is indispensable in order to *name the unnameable*, to break the censorships, institutionalized or internalized, which prohibit the return of the repressed; and first of all in the heresiarch himself.

But it is in the constitution of groups that the effectiveness of representations is most apparent, and particularly in the words, slogans and theories which help to create the social order by imposing principles of di-vision and, more generally, the symbolic power of the whole political theatre which actualizes and officializes visions of the world and political divisions. The political labour of representation (not only in words or theories but also in demonstrations, ceremonies or any other form of symbolization of divisions or oppositions) gives the objectivity of public discourse and exemplary practice to a way of seeing or of experiencing the social world that was previously relegated to the state of a practical disposition of a tacit and often confused experience (unease, rebelliousness, etc.). It thus enables agents to discover within themselves common properties that lie beyond the diversity of particular situations which isolate, divide and demobilize, and to construct their social identity on the basis of characteristics or experiences that seemed totally dissimilar so long as the principle of pertinence by virtue of which they could be constituted as indices of membership of the same class was lacking.

The transition from the state of being a practical group to the state of being an instituted group (class, nation, etc.) presupposes the construction of the principle of classification capable of producing the set of distinctive properties which characterize the set of members in this group, and capable also of annulling the set of non-pertinent properties which part or all of its members possess in other contexts (e.g. properties of nationality, age or sex), and which might serve as a basis for other constructions. The struggle lies therefore at the very root of the construction of the class (social, ethnic, sexual, etc.): every group is the site of a struggle to impose a legitimate principle of group construction, and every distribution of properties, whether it concerns sex or age, education or wealth, may serve as a basis for specifically political divisions or struggles. The construction of dominated groups on the basis of such and such specific difference is inseparable from the deconstruction of groups established on the basis of generic properties or qualities (men, the old, the French, Parisians, citizens, patriots, etc.) which, in another state of symbolic relations of power, defined the social identity, and sometimes even the legal identity, of the agents concerned. Indeed, any attempt to institute a new division must reckon with the resistance of those who, occupying a dominant position in the space thus divided, have an interest in perpetuating a doxic relation to the social world which leads to the acceptance of established divisions as natural or to their symbolic denial through the affirmation of a higher unity (national, familial, etc).[1] In other words, dominant individuals favour the consensus, a fundamental agreement concerning the meaning or sense of the social world (thus converted into the doxic, natural world) which is based on agreement concerning the principles of di-vision.

The propulsive force of heretical criticism is met by the resistant force of orthodoxy. Dominated individuals make common cause with discourse and consciousness, indeed with science, since they cannot constitute themselves as a separate group, mobilize themselves or mobilize their potential power unless they question the categories of perception of the social order which, being the product of that order, inclined them to recognize that order and thus submit to it.

Dominated individuals are less likely to bring about a symbolic revolution – which is the condition for the reappropriation of the social identity of which their acceptance of dominant taxonomies has deprived them (even subjectively) – when the subversive force and critical competence accumulated in the course of previous struggles is relatively slight, and consequently when the consciousness of the positive or, more likely, negative properties which define them is relatively weak. Thus dispossessed of the economic and cultural conditions necessary for their awareness of the fact that they are dispossessed and enclosed within the limits of the knowledge authorized by their instruments of knowledge, the utterances and the actions that sub-proletarians and proletarianized peasants produce, in order to subvert the social order of which they are the victims, are organized according to the principles of logical division which are at the very root of this order (cf. wars of religion).

In contrast to this, dominant individuals, in the absence of being able to restore the *silence of the doxa*, strive to produce, through a purely reactionary discourse, a substitute for everything that is threatened by the very existence of heretical discourse. Finding nothing for which to reproach the social world as it stands, they endeavour to impose universally, through a discourse permeated by the simplicity and transparency of common sense, the feeling of obviousness and necessity which this world imposes on them; having an interest in leaving things as they are, they attempt to undermine politics in a depoliticized political discourse, produced through a process of neutralization or, even better, of negation, which seeks to restore the doxa to its original state of innocence and which, being oriented towards the naturalization of the social order, always borrows the language of nature.

This politically unmarked political language is characterized by a rhetoric of impartiality, marked by the effects of symmetry, balance, the golden mean, and sustained by an ethos of propriety and decency, exemplified by the avoidance of the most violent polemical forms, by discretion, an avowed respect for adversaries, in short, everything which expresses the negation of political struggle as struggle. This strategy of (ethical) neutrality is naturally accomplished in the rhetoric of scientificity.

This nostalgic yearning for the protodoxa is expressed with utter naïvety in the admiration that all conservatisms display for 'decent people' (most often personified by the peasant), whose essential property is designated clearly by the euphemisms ('simple folk', 'working people') which feature in orthodox discourse: their submission to the established order. In fact, the struggle between orthodoxy and heterodoxy that occurs in the political field conceals the opposition between the set of political propositions taken as a whole (whether orthodox or heterodox), that is, the sphere of what is politically utterable in the political field, on the one hand, and, on the other, everything that remains beyond discussion (in the field), that is, beyond the reach of discourse and which, relegated to the state of doxa, is accepted tacitly without discussion or examination by the very people who confront one another at the level of declared political choices.

The struggle in which knowledge of the social world is at stake would be pointless if each agent could find, within himself, the source of an infallible knowledge of the truth of his condition and his position in the social space, and it would be equally pointless if the same agents could not recognize themselves in different discourses and classifications (according to class, ethnicity, religion, sex, etc.), or in opposing evaluations of the products resulting from the same principles of classification. But the effects of this struggle would be totally unpredictable if there were no limit to allodoxia, to errors in perception and above all in expression, and if the propensity to recognize oneself in the different discourses and classifications offered were equally probable among all agents, whatever their position in the social space (and hence their dispositions), and whatever the structure of that space, the form of the distributions and the nature of the divisions according to which it is actually organized.

The pre-vision or theory effect (understood as the effect of imposition of the principles of di-vision which occurs whenever an attempt is made to make something explicit) operates in the margin of uncertainty resulting from the discontinuity between the silent and self-evident truths of the ethos and the public expressions of the logos: thanks to the allodoxia made possible by the distance between the order of practice and the order of discourse, the same dispositions may be recognized in very different, sometimes opposing stances. This means that science is destined to exert a theory effect, but one which takes a very particular form: by expressing in a coherent and empirically valid discourse what was previously ignored, i.e. what was (according to the case in question) implicit or repressed, it transforms the representation of the social world as well as simultaneously transforming the social world itself, at least to the extent that it renders possible practices that conform to this transformed representation. Thus, if it is true that one can trace (virtually as far back in history as one wishes) the first manifestations of class struggle, and even the first more or less elaborated expressions of a 'theory' of class struggle (by speaking of 'precursors'), the fact remains that it is only after Marx, and indeed only after the creation of parties capable of imposing (on a large scale) a vision of the social world organized according to the theory of class struggle, that one could refer, strictly speaking, to classes and class struggle. Those who, in the name of Marxism, search for classes and class struggle in pre-capitalist (and pre-Marxist) societies are committing a theoretical error which is altogether typical of the combination of scientistic realism and economism which always inclined the Marxist tradition to look for classes in the very reality of the social world, often reduced to its economic dimension:[2] paradoxically, Marxist theory, which has exercised a theory effect unrivalled in history, devotes no space to the theory effect in its theory of history and of class.

Reality and will: class (or the class struggle) is reality to the extent that it is will and will to the extent that it is reality. Political practices and political representations (and in particular the representations of the division into classes), of the kind that can be observed and measured at a given moment in time in a society which has had a long exposure to the theory of class struggle, are partly the product of the theory effect – it being understood that this effect has owed a measure of its symbolic effectiveness to the fact that the theory of class struggle was objectively rooted in objective and incorporated properties, and as a consequence encountered the complicity of political dispositions. The categories according to which a group envisages itself, and according to which it represents itself and its specific reality, contribute to the reality of this group. This implies that the whole history of the working-class movement and of the theories through which it has constructed social reality is present in the reality of this movement considered at a particular moment in time. It is in the struggles which shape the history of the social world that the categories of perception of the social world, and the groups produced according to these categories, are simultaneously constructed.[3]

Even the most strictly constative scientific description is always open to the possibility of functioning in a prescriptive way, capable of contributing to its own verification by exercising a theory effect through which it helps to bring about that which it declares. Like the phrase, 'the meeting is open', the thesis, 'there are two classes', may be understood as a constative utterance or a performative utterance. This is what creates the intrinsic indeterminacy of all political theses which, like the affirmation or negation of the existence of classes, regions or nations, take a clear stand on the reality of different representations of reality, or on their ability to make reality. The science which may be tempted to cut through these debates by providing an objective measure of the degree of realism of the respective positions must, if it is to proceed in a logical way, describe the space in which these struggles take place and where what is at stake, among other things, is the representation of the forces engaged in the struggle and their chances of success – and it must do so without ignoring the fact that any 'objective' evaluation of those aspects of reality which are at stake in the struggles in reality is likely to exert effects that are entirely real. How can one fail to see that a prediction may have a role not only in its author's intentions, but also in the reality of its social realization, either as a *self-fulfilling prophecy*, a performative representation capable of exerting a specifically political effect of consecrating the established order (and all the more so the more recognized it is), or as an *exorcism*, capable of eliciting the actions likely to refute it? As Gunnar Myrdal has clearly demonstrated, the key words in the vocabulary of economics, not only terms like 'principle', 'equilibrium', 'productivity', 'adjustment', 'function', etc., but also more central and unavoidable concepts like 'utility', 'value', 'real' or 'subjective' costs, etc., not to mention notions like 'economic', 'natural', 'equitable' (to which one should add 'rational'), are always simultaneously descriptive and prescriptive.[4]

The most neutral science exerts effects which are anything but neutral. Thus, simply by establishing and publishing the value assumed by the probability function of an event, i.e., as Popper suggests, the force of the *propensity* of this event to occur, an objective property inherent in the nature of things, one may help to reinforce this event's 'claim to exist', as Leibniz used to say, by determining agents to prepare for it and to submit to it, or, conversely, by inciting them to mobilize in an effort to prevent it by using their knowledge of its probability in order to make its occurrence more difficult, if not impossible. Equally, it is not enough to replace the academic opposition between two ways of conceiving social differentiation, as a set of hierarchical strata or as a set of antagonistic strata, with the question – which is of capital importance for any revolutionary strategy – of whether, at the moment in question, the dominated classes constitute an antagonistic power capable of defining its own objectives, in short, a mobilized class, or, on the contrary, a stratum situated at the lowest point in a hierarchized space and defined by its distance from the dominant values; or, in other words, whether the struggle between the classes is a revolutionary struggle, aimed at overturning the established order, or a competitive struggle, a kind of race in which the dominated endeavour to appropriate the properties of the dominant. Nothing would be more open to refutation by reality, and therefore less scientific, than an answer to this question which, considering exclusively the practices and dispositions of the agents at the moment in question, failed to take into account the existence or non-existence of agents or organizations capable of working to confirm or invalidate one vision or the other, on the basis of more or less realistic pre-visions or predictions of the objective prospects for one possibility or the other, predictions and prospects that are themselves liable to be affected by scientific knowledge of reality.

All the indications are that the *theory effect*, which may be exerted, in reality itself, by agents and organizations capable of imposing a principle of division or, if you like, of producing or reinforcing symbolically the systematic propensity to favour certain aspects of reality and ignore others, is all the more powerful and above all durable when the processes of objectification and of rendering things explicit are rooted in reality, and hence the divisions in thought correspond more precisely to real divisions. In other words, the potential force which is mobilized by symbolic constitution is all the more important when the *classificatory properties* through which a group is explicitly characterized, and in which it *recognizes* itself, encompass more completely the properties with which the agents constitutive of the group are objectively endowed (and which define their position in the distribution of the instruments of appropriation of the accumulated social product).

The science of the social mechanisms which, like the mechanisms of cultural heredity linked to the functioning of the educational system, or the mechanisms of symbolic domination linked to the unification of the market in economic and cultural goods, tend to ensure the reproduction of the established order can be put to the service of an opportunistic, *laisser-faire* approach committed to *rationalizing* (in both senses) the way these mechanisms function. But this science may just as easily serve as a foundation for a politics oriented towards completely different ends which, breaking just as much with the voluntarism of ignorance or despair as with the *laisser-faire* approach, would arm itself with the knowledge of these mechanisms in order to try and neutralize them; and which would find, in the knowledge of the probable, not an incitement to fatalistic resignation or irresponsible utopianism, but the foundation for a rejection of the probable based on the scientific mastery of the laws of production governing the eventuality rejected.

6

Censorship and the Imposition of Form

Louche *[skewed]. This word is used, in grammatical contexts, to indicate expressions which seem at first to introduce one meaning but which go on to determine an entirely different one. It is used in particular of phrases whose construction is equivocal to the point of disturbing their clarity of expression. What renders a phrase* skewed *arises therefore in the specific disposition of the words which compose it, when they seem at first glance to create a certain relation, although in fact they enjoy a different one: just as* skew-eyed *people seem to look in one direction, while they are actually looking somewhere else.*

M. Beauzée, Encyclopédie méthodique,
grammaire et littérature, vol. 2

The specialized languages that schools of specialists produce and reproduce through the systematic alteration of the common language are, as with all discourses, the product of a *compromise* between an *expressive interest* and a *censorship* constituted by the very structure of the field in which the discourse is produced and circulates. This 'compromise formation', in the Freudian sense, is more or less 'successful' depending on the *specific competence* of the producer, and is the product of *strategies of euphemization* that consist in imposing form as well as observing formalities. These strategies tend to guarantee the satisfaction of the expressive interest, biological drive or political interest (in the broad sense of the term), within the limits of the *structure of opportunities for material or symbolic profit* which the different forms of discourse can procure for different producers according to their position in the field, that is, in the structure of the distribution of the specific capital which is at stake in this field.[1]

The metaphor of censorship should not mislead: it is the structure of the field itself which governs expression by governing both access to expression and the form of expression, and not some legal proceeding which has been specially adapted to designate and repress the transgression of a kind of linguistic code. This structural censorship is exercised through the medium of the sanctions of the field, functioning as a market on which the prices of different kinds of expression are formed; it is imposed on all producers of symbolic goods, including the authorized spokesperson, whose authoritative discourse is more subject to the norms of official propriety than any other, and it condemns the occupants of dominated positions either to silence or to shocking outspokenness. The need for this censorship to manifest itself in the form of explicit prohibitions, imposed and sanctioned by an institutionalized authority, diminishes as the mechanisms which ensure the allocation of agents to different positions (and whose very success ensures their anonymity) are increasingly capable of ensuring that the different positions are occupied by agents able and inclined to engage in discourse (or to keep silent) which is compatible with the objective definition of the position. (This explains the importance which co-optation procedures always grant to the apparently insignificant indices of the disposition to observe formalities.) Censorship is never quite as perfect or as invisible as when each agent has nothing to say apart from what he is objectively authorized to say: in this case he does not even have to be his own censor because he is, in a way, censored once and for all, through the forms of perception and expression that he has internalized and which impose their form on all his expressions.

Among the most effective and best concealed censorships are all those which consist in excluding certain agents from communication by excluding them from the groups which speak or the places which allow one to speak with authority. In order to explain what may or may not be said in a group, one has to take into account not only the symbolic relations of power which become established within it and which deprive certain individuals (e.g. women) of the possibility of speaking or which oblige them to conquer that right through force, but also the laws of group formation themselves (e.g. the logic of conscious or unconscious exclusion) which function like a prior censorship.

Symbolic productions therefore owe their most specific properties to the social conditions of their production and, more precisely, to the position of the producer in the field of production, which governs, through various forms of mediation, not only the expressive interest, and the form and the force of the censorship which is imposed on it, but also the competence which allows this interest to be satisfied within the limits of these constraints. The *dialectical* relation which is established between the expressive interest and censorship prevents us from distinguishing in the *opus operatum* between form and content, that is, between what is said and the manner of saying it or even the manner of hearing it. By imposing form, the censorship exercised by the structure of the field determines the form – which all formalist analyses attempt to detach from social determinisms – and, necessarily, the content, which is inseparable from its appropriate expression and therefore literally unthinkable outside of the known forms and recognized norms. Censorship also determines the form of reception: to produce a philosophical discourse of a duly formal nature, that is, bearing the set of agreed signs (a certain use of syntax, vocabulary, references, etc.) by which philosophical discourse is recognized and through which it secures recognition as philosophical,[2] is to produce a product which demands to be received with due formality, that is, with due respect for the forms it has adopted or, as we see in literature, *for its nature as form*. Legitimate works thus exercise a violence which protects them from the violence which would be needed if we were to perceive the expressive interest which they express only in forms which deny it: the histories of art, literature and philosophy testify to the efficacy of strategies of the imposition of form through which consecrated works impose the terms of their own perception; and 'methods' like structural or semiological analysis, which purport to study structures independently of functions, are no exception to this rule.

It follows that a work is tied to a particular field no less by its form than by its content: to imagine what Heidegger would have said in another form, such as the form of philosophical discourse employed in Germany in 1890, or the form assumed nowadays by political science articles from Yale or Harvard, or any other form, is to imagine an *impossible* Heidegger (e.g. a philosophical 'vagrant', or an oppositional immigrant in 1933), or a field of production that was no less impossible in Germany at the time when Heidegger was active. The form through which symbolic productions share most directly in the social conditions of their production is also the means by which their most specific social effect is exercised: specifically symbolic violence can only be exercised by the person who exercises it, and endured by the person who endures it, in a form which results in its misrecognition as such, in other words, which results in its recognition as legitimate.

THE RHETORIC OF THE FALSE BREAK

The 'special language' distinguishes itself from scientific language in that it conceals heteronomy behind the appearance of autonomy: being unable to function without the aid of ordinary language, it must produce the illusion of independence through strategies which create a false break, using procedures that differ according to the field and, when in the same field, according to positions and moments. This language can, for example, mimic the fundamental property of all scientific language: the determination of an element through its membership of a system.[3] The words which pure science borrows from ordinary language derive their entire meaning from the system constructed, and the option (often inevitable) of resorting to a common word rather than a neologism or a pure and arbitrary symbol can only be chosen – in keeping with a correct methodology – through the desire to utilize the capacity sometimes possessed by language to portray hitherto unsuspected relations, when it functions as a depository for a collective endeavour.[4] The word 'group' used by mathematicians is a perfectly self-sufficient symbol because it is entirely defined by the operations and the relations which define its specific structure and which are the source of its properties. Conversely, most of the special usages of the word that are listed by dictionaries (e.g. in painting, 'the gathering of several characters constituting an organic unity in a work of art', or in economics, 'a set of enterprises united by diverse links') have only a low level of autonomy in relation to the first meaning and would remain unintelligible for anyone who did not have a working knowledge of that meaning.

The Heideggerian words that are borrowed from ordinary language are numberless, but they are transfigured by the process of imposing form which produces the apparent autonomy of philosophical language by inserting them, through the systematic accentuation of morphological relations, into a *network of relations* manifested in the concrete form of the language and thereby suggesting that each element of the discourse depends on the others *simultaneously* as signifier and as signified. Thus a word as ordinary

as *Fürsorge* (solicitude), becomes *palpably* attached by its very form
to a whole set of words from the same family: *Sorge* (care), *Sorgfalt*
(carefulness), *Sorglosigkeit* (negligence, carelessness), *sorgenvoll*
(concerned), *besorgt* (preoccupied), *Lebenssorge* (concern for life),
Selbstsorge (self-interest). The play on words of the same root –
which is very common in the dictums and proverbs found in all
popular wisdom – is only one of the formal means, if doubtless the
most reliable, of giving the impression that there is a necessary
relation between two signifieds. The association by alliteration or by
assonance, which establishes quasi-material relations of resemblance
of form and of sound, can also produce formally necessary associations likely to bring to light a hidden relation between the signifieds
or, more probably, to bring it into existence solely by virtue of the
play on forms: it is, for example, the philosophical puns of the later
Heidegger, *Denken* = *Danken* (thinking = thanking), or the sequence of plays on words relating to *Sorge als besorgende Fürsorge*, the
notion of 'care as concernful solicitude', which would elicit accusations of verbalism were it not for the pattern of morphological
allusions and etymological cross-references creating the illusion of a
global coherence of form, and therefore of sense, and, as a consequence, the illusion of the necessity of discourse: '*Die Entschlossenheit
aber ist nur die in die Sorge gesorgte und als Sorge mögliche
Eigentlichkeit dieser selbst*' ('Resoluteness, however, is only that
authenticity which, in care, is the object of care, and which is
possible as care – the authenticity of care itself').[5]

All the potential resources of ordinary language are used to create
the impression that there exists a necessary link between all signifiers
and that the relationship between signifiers and signifieds is established solely through the mediation of the system of philosophical
concepts, 'technical' words which are ennobled forms of ordinary
words (*Entdeckung*, discovery or uncovering, *Entdeckheit*, disco-
veredness or uncoveredness), traditional notions (*Dasein*, a word
used in common by Heidegger, Jaspers and some others) which are
used in a way that implies a slight discrepancy, destined to mark an
allegorical deviation (ontological, metaphysical, etc.), neologisms
recast to constitute purportedly unpremeditated distinctions or at
least to produce an impression of radical overcoming (*existentiel* and
existential; *zeitlich*, timely, and *temporal*, temporal – an opposition
which moreover plays no effective role in *Being and Time*).

The imposition of form produces the illusion of systematicity and,
by virtue of this and the break between specialized and ordinary
language which it brings about, it produces the illusion of the

autonomy of the system. By being inserted into the network of words that are both morphologically similar and etymologically related, and being woven thereby into the tissue of the Heideggerian vocabulary, the word *Fürsorge* (solicitude) is divested of its primary meaning, which is unambiguously conveyed in the expression *Sozial-fürsorge* (social welfare). Once transformed and transfigured in this way, the word loses its social identity and its ordinary meaning in order to assume a distorted meaning (which might be rendered more or less by the word 'procuration', taken in its etymological sense). Thus the social phantasm of (social) assistance, symbolic of the 'welfare state' or the 'insurance state' denounced by Carl Schmitt or Ernst Jünger in a less euphemized language, can manifest itself in legitimate discourse (*Sorge* and *Fürsorge* are central to the theory of temporality), but in a form such that it does not appear to be there, such that effectively it is not there.

It is the incorporation of a word into the system of philosophical language that brings about the *negation* of its primary meaning, that is the meaning which the tabooed word assumes with reference to the system of ordinary language and which, although officially banished from the overt system, continues to lead a clandestine existence. This negation is the source of the duplicity authorized by the dual message registered in each element of discourse, always defined by belonging simultaneously to two systems, the overt system of the philosophical idiolect and the latent system of ordinary language.

If one wishes to prise the expressive interest away from the unsayable and the unnameable, and subject it to the transformation necessary for it to accede to the order of what is sayable in a given field, then one must do more than simply substitute one word for another, an acceptable one for a censored one. This elementary form of euphemization hides another much more subtle one which uses the essential property of language – the primacy of relations over elements, of form over substance, according to the opposition established by Saussure – to conceal the repressed elements by integrating them into a network of relations which modify their *value* without modifying their 'substance'.[6] It is only in the case of specialized languages, produced by specialists with an explicitly systematizing intention, that the effect of concealment through the imposition of form is fully exercised. In this case, as in all cases of camouflage through form and in *all due form*, as it is analysed by *Gestalttheorie*, the tabooed meanings, though recognizable in theory, remain misrecognized in practice; though present as substance they are absent as form, like a face hidden in the bush. The role of this kind of expression is to mask the primitive experiences of the social world and the social phantasms which are its source, as much as to reveal them; to allow them to speak, while using a mode of expression which suggests that they are not being said. These specialized languages can articulate such experience only in forms of expression which render it misrecognizable, because the specialist is unable to recognize the fact that he is articulating it. Subject to the tacit or explicit norms of a particular field, the primitive substance is, as it were, dissolved in the form; through the imposition of form and the observance of formalities it becomes form. This imposition of form is both a transformation and a transubstantiation: the substance signified *is* the signifying form in which it is realized.

The imposition of form makes it both justified and unjustified to reduce *negation* to what it negates, to the social phantasm which is its source. Because of the fact that this 'lifting [*Aufhebung*] of repression' – as Freud called it, using a Hegelian term – simultaneously denies and maintains both the repression and the repressed, it allows for a doubling of profits: the profit of saying and the profit of denying what is said by the way of saying it. It is clear that the opposition between 'authenticity' (*Eigentlichkeit*) and 'inauthenticity' (*Uneigentlichkeit*), which Heidegger calls the 'primordial modes of *Dasein*' and around which his whole work is organized (even from the viewpoint of the most strictly internal readings), is simply a particular and particularly subtle form of the general opposition between the 'elite' and the 'masses'. 'They' (*das Man*, literally 'one') are tyrannical (the dictatorship of the 'they'), inquisitorial (the 'they' gets involved in everything) and reduce everything to its lowest level; 'they' shirk responsibility, opt out of their freedom and slide into a tendency to take things easy and make them easy; in short 'they' behave like irresponsible welfare recipients who live off society.

One could list the commonplaces of academic aristocratism which recur throughout this oft-cited passage,[7] replete with *topoi* on the *agora* as an antithesis of *scholè*, leisure versus school; the horror of statistics (the notion of the 'average'), which symbolizes all the 'levelling-down' operations which threaten the 'person' (here called *Dasein*) and its most precious attributes, its 'originality' and its 'privacy'; contempt for all the 'levelling' forces (which others have termed 'massifying'), first and foremost the egalitarian ideologies which threaten what is achieved through effort ('the fruits of hard work'), meaning culture (which is the specific capital of the mandarin, who is the son of his works), ideologies which encourage the easy-going attitudes of the 'masses'; a rejection of social mechanisms like public opinion, the philosopher's hereditary enemy, and which is conveyed once more by the play on *öffentlich* and *Öffentlichkeit*, on 'public' and 'publicness', and of all the things symbolized by 'social assistance', like democracy, political parties, paid holidays (which threaten the monopoly of *scholè* and meditative seclusion in nature), 'culture for the masses', television and paperback editions of Plato.[8] Heidegger was to put all this much better in his inimitable *pastoral* style when, in *An Introduction to Metaphysics*, written in 1935, he tried to show how the triumph of the spirit of science and technology in Western civilization is accomplished and perfected in 'the flight of the gods, the destruction of the earth, the transformation of men into a mass, the hatred and suspicion of everything free and creative' (*'die Flucht der Götter, die Zerstörung der Erde, die Vermassung der Menschen, der Vorrang des Mittelmässigen'*).[9]

But it is equally clear that among philosophically distinguished minds the opposition between the distinguished and the vulgar cannot take on a vulgar form. Academic aristocratism distinguishes between the distinguished and the vulgar forms of aristocratism. It is this sense of philosophical distinction[10] which frustrates the attempts of Heidegger's critics to find blatantly Nazi theses in his works and political writings, and which Heidegger's supporters will always call upon to prove his wish to distance himself from the most marked forms of contempt for the masses.[11] What may be called this 'primary' (in both senses) opposition can function in his work only in the form in which it was initially and permanently introduced, and which constantly transforms itself as his otherwise static system evolves, taking on new but always highly sublimated forms.

The imposition of form is in itself a warning: by its elevated nature it indicates its sovereign distance from all determinations, even from those 'isms' which reduce the irreducible unity of a thought system to the uniformity of a logical class; it also indicates its distance from all determinisms and especially the social determinisms which reduce the priceless individuality of a thinker to the banality of a (social) class. It is this distance, this *difference* which is explicitly instituted at the core of philosophical discourse in the form of the opposition between the ontological and the ontic (or anthropological) and which provides the already euphemized discourse with a second and impregnable line of defence: henceforth every word carries the indelible trace of the *break* which separates the authentically ontological sense from the ordinary and vulgar one, and which is sometimes inscribed in the signifying substance by one of the phonological games (*existentiell/existenzial*) which have since been so often imitated. Thus the double-sided play with double-edged words is naturally extended to the warnings against 'vulgar' and 'vulgarly anthropological' readings attempting to highlight the meanings that are negated but not refuted, and doomed by *philosophical sublimation* to the absent presence of a spectral existence: 'The term "concern" has, in the first instance, its colloquial [*vorwissenschaftliche*] signification, and can mean to carry out something, to get it done [*erledigen*], to "straighten it out". It can also mean to "provide oneself with something". We use the expression with still another characteristic turn of phrase when we say "I am concerned for the success of the undertaking". Here "concern" means something like apprehensiveness. *In contrast to these colloquial ontical significations, the expression "concern" will be used in this investigation as an ontological term for an existentiale*, and will designate the Being of a possible way of Being-in-the-world. This term has been chosen not because *Dasein* happens to be proximally and to a large extent "practical" and economic, but because the Being of *Dasein* itself is to be made visible as *care*. This expression too is to be taken as an *ontological structural concept*. It has *nothing to do* with "tribulation", "melancholy", or "the cares of life", though ontically one can come across these in every *Dasein*.'[12]

The imposition of a sharp divide between sacred and profane knowledge, which underlies the claims of all groups of specialists seeking to secure a monopoly of knowledge or sacred practice by constituting others as profane, thus takes on an original form: it is omnipresent, dividing each word against itself, as it were, by making it signify that it does not signify what it appears to signify, by inscribing within it – by placing it between inverted commas or significantly distorting its substantive meaning, or just setting it etymologically or phonologically within a tendentious lexical cluster – the distance which separates the 'authentic' from the 'vulgar' or 'naïve' sense.[13] By discrediting the primary meanings which continue to function as a hidden prop for a number of relations constitutive of the overt system, one provides oneself with the possibility of taking the double-dealing a step further. Indeed, despite the anathema that is poured upon them, these negated meanings still fulfil a philosophical function, since they act at least as a negative referent in relation to which philosophical distance is established, the 'ontological difference' which separates the 'ontological' from the 'ontic', i.e. the initiated from the lay person who alone is responsible, through his ignorance and perversity, for the culpable evocation of vulgar meanings. By using ordinary words in other ways, by reviving the subtle truth, the *etumon*, which has been lost by routine usage, one turns the correct relation between words into the principle by which philological/philosophical alchemy stands or falls: 'If an alchemist, uninitiated in heart and soul, fails in his experiments, it is not only because he uses impure elements but above all because he thinks with the common *properties* of these impure elements and not with the *virtues* of ideal elements. Thus, once the complete and absolute duplication has been achieved, *ideality* can be fully experienced.'[14] Language, too, has its subtle elements, liberated by philological/philosophical subtlety, such as the grammatical duality of the Greek word *on* (being), both a noun and a verbal form, which prompted Heidegger to remark: 'What is here set forth, which at first may be taken for grammatical hair-splitting, is in truth the riddle of Being.'[15]

Thus assured of the effectiveness of philosophical negation, we can even recall censored meanings and find a supplementary effect in the complete reversal of the relationship between the overt system and the hidden system which is provoked by this *return of the repressed*: indeed, it is difficult not to see this as proof of the powerful ability of 'essential thought' to ground in Being such realities as the derisorily contingent 'social security' – so unworthy of thought that they are named in inverted commas.[16] Thus, in this 'upside-down world', where the event is never more than the illustration of the 'essence', the grounding is grounded by what it grounds.[17] 'For example, "welfare work" [*Fürsorge*], as a factical social arrangement, is grounded in *Dasein*'s state of Being as Being-with. Its factical urgency gets its motivation in that *Dasein* maintains itself proximally and for the most part in the deficient modes of solicitude.'[18] This blatant and invisible reference, invisible because it is blatant, helps, by its audacity, to disguise the fact that *continuous mention is made of social welfare* in an entire work *ostensibly* devoted to an ontological property of *Dasein* whose 'empirical [i.e. ordinary, vulgar and banal] need' for assistance is only a contingent manifestation. The paradigm of the stolen letter, which Lacan illustrates with the anecdote, 'Why do you tell me you are going to Cracow so I'll believe you are going to Lvov, when you really are going to Cracow?',[19] is used by Heidegger to encourage the belief, by proclaiming what he is really doing, that he is not really doing what he has always done. There is, in fact, no doubt: 'social welfare, *Sozialfürsorge*, is indeed 'concern for' and 'on behalf of' those in receipt of aid, which disburdens them of concern for themselves and authorizes their inclination to be 'careless', to 'take things easily and make things easy', just as philosophical solicitude (*Fürsorge*), which is the sublime variant of the former, disburdens *Dasein* of concern, or as Sartre said (or might have said) in 1943, frees the *Pour-soi* (self-conscious being) from its freedom, thus dooming it to 'bad faith' and the 'serious-mindedness' of an 'inauthentic' existence. 'Thus the particular *Dasein* in its everydayness is *disburdened* by the "they". Not only that; by thus disburdening it of its Being, the "they" accommodates *Dasein* if *Dasein* has any tendency to take things easily and make them easy. And because the "they" constantly accommodates the particular *Dasein* by disburdening it of its being, the "they" retains and enhances its stubborn dominion.'[20]

The play with the palpable forms of language is most accomplished when it bears on pairs of terms rather than isolated words, i.e. on the relations between contradictory terms. In contrast to straightforward philosophical puns based on assonance and alliteration, 'primordial' puns, those which orient and organize Heidegger's thought in depth, play on verbal forms to exploit them both as palpable forms and as forms of classification. These total forms, which reconcile the independent necessities of sound and sense in the miracle of an expression that is doubly necessary, are the transformed form of a linguistic fabric that is already moulded politically, that is, moulded by objectively political principles of opposition, and which is recorded and preserved in ordinary language. There is no other way of explaining the predilection of scholarly languages for *binary thinking*: what in this case is censored and repressed is not a taboo term taken in isolation, but a relation of opposition between words which always alludes to a relation of opposition between social groups.[21]

Ordinary language is not only an infinite store of palpable forms available for poetical or philosophical games, or, as with the later Heidegger and his followers, for free associations in what Nietzsche called a *Begriffsdichtung*; it is also a reservoir of forms of apperception of the social world and of commonplace expressions, in which the principles which govern the vision of the social world common to an entire group are deposited (Germanic/Romance or Latin, ordinary/distinguished, simple/complicated, rural/urban, etc.). The structure of class relations is only ever named and grasped through the forms of classification which, even in the case of those conveyed by ordinary language, are never independent of this structure (something forgotten by the ethnomethodologists and all the *formalist*

analyses of these forms). Indeed, although the most socially
'marked' (vulgar/distinguished) oppositions may receive very different meanings according to usage and users, ordinary language, as
the product of the accumulated labour of thought dominated by the
relations of power between classes, and *a fortiori* scholarly language,
as the product of fields dominated by the interests and values of the
dominant classes, are in a way primary ideologies which lend
themselves more 'naturally' to usages conforming to the values and
interests of the dominant classes.[22] But whereas the ordinary practice of euphemization (as it is pursued in 'political science', for
example) substitutes one word for another, or visibly neutralizes the
ordinary meaning of an excessively marked word by an explicit
caution (inverted commas, for instance) or a distinctive definition,
Heidegger proceeds in a manner that is infinitely more complex: by
using the ordinary word, but in a network of morphologically
interconnected words, he invites a philological and polyphonic
reading that is able to evoke and revoke the ordinary sense simultaneously, able to suggest it while ostensibly repressing it, along with
its pejorative connotations, into the order of vulgar and vulgarly
'anthropological' understanding.[23]

The philosophical imagination – which, like mythical thought, rejoices
when the purely linguistic relation, materially exemplified by
homophony, is superimposed on a relation of sense – plays on linguistic
forms which are also classificatory forms. Thus, in the essay *The Essence
of Truth* (*Von Wesen der Wahrheit*), the opposition between the 'essent'
(*Wesen*) and the 'non-essent' (*Un-wesen*) is superimposed on the underlying opposition, simultaneously evoked and revoked, between order – a
kind of phantom term – and disorder, one of the possible senses of
non-essent. The parallel oppositions, unequally euphemized variants of
certain 'primordial' oppositions, themselves roughly reducible to one
another, numerous examples of which appear in Heidegger's work subsequent to his 'reversal', reaffirm – in a form which is sublimated and
which, the more it is rooted in misrecognition, is all the more universal in
its applications (like the opposition between the ontic and the ontological) – the founding opposition, itself subject to taboo. In so doing, they
constitute that opposition by inscribing it in Being (the ontologizing
effect) while denying it symbolically, *either* by reducing an absolute, total
and clear-cut opposition to one of the superficial and partial secondary
oppositions that can be derived from it, or even one of the most easily
manipulated terms of a secondary opposition (as in the example above of
the non-essent), *or*, by a strategy that does not exclude the former,
simply and purely by denying the founding opposition through a fictitious
universalization of one of the terms of the relation – in the way that

'infirmity' and 'powerlessness' (*Ohnmacht*) are inscribed in the universality of *Dasein*, grounding a form of equality and solidarity in distress. The puns on the non-essent harness these effects and achieve a reconciliation between opposites that can only be compared with what occurs in magic: rendering absolute the *established order* (conjured up only by its opposite, in the way that, in dreams, clothes can signify nudity) which coincides with the symbolic negation, through universalization, of the only visible term in the relation of domination which establishes this order.[24]

Everything is thus arranged so as to rule out as indecent any attempt to apply to the text the *violence* whose legitimacy Heidegger himself recognized when he applied it to Kant, and which alone allows one to 'grasp the sense beyond the obstinate silence of language'. Any exposition of the originary thought which rejects the inspired paraphrase of the untranslatable idiolect is condemned in advance by the guardians of the sanctuary.[25] The only way of saying what words *mean to say*, when they refuse to say innocently what they mean or, what amounts to the same thing, when they keep saying it but only indirectly, is to reduce the irreducible, to translate the untranslatable, to say what they mean in the naïve terms which their primary function is precisely to deny. 'Authenticity' is not a naïve designation of the exclusive quality of a socially designated 'elite'. It indicates a universal potential – like 'inauthenticity' – but one which only really belongs to those who manage to appropriate it by apprehending it for what it is and at the same time by managing to 'tear themselves away' from 'inauthenticity', a kind of original sin, thus stigmatized as a fault guilty of its own failing, since the chosen few are capable of being converted. This is clearly stated by Jünger: 'Whether to assume one's own destiny, or to be treated like an object: that is the dilemma which everyone, nowadays, is certain to have to resolve, but to have to decide alone . . . Consider man in his pristine state of freedom, as created by God. He is not the exception, nor is he one of an elite. Far from it: for the free man is hidden within every man, and differences exist only in so far as each individual is able to develop that freedom which was his birthright.'[26]

Though equally free, human beings are unequal in their ability to use their freedom authentically and only an 'elite' can appropriate the opportunities which are universally available for acceding to the freedom of the 'elite'. This ethical voluntarism – pushed to its limit by Sartre – converts the objective duality of social destinies into a duality of relations to existence, making authentic existence an 'existential modification' of the ordinary way of apprehending every-

day existence, that is, in plain speaking, a revolution in thought.[27]
When Heidegger makes authenticity begin with the perception of
inauthenticity, in that moment of truth where *Dasein* is revealed
through anxiety as projecting order into the world through its
decision (a kind of Kierkegaardian 'leap' into the unknown),[28] or,
conversely, when he describes man's reduction to the state of an
instrument, another way of apprehending 'everyday existence',
the way which 'they' adopt when they treat themselves as tools and
'care about' tools for their instrumental utility, and thus become
instruments themselves, adapting themselves to others as an instrument adapts to other instruments, fulfilling a function which others
could fulfil just as well and, once reduced in this way to the state of
an interchangeable element in a set, forget themselves in the
fulfilment of their function – when Heidegger discusses existence in
terms of this alternative, he reduces the objective duality of social
conditions to the duality of the modes of existence they obviously
encourage in a very unequal manner; and he thereby considers both
those who ensure their access to 'authentic' existence and those who
'abandon themselves' to an 'inauthentic' existence to be responsible
for what they are, the former for their 'resolution'[29] in tearing
themselves away from everyday existence in order to exploit their
potential, the latter for their 'resignation' which dooms them to
'degradation' and 'social welfare'.

This social philosophy fits perfectly with the form in which it is
expressed. In fact, one has only to resituate Heideggerian language
in the space of contemporary languages where its distinction and
social value are objectively defined in order to see that this particularly improbable stylistic combination is rigorously homologous to
the ideological combination it is responsible for conveying: that is, to
highlight the pertinent points only, the conventional and hieratic
language of post-Mallarmé poetry in the style of Stefan George,
the academic language of neo-Kantian rationalism in the style of
Cassirer, and lastly the language of the 'theorists' of the 'conservative revolution' like Möller van den Bruck[30] or, certainly closer to
Heidegger politically, Ernst Jünger.[31] In opposition to the highly
ritualized and purified language (above all in its vocabulary) of
post-Symbolist poetry, Heideggerian language, which is its trans-
position in the philosophical order, welcomes, thanks to the freedom
implied in the strictly conceptual logic of the *Begriffsdichtung*, words
(e.g. *Fürsorge*) and themes which are excluded from the esoteric
discourse of great experts[32] as well as the highly neutralized language
of academic philosophy. Taking his cue from the philosophical

tradition which encourages the exploitation of the infinite potentialities of thought contained in ordinary language[33] and common-sense proverbs, Heidegger introduced words and things into academic philosophy (according to the parable of Heraclitus' oven, which he relates with self-satisfaction) that had previously been banned, but by conferring a new nobility on them through the imposition of all the problems and emblems that characterize the philosophical tradition, and by integrating them into the fabric woven by the verbal games of conceptual poetry. The difference between the spokespersons of the 'conservative revolution' and Heidegger, who introduced virtually all of their theses and many of their words into philosophy, lies entirely in the form which renders them misrecognizable. But the specificity of Heideggerian discourse would doubtless be lost if the totally original combination of distance and proximity, of loftiness and simplicity, which is realized in this pastoral variant of professorial discourse, were reduced to one or other of its antagonistic aspects: this bastard language embraces perfectly the purpose of the elitism which is within reach of the masses and which offers the most 'ordinary' people the promise of philosophical salvation, provided they are capable of hearing, above the corrupt messages of wicked pastors, the 'authentic' thoughts of a philosophical *Führer* who is never more than a *Fürsprecher*, a humble advocate serving the sacred word and thereby made sacred.

INTERNAL READING AND THE RESPECT FOR FORMS

Fritz Ringer was no doubt right to identify the truth about the reaction of the German 'mandarins' to National Socialism in the words of Spranger, who, in 1932, believed that 'the national students' movement is still authentic in its *content*, but undisciplined in its *form*'.[34] For academic logocentrism, whose limit is set by the verbal fetishism of Heideggerian philosophy – the philo-logical philosophy *par excellence* – it is good form which makes good sense. The truth of the relation between philosophical aristocratism (the supreme form of academic aristocratism) and any other type of aristocratism – including the authentically aristocratic aristocratism of the Junkers and their spokespersons – is expressed in the imposition of form and the prohibition against any kind of 'reductionism', that is, against any destruction of form aimed at *restoring discourse to its simplest expression* and, in so doing, to the social conditions of its production. The only proof one needs of this is the form taken by Habermas' reflections on Heidegger: 'Since 1945 the issue of Heidegger's fascism has been raised in diverse quarters. It is essentially the rectoral address of 1933, when Heidegger celebrated the "upheaval in Germany's existence", which has been at the heart of the debate. Any criticism which stops there, however, remains schematic. What is much more interesting, on the other hand, is to discover how the author of *Being and Time* (the most important philosophical event since Hegel's *Phenomenology*), *how such a great thinker could stoop to such an obviously elementary mode of thought*, which any lucid analysis can discern in the *unstylized pathos* of this call for the self-assertion of German universities.'[35] It is clearly not enough to guard against the 'elevated' quality of 'Martin Heidegger's linguistic posture as a writer'[36] in order to break with the concern for the 'elevation' of discourse, that sense of philosophical dignity which is fundamentally expressed in the philosopher's relation to language.

The 'elevated' style is not merely a contingent property of philosophical discourse. It is the means by which a discourse declares itself to be *authorized*, invested, by virtue of its very conformity, with the authority of a body of people especially mandated to exercise a kind of conceptual magistrature (predominantly logical or moral depending on the authors and the eras). It also ensures that certain things which have no place in the appropriate discourse, or which cannot find the spokespersons capable of putting them in the correct form, are not said, whereas others are said and understood which would otherwise be unsayable and unacceptable. In ordinary speech as in learned discourse, styles are hierarchical and hierarchizing; an 'elevated' language is appropriate for a 'top-level thinker', which is what made the 'unstylized pathos' of Heidegger's 1933 address seem so inappropriate in the eyes of all those who have a sense of philosophical dignity, namely, a sense of their dignity as philosophers: the same people who acclaimed the philosophically stylized pathos of *Being and Time* as a philosophical event.

It is through the 'elevated' style of a discourse that its status in the hierarchy of discourses and the respect due to its status are invoked. A phrase such as, 'The real dwelling plight lies in this, that mortals ever search anew for the essence of dwelling, that they must ever learn to dwell,'[37] is not treated in the same way as a statement in ordinary language, such as, 'the housing crisis is worsening,' or even a proposition in technical language, such as, 'In the *Hausvogteiplatz*, the business district of Berlin, the price of land per square metre was 115 Marks in 1865, 344 Marks in 1880 and 990 Marks in 1985.'[38] As a discourse with its own *form*, philosophical discourse dictates the conditions of its perception.[39] The imposition of form which keeps the lay person at a respectful distance protects the text from 'trivialization' (as Heidegger calls it), by reserving it for an *internal reading*, in both senses: that of a reading confined within the limits of the text itself, and concomitantly, that of a reading reserved for the closed group of professional readers who accept as self-evident an 'internalist' definition of reading. We have only to observe social custom to see that the philosophical text is defined as one which can only be read (in fact) by 'philosophers', i.e. by readers who are ready to recognize and grant recognition to a philosophical discourse, and to read it as it demands to be read: 'philosophically', in accordance with a pure and purely philosophical intention, excluding all reference to anything other than the discourse itself, which, being its own foundation, admits of nothing outside of itself.

The institutionalized circle of collective misrecognition, which is the basis of belief in the value of an ideological discourse, is established only when the structure of the field of production and circulation of this discourse is such that the *negation* it effects (by saying what it says only in a form which suggests that it is not saying it) is brought together with interpreters who are able, as it were, to *misrecognize again* the negated message; in other words, the circle is established only when what is denied by the form is 're-misrecognized', that is, known and recognized in the form, and only in the form, in which it is realized by denying itself. In short, a discourse of denial calls for a formal (or formalist) reading which recognizes and reproduces the initial denial, instead of denying it in order to discover what it denies. The symbolic violence that any ideological discourse implies, in so far as it based on misrecognition which calls for re-misrecognition, is only operative inasmuch as it is able to make its addressees treat it the way it demands to be treated, namely, with all due respect, observing the proper formalities required by its formal properties. Ideological production is all the more successful when it is able to *put in the wrong* anyone who attempts to *reduce* it to its objective truth. The ability to accuse the science of ideology of being ideological is a specific characteristic of the dominant ideology: uttering the hidden truth of a discourse is scandalous because it says something which was 'the last thing to be said'.

The most sophisticated symbolic strategies can never produce completely the conditions of their own success and would be doomed to failure if they could not count on the active complicity of a whole body of individuals who defend orthodoxy and orchestrate – by amplifying it – the initial condemnation of reductive readings.[40]

> Heidegger need only assert that 'philosophy is *essentially* untimely because it is one of the few things that can never find an immediate echo in the present',[41] or, as he suggests in his introduction to Nietzsche, that 'it belongs to the essence of every genuine philosophy that its contemporaries invariably misunderstand it'[42] – variations on the theme of the 'accursed philosopher' which are particularly colourful in his account – for all the commentators immediately to follow suit:[43] 'It is the fate of all philosophical thought, once it has achieved a certain degree of strength and rigour, to be misunderstood by the contemporaries it challenges. To classify as an apostle of pathos, an advocate of nihilism and an opponent of logic and of science, a philosopher whose unique and constant concern has been the problem of truth, is one of the strangest travesties of which a frivolous age is guilty.'[44] 'His thought appears as something alien to our times and everything contemporary.'[45]
>
> Thus the 'Letter on humanism', most striking and most quoted of all the interventions aimed at strategically manipulating the relation between overt and latent systems, and thereby manipulating the public image of the work, has functioned as a kind of pastoral letter, an infinite source of commentaries enabling the simple evangelists of Being to reproduce for themselves the precautions inscribed in each of the master's warnings and thus to stand on the right side of the barrier between the sacred and the profane, between the initiated and the lay person. As the waves of dissemination progress, expanding in ever-widening circles from authorized interpretations and inspired commentaries to scholarly theses, introductory studies and finally textbooks, as one slides down the scale of interpretations, matched by the decline in the loftiness of the phrasing or paraphrasing, the exoteric discourse tends increasingly to return to basic truths; but, as in emanationist philosophies, this dissemination is accompanied by a loss of value, if not of substance, and the 'trivialized' and 'vulgarized' discourse carries the mark of its degradation, thus adding even more to the value of the original or founding discourse.

The relations which are established between the work of a great interpreter and the interpretations or over-interpretations it *solicits*, or between the self-interpretations aimed at correcting and preventing misinformed or malicious interpretations and legitimizing authorized ones, resemble perfectly – apart from their lack of a sense of humour – those which, since Duchamp, have developed between the artist and the group of his interpreters: in both cases, the production anticipates the interpretation, and, in the double-guessing game played by its interpreters, invites over-interpretation, while still reserving the right to repudiate this in the name of the essential inexhaustibility of the work, which may lead one to accept or, equally, to reject any interpretation, by virtue of the transcendent power of its creative force, which is also expressed as a power of criticism and self-criticism. Heidegger's philosophy is unquestionably the first and the most accomplished of the *ready-made* philosophical creations, works *made to be* interpreted and *made by* interpretation or, more precisely, by the interactions between the interpreter who necessarily proceeds *by excess* and the producer who, through his refutations, amendments and corrections, establishes an unbridgeable gulf between the work and any particular interpretation.[46]

The analogy is less artificial than it appears at first sight: by establishing that the sense of the 'ontological difference' which separates his thought from all previous thought[47] is also what separates 'popular', pre-ontological and naïvely 'anthropological' interpretations (as is Sartre's, according to Heidegger) from authentic ones, Heidegger places his work out of reach and condemns in advance any reading which, whether intentionally or not, would limit itself to its vulgar meaning and which would, for example, reduce the analysis of 'inauthentic' existence to a sociological description, as some well-intentioned but wrong-headed interpreters have done, and as the sociologist also does, but with a totally different purpose. By positing within the work itself a distinction between two different readings of it, Heidegger finds himself well placed to persuade the consenting reader, when faced with the most disconcerting puns or the most blatant platitudes, to seek guidance from the master. The reader may of course understand only too well, but he is persuaded to doubt the authenticity of his own understanding, and to prohibit himself from judging a work which has been set up once and for all as the yardstick of its own comprehension. Like a priest who, as Weber observes, has the means to make the lay person carry the responsibility for the failure of the cultural enterprise, the great priestly prophecy thus guarantees the complicity of the interpreters who have no option but to pursue and recognize the necessity of the work, even through accidents, shifts and lapses, or find themselves cast out into the darkness of 'error' or, even better, 'errance'.

Here, in passing, is a remarkable example of interpretation mania, calling on the combined resources of the international interpreters' guild, in order to avoid the simplistic, as denounced in advance by a magisterial pun: 'In English this term (errance) is an artefact with the following warrant: The primary sense of the Latin *errare* is "to wander", the secondary sense "to go astray" or "to err", in the sense of "to wander from the right path". This double sense is retained in the French *errer*. In English, the two senses are retained in the adjectival form, "errant": the first sense ("to wander") being used to describe persons who wander about searching for adventure (vg. "knights errant"); the second sense signifying "deviating from the true or correct", "erring". The noun form, "errance", is not justified by normal English usage, but we introduce it ourselves (following the example of the French translators, pp. 96 ff.), intending to suggest both nuances of "wandering about" and of "going astray" ("erring"), the former the fundament of the latter. This seems to be faithful to the author's intentions and *to avoid as much as possible the simplest interpretations* that would spontaneously arise by translating as "error".'[48]

As the source of authority and guarantees, texts are naturally the object of strategies which, in these domains, are effective only if they are concealed as such, and especially – that is the function of belief – in the eyes of their own authors; sharing in their symbolic capital is granted in exchange for that respect for the proprieties which define in each case, according to the objective distance between the work and the interpreter, the style of the relation to be established between them. What is required is a more complete analysis, in each particular case, of the specific interests of the interpreter, whether researcher, official spokesperson, inspired commentator or straight-forward teacher, according to the relative position of the work being interpreted and the interpreter in their respective hierarchies at a given moment; and to determine how and where they guide the interpretation. It would thus be very difficult to understand a position as apparently paradoxical as that of the French Heidegge-rian Marxists – followers of Marcuse[49] and Hobert[50] – without bearing in mind that the Heideggerian whitewashing exercise came just in time to meet the expectations of those Marxists who were most concerned to let themselves off the hook by linking the *pleibeia philosophia par excellence*, then strongly suspected of being 'trivial', with the most prestigious of contemporary philosophies.[51] Of all the manipulative devices hidden in the 'Letter on humanism',[52] none was able to influence 'distinguished' Marxists more effectively than the second-degree strategy which involved re-interpreting for a new political context – committed to talking the language of 'a fruitful dialogue with Marxism' – the typically Heideggerian strategy of an (artificial) *overcoming through radicalization* which the early Heidegger directed against the Marxist concept of alienation (*Ent-*

fremdung): 'the fundamental ontology' which grounds what Marx described as 'the experience of alienation' (albeit in a manner that remained too 'anthropological') in the most radical and fundamental alienation of human beings, i.e. their forgetting of the truth of Being, surely represents the *nec plus ultra* of radicalism.[53]

> One only has to reread the account of a discussion between Jean Beaufret, Henri Lefebvre and Kostas Axelos[54] in order to convince oneself that this unexpected philosophical combination owes little to what may be called strictly 'internal' arguments: 'I was *enchanted* and seized by a vision – not a particularly exact description – that was all the more striking for the way it *contrasted with the triviality* of most of the philosophical texts that have appeared over the years' (H. Lefebvre); 'There is *no antagonism* between Heidegger's cosmic-historical vision and Marx's historical–practical conception' (H. Lefebvre); 'What provided the common ground and I believe links Marx and Heidegger is the era itself in which we live, the era of highly advanced industrial civilization and of the global diffusion of technology . . . Ultimately, the two thinkers do at least share the same objective . . . Unlike, for example, the sociologists who analyse only specific manifestations here and there' (F. Châtelet);[55] 'Marx and Heidegger *both* proceed to a *radical critique* of the world of the present as well as the past, and they share a common concern to plan for the future of the planet' (K. Axelos); 'Heidegger's essential contribution is to help us understand what Marx has said' (J. Beaufret); 'The impossibility of being Nazi is part and parcel of the reversal between *Being and Time* and *Time and Being*. If *Being and Time* did not preserve Heidegger from Nazism, *Time and Being*, which is not a book but the sum of his reflections since 1930 and his publications since 1946, distanced him from it for good' (J. Beaufret); 'Heidegger is *well and truly materialistic*' (H. Lefebvre); 'Heidegger, in a very different style, continues Marx's work' (F. Châtelet).

The specific interests of the interpreters, and the very logic of the field which conveys the most prestigious works to the readers with the greatest vocation and talent for hermeneutic hagiography, do not explain how, at a certain point, Heideggerian philosophy came to be recognized in the most diverse sectors of the philosophical field as the most *distinguished* fulfilment of the philosophical ambition. This social destiny could only be realized on the basis of a pre-existing affinity of dispositions, itself deriving from the logic of recruitment and training of the body of philosophy professors and from the position of the philosophical field in the structure of the university field and intellectual field, etc. The petit-bourgeois elitism of this 'cream' of the professorial body constituted by philosophy professors

(who have often come from the lower strata of the petite bourgeoisie
and who, by their academic prowess, have conquered the peaks of
the hierarchy of humanist disciplines to reach the topmost ivory
tower of the educational system, high above the world and any
worldly power) could hardly fail to resonate harmoniously with
Heidegger's thought, that exemplary product of an homologous
disposition.

All of the effects which appear most specific to Heideggerian
language, notably all of the effects which constitute the *flabby
rhetoric of the homily*, a variation on the words of a sacred text which
serves as the source of an unending and unremitting commentary,
guided by the intention to exhaust a subject which is by definition
inexhaustible, represent the exemplary limit and therefore the
absolute legitimation of the professional tics and tricks which allow
the 'ex-cathedra prophets' (*Kathederpropheten*), as Weber called
them, to re-produce mundanely the illusion of being above the
mundane. These effects of priestly prophecy therefore succeed fully
only if they rest on the profound complicity that links the author and
his interpreters in an acceptance of the presuppositions implied by a
sociological definition of the function of 'the lesser ministerial
prophet', as Weber again put it; and none of these presuppositions
serves Heidegger's interests better than the *divinization of the text*
conferred by any self-respectingly literate reader. It required a
transgression of the academic imperative of neutrality as extraordinary as enrolment in the Nazi Party for the question of Heidegger's
'political thought' to be raised, and then it was immediately set aside
again, as it seemed an improper suggestion, which is yet another
form of neutralization: the definition which excludes any overt
reference to politics in philosophy has been so profoundly internalized by professors of philosophy that they have managed to forget
that Heidegger's philosophy is political from beginning to end.

But comprehension within established forms would remain empty
and formal if it did not often mask a kind of understanding which is
both more profound and more obscure, and which is built on the
more or less perfect homology of positions and the affinity of the
habitus. To understand also means to understand without having to
be told, to read between the lines, by re-enacting in the mode of
practice (in most cases unconsciously) the linguistic associations and
substitutions initially set up by the producer: this is how a solution is
found to the specific contradiction of ideological discourse, which
draws its efficacy from its duplicity, and can only legitimately express
social interest in forms which dissimulate or betray it. The homology

of positions and the largely successful orchestration of divergent habitus encourage a practical recognition of the interests which the reader represents and the specific form of censorship which prohibits their direct expression, and this recognition gives direct access, independently of any conscious act of decoding, to what discourse *means*.[56] This pre-verbal understanding is engendered by the encounter between an as yet unspoken, indeed repressed, expressive interest, and its accepted mode of expression, which is already articulated according to the norms of a field.[57]

Part III

Symbolic Power and the Political Field

7

On Symbolic Power

This text, which was written as part of an attempt to present an assessment of a number of investigations of symbolism in an academic situation of a particular type – that of the lecture in a foreign university (Chicago, April 1973) – must not be read as a history, even an academic history, of theories of symbolism, and especially not as a sort of pseudo-Hegelian reconstruction of a procedure which would have led, by successive acts of dialectical transcendence, to the 'final theory'.

If the 'immigration of ideas', as Marx puts it, rarely happens without these ideas incurring some damage in the process, this is because such immigration separates cultural productions from the system of theoretical reference points in relation to which they are consciously or unconsciously defined, in other words, from the field of production, sign-posted by proper names or concepts ending in '-ism', a field which always defines them far more than they contribute to defining it. That is why 'immigration' situations make it particularly necessary to bring to light the horizon of reference which, in ordinary situations, may remain implicit. But it is self-evident that the fact of *repatriating* this exported produce involves great dangers of naïvety and simplification – and also great risks, since it provides us with an instrument of objectification.

None the less, in a state of the field in which power is visible everywhere, while in previous ages people refused to recognize it even where it was staring them in the face, it is perhaps useful to remember that, without turning power into a 'circle whose centre is everywhere and nowhere', which could be to dissolve it in yet another way, we have to be able to discover it in places where it is least visible, where it is most completely misrecognized – and thus, in fact, recognized. For symbolic power is that invisible power which can be exercised only with the complicity of those who do not want to know that they are subject to it or even that they themselves exercise it.

'Symbolic Systems' (Art, Religion, Language) as Structuring Structures

The neo-Kantian tradition (Humboldt–Cassirer or, in its American variant, Sapir–Whorf, as far as language is concerned) treats the different symbolic universes (myth, language, art and science) as instruments for knowing and constructing the world of objects, as 'symbolic forms', thus recognizing, as Marx notes in his *Theses on Feuerbach*, the 'active aspect' of cognition. In the same tradition, but with a more properly historical intent, Panofsky treats perspective as a *historical form*, without however going so far as to reconstruct systematically its *social conditions* of production.

Durkheim explicitly includes himself in the Kantian tradition. None the less, by virtue of the fact that he endeavours to give a 'positive' and 'empirical' answer to the problem of knowledge by avoiding the alternative of apriorism and empiricism, he lays the foundations of a *sociology of symbolic forms* (Cassirer was to say expressly that he uses the concept of 'symbolic form' as an equivalent of form of classification).[1] With Durkheim, the forms of classification cease to be universal (transcendental) forms and become (as is implicitly the case in Panofsky) *social forms*, that is, forms that are arbitrary (relative to a particular group) and socially determined.[2]

In this idealist tradition, the objectivity of the meaning or sense of the world is defined by the consent or agreement of the structuring subjectivities (sensus = consensus).

'Symbolic Systems' as Structured Structures (Susceptible to Structural Analysis)

Structural analysis constitutes the methodological instrument which enables the neo-Kantian ambition of grasping the specific logic of each of the 'symbolic forms' to be realized. Proceeding, in accordance with Schelling's wish, to a properly *tautegorical* (in opposition to *allegorical*) reading which refers the myth to nothing outside itself, structural analysis aims at laying bare the structure immanent in each symbolic production. But, unlike the neo-Kantian tradition,

Figure 1

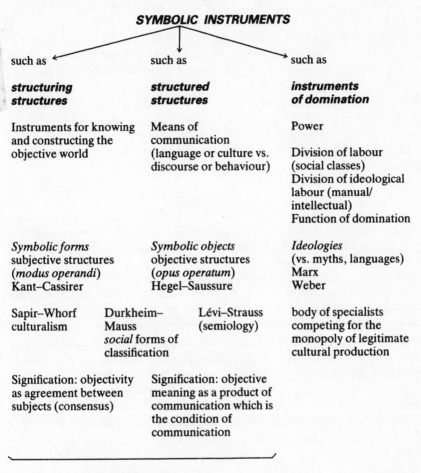

SYMBOLIC INSTRUMENTS

such as ←   such as   → such as

structuring structures	*structured structures*	*instruments of domination*
Instruments for knowing and constructing the objective world	Means of communication (language or culture vs. discourse or behaviour)	Power
		Division of labour (social classes)
		Division of ideological labour (manual/ intellectual)
		Function of domination
Symbolic forms subjective structures (*modus operandi*) Kant–Cassirer	*Symbolic objects* objective structures (*opus operatum*) Hegel–Saussure	*Ideologies* (vs. myths, languages) Marx Weber
Sapir–Whorf culturalism	Durkheim– Mauss *social* forms of classification Lévi–Strauss (semiology)	body of specialists competing for the monopoly of legitimate cultural production
Signification: objectivity as agreement between subjects (consensus)	Signification: objective meaning as a product of communication which is the condition of communication	

sociology of symbolic forms:
contribution of symbolic power to
the gnoseological order:
sense = consensus, i.e. *doxa*

Ideological power as specific contribution
of symbolic violence (orthodoxy) to
political violence (domination)

Division of the labour of domination

which emphasized the *modus operandi* or productive activity of consciousness, the structuralist tradition emphasizes the *opus operatum* or structured structures. This is evident in the way Saussure, the founder of this tradition, views language: as a structured system, language (*langue*) is fundamentally treated as the condition of intelligibility of speech (*parole*), as the structured medium which has to be reconstructed in order to account for the constant relation between sound and meaning. (In the opposition he establishes between iconology and iconography, and which is the exact equivalent of the opposition between phonology and phonetics, Panofsky – and that entire aspect of his work which aims at laying bare the deep structures of works of art – is part of this tradition.)

First synthesis

As instruments of knowledge and communication, 'symbolic structures' can exercise a structuring power only because they themselves are structured. Symbolic power is a power of constructing reality, and one which tends to establish a *gnoseological* order: the immediate meaning of the world (and in particular of the social world) depends on what Durkheim calls *logical conformism*, that is, 'a homogeneous conception of time, space, number and cause, one which makes it possible for different intellects to reach agreement'. Durkheim – and, after him, Radcliffe-Brown, who makes 'social solidarity' dependent on the sharing of a symbolic system – has the merit of designating the *social function* (in the sense of structural-functionalism) of symbolism in an explicit way: it is an authentic political function which cannot be reduced to the structuralists' function of communication. Symbols are the instruments *par excellence* of 'social integration': as instruments of knowledge and communication (cf. Durkheim's analysis of the festivity), they make it possible for there to be a *consensus* on the meaning of the social world, a consensus which contributes fundamentally to the reproduction of the social order. 'Logical' integration is the precondition of 'moral' integration.[3]

SYMBOLIC PRODUCTIONS AS INSTRUMENTS OF DOMINATION

The Marxist tradition lays great emphasis on the *political functions* of 'symbolic systems', to the detriment of their logical structure and gnoseological function (although Engels talks of 'systematic expression' in relation to law). This functionalism (which has nothing in common with the structural-functionalism of Durkheim or Radcliffe-Brown) explains symbolic productions by relating them to the interests of the dominant class. Unlike myth, which is a collective and collectively appropriated product, ideologies serve particular interests which they tend to present as universal interests, shared by the group as a whole. The dominant culture contributes to the real integration of the dominant class (by facilitating the communication between all its members and by distinguishing them from other classes); it also contributes to the fictitious integration of society as a whole, and thus to the apathy (false consciousness) of the dominated classes; and finally, it contributes to the legitimation of the established order by establishing distinctions (hierarchies) and legitimating these distinctions. The dominant culture produces this ideological effect by concealing the function of division beneath the function of communication: the culture which unifies (the medium of communication) is also the culture which separates (the instrument of distinction) and which legitimates distinctions by forcing all other cultures (designated as sub-cultures) to define themselves by their distance from the dominant culture.

Second synthesis

In criticizing all forms of the 'interactionist' error which consists in reducing relations of power to relations of communication, it is not enough to note that relations of communication are always, inseparably, power relations which, in form and content, depend on the material or symbolic power accumulated by the agents (or institutions) involved in these relations and which, like the gift or the potlatch, can enable symbolic power to be accumulated. It is as structured and structuring instruments of communication and knowledge that 'symbolic systems' fulfil their political function, as instruments which help to ensure that one class dominates another (symbolic violence) by bringing their own distinctive power to bear on the relations of power which underlie them and thus by contributing, in Weber's terms, to the 'domestication of the dominated'.

The different classes and class fractions are engaged in a symbolic struggle properly speaking, one aimed at imposing the definition of the social world that is best suited to their interests. The field of ideological stances thus reproduces in transfigured form the field of social positions.[4] These classes can engage in this struggle either directly, in the symbolic conflicts of everyday life, or else by proxy, via the struggle between the different specialists in symbolic production (full-time producers), a struggle over the monopoly of legitimate symbolic violence (cf. Weber), that is, of the power to impose (or even to inculcate) the arbitrary instruments of knowledge and expression (taxonomies) of social reality – but instruments whose arbitrary nature is not realized as such. The field of symbolic production is a microcosm of the symbolic struggle between classes; it is by serving their own interests in the struggle within the field of production (and only to this extent) that producers serve the interests of groups outside the field of production.

The dominant class is the site of a struggle over the hierarchy of the principles of hierarchization. Dominant class fractions, whose power rests on economic capital, aim to impose the legitimacy of their domination either through their own symbolic production, or through the intermediary of conservative ideologues, who never really serve the interests of the dominant class except *as a side-effect* and who always threaten to appropriate for their own benefit the power to define the social world that they hold by delegation. The dominated fraction (clerics or 'intellectuals' and 'artists', depending on the period) always tends to set the specific capital, to which it owes its position, at the top of the hierarchy of the principles of hierarchization.

SOURCES AND EFFECTS OF SYMBOLIC POWER

As instruments of domination that are structuring because they are structured, the ideological systems that specialists produce in and for the struggle over the monopoly of legitimate ideological production reproduce in a misrecognizable form, through the intermediary of the homology between the field of ideological production and the field of social classes, the structure of the field of social classes.

'Symbolic systems' are fundamentally distinguishable according to whether they are produced and thereby appropriated by the group as a whole or, on the contrary, produced by a body of *specialists* and, more precisely, by a relatively autonomous field of production and circulation. The history of the transformation of myth into religion (ideology) cannot be separated from the history of the constitution of a body of specialized producers of religious rites and discourse, i.e. from the development of the *division of religious labour*, which is itself a dimension of the development of the division of social labour, and thus of the division into classes. This religious division leads, among other consequences, to members of the laity being *disposses-sed* of the instruments of symbolic production.[5]

Ideologies owe their structure and their most specific functions to the social conditions of their production and circulation, that is, first, to the functions they perform for specialists competing for a monopoly over the competence under consideration (religious, artistic, etc); and second, and as a by-product of this, to the functions they perform for non-specialists. We must remember that ideologies are always *doubly determined*, that they owe their most specific characteristics not only to the interests of the classes or class fractions they express (the function of sociodicy), but also to the specific interests of those who produce them and to the specific logic of the field of production (commonly transfigured into the form of an ideology of 'creation' and of the 'creative artist'). This provides us with a means of avoiding the brutal reduction of ideological products to the interests of the classes which they serve (this 'short-circuit' effect is common in Marxist criticism) without succumbing to the idealist illusion which consists in treating ideological productions as self-sufficient, self-created totalities amenable to a pure and purely internal analysis (semiology).[6]

The properly ideological function of the field of ideological production is performed almost automatically on the basis of the structural homology between the field of ideological production and the field of class struggle. The homology between the two fields means that struggles over the specific objects of the autonomous field automatically produce *euphemized* forms of the economic and political struggles between classes: it is in the correspondence of structure to structure that the properly ideological function of the dominant discourse is performed. This discourse is a structured and structuring medium tending to impose an apprehension of the established order as natural (orthodoxy) through the disguised (and thus misrecognized) imposition of systems of classification and of mental structures that are objectively adjusted to social structures. The fact that the correspondence can be effected only from system to system conceals, both from the eyes of the producers themselves and from the eyes of non-professionals, the fact that internal systems of classification reproduce overt political taxonomies in misrecogniz-able form, as well as the fact that the specific axiomatics of each specialized field is the transformed form (in conformity with the laws specific to the field) of the fundamental principles of the division of labour. (For example, the university system of classification, which mobilizes in misrecognizable form the objective divisions of the social structure and especially the division of labour, in both theory and practice, converts social properties into natural properties.) The truly ideological effect consists precisely in the imposition of political systems of classification beneath the legitimate appearance of philosophical, religious, legal (etc.) taxonomies. Symbolic systems owe their distinctive power to the fact that the relations of power expressed through them are manifested only in the misrecognizable form of relations of meaning (displacement).

Symbolic power – as a power of constituting the given through utterances, of making people see and believe, of confirming or transforming the vision of the world and, thereby, action on the world and thus the world itself, an almost magical power which enables one to obtain the equivalent of what is obtained through force (whether physical or economic), by virtue of the specific effect of mobilization – is a power that can be exercised only if it is *recognized*, that is, misrecognized as arbitrary. This means that symbolic power does not reside in 'symbolic systems' in the form of an 'illocutionary force' but that it is defined in and through a given relation between those who exercise power and those who submit to it, i.e. in the very structure of the field in which *belief* is produced and reproduced.[7] What creates the power of words and slogans, a power capable of maintaining or subverting the social order, is the belief in the legitimacy of words and of those who utter them. And words alone cannot create this belief.

Symbolic power, a subordinate power, is a transformed, i.e. misrecognizable, transfigured and legitimated form of the other forms of power. One can transcend the alternative of energetic models, which describe social relations as relations of force, and cybernetic models, which turn them into relations of communication, only by describing the laws of transformation which govern the transmutation of the different kinds of capital into symbolic capital, and in particular the labour of dissimulation and transfiguration (in a word, of *euphemization*) which secures a real transubstantiation of the relations of power by rendering recognizable and misrecognizable the violence they objectively contain and thus by transforming them into symbolic power, capable of producing real effects without any apparent expenditure of energy.[8]

8

Political Representation

Elements for a Theory of the Political Field

To the Memory of Georges Haupt

The silence that weighs on the conditions which force citizens, all the more brutally the more economically and culturally deprived they are, to face the alternative of having to abdicate their rights by abstaining from voting or being dispossessed by the fact that they delegate their power, bears the same relation to 'political science' as the silence that weighs on the economic and cultural conditions of 'rational' economic behaviour bears to economics. If it is going to avoid *naturalizing* the social mechanisms which produce and reproduce the gap between politically 'active' agents and politically 'passive' agents[1] and setting up as eternal laws historical regularities that are valid within the limits of a given state of the structure of the distribution of capital, and cultural capital in particular, any analysis of the political struggle must be based on the social and economic determinants of the division of political labour.[2]

The political field, understood both as a field of forces and as a field of struggles aimed at transforming the relation of forces which confers on this field its structure at any given moment, is not an *imperium in imperio*: the effects of external necessity make their presence felt in it by virtue, above all, of the relation which those who are represented, through their differential distance from the instruments of political production, have with those who represent them, and of the relation that the latter, through their own dispositions, have with their organizations. The unequal distribution of the instruments of production of an explicitly formulated representation of the social world means that political life can be described in terms of the logic of supply and demand: the political field is the site in which, through the competition between the agents involved in it, political products, issues, programmes, analyses, commentaries, concepts and events are created – products between which ordinary citizens, reduced to the status of 'consumers', have to choose, thereby running a risk of misunderstanding that is all the greater the further they are from the place of production.

THE MONOPOLY OF THE PROFESSIONALS

Without repeating here the analysis of the social conditions constitutive of the social and technical competence demanded by active participation in 'politics',[3] we must at least remember that the effects created by the morphological obstacles that the size of political units and the number of citizens put in the way of any form of direct government are, so to speak, reinforced by the effects of economic and cultural dispossession: the concentration of political capital in the hands of a small number of people is something that is prevented with greater difficulty – and thus all the more likely to happen – the more completely ordinary individuals are divested of the material and cultural instruments necessary for them to participate actively in politics, that is, above all, *leisure time* and *cultural capital*.[4]

Because the products offered by the political field are instruments for perceiving and expressing the social world (or, if you like, principles of di-vision), the distribution of opinions in a given population depends on the state of the instruments of perception and expression available and on the access that different groups have to these instruments. This means that the political field in fact produces an effect of censorship by limiting the universe of political discourse, and thereby the universe of what is politically thinkable, to the finite space of discourses capable of being produced or reproduced within the limits of the political *problematic*, understood as a space of stances effectively adopted within the field – i.e. stances that are socio-logically possible given the laws that determine entry into the field. The boundary between what is politically sayable or unsayable, thinkable or unthinkable, for a class of non-professionals is determined by the relation between the expressive interests of that class and the capacity to express these interests, a capacity which is secured by its position in the relations of cultural and thus political production. 'An intention', observes Wittgenstein, 'is embedded in its situation, in human customs and institutions. If the technique of the game of chess did not exist, I could not intend to play a game of chess. In so far as I do intend the construction of a sentence in advance, that is made possible by the fact that I can speak the language in question.'[5] A political intention can be constituted only in one's relation to a given state of the political game and, more precisely, of the universe of the techniques of action and expression it offers at any given moment. In this and other cases, moving from the implicit to the explicit, from one's subjective impression to objective expression, to public manifestation in the form of a discourse or public act, constitutes in itself an act of *institution* and thereby represents a form of officialization and legitimation: it is no coincidence that, as Benveniste observes, all the words relating to the law have an etymological root meaning *to say*. And the institution, understood as that which is already instituted, already made explicit, creates at one and the same time an effect of public care and lawfulness and an effect of closure and dispossession.

Given the fact that, at least outside periods of crisis, the production of politically effective and legitimate forms of perception and expression is the monopoly of professionals, and is thus subjected to the constraints and limitations inherent in the functioning of the political field, it is evident that the effects of the kind of property-based electoral logic (which in fact controls access to the choice between the political products on offer) are intensified by the effects of the oligopolistic logic which governs the supply of products. This monopoly of production is left in the hands of a body of professionals, in other words, of a small number of units of production, themselves supervised by professionals; these constraints weigh heavily on the choices made by consumers, who are all the more dedicated to an unquestioned *loyalty* to recognized brands and to an unconditional delegating of power to their representatives the more they lack any *social competence* for politics and any of their own instruments of production of political discourse or acts. The market of politics is doubtless one of the least free markets that exist.

The constraints of the market weigh first and foremost on those members of the dominated classes who have no choice but to abdicate or hand over their power to the party, a permanent organization which has to produce the *representation* of the continuity of the class, which always risks lapsing into the discontinuity of atomized existence (falling back into private life and the quest for individual paths to salvation) or into the particularity of strictly protest struggles.[6] This means that, more than the members of the dominant classes, who can satisfy themselves with associations, pressure groups or party associations,[7] they need parties understood as *permanent* organizations whose aim is to win power, and offering their militants and their electors not only a doctrine but a *programme* of thought and action, and thereby demanding in advance total support. As Marx notes in *The Poverty of Philosophy*, one can date the birth of a social group from the moment the members of its representative organizations do not struggle merely for the defence of the economic interests of their supporters and members but for the defence and development of the organization itself. But how can one fail to see that, if the existence of a permanent organization, relatively independent of corporate and conjunctural interests, is a precondition of the permanent and properly political *representation* of the class, it also carries the threat that the 'ordinary' members of the class will be dispossessed? The antinomy of the 'established revolutionary power', as Bakunin calls it, is quite similar to that of the reformed church as described by Troeltsch. The *fides implicita*, a total and comprehensive delegating of power through which the most deprived people grant, *en bloc*, a sort of unlimited credit to the party of their choice, gives free rein to the mechanisms which tend to divest them of any control over the apparatus. This means that, by a strange irony, the concentration of political capital is at its greatest – in the absence of a deliberate (and improbable) intervention against this trend – in parties whose aim is to struggle against the concentration of economic capital.

Gramsci often referred to the tendency observable in communist parties to treat the party and its bosses with a kind of millenarian fideism, as if they were to be as revered as providence itself: 'In our party, we have had another aspect of the danger to lament: the withering of all individual activity; the passivity of the mass of members; the stupid confidence that there is always somebody else who is thinking of everything and taking care of everything.' 'Disturbed by their condition of absolute inferiority, lacking any constitutional education, the masses abdicated completely all sovereignty and all power. The organization became identified for them with the organizer as an individual, just as for an army in the field the individual commander becomes the protector of the safety of all, the guarantor of success and victory.'[8] And one could also quote, *a contrario*, Rosa Luxemburg, when she describes (with a good deal of wishful thinking) a party which itself limits its own power by the conscious and constant effort of its bosses to strip themselves of power so as to act as the executors of the will of the masses. 'The only role of the so-called "leaders" of social-democracy consists in enlightening the masses concerning their historic mission. The authority and influence of the "bosses" in a democracy increase only in proportion to the educative activity they perform towards this end. In other words, their prestige and their influence increase only in so far as the bosses destroy what was hitherto the function of the leaders, the blindness of the masses, in so far as they strip themselves of their status as bosses, and in so far as they turn the masses themselves into the leaders and turn themselves into the *executive* organs of the conscious action of the masses.'[9] It would be interesting to determine what, in the positions on this problem adopted by the different 'theoreticians' (who, like Gramsci, can swing from the spontaneism of *Ordine Nuovo* to the centralism of his article on the Communist Party)[10] stems from objective factors (such as the level of the general and political education of the masses), in particular from the direct experience of the attitudes of the masses in a given set of historical circumstances, and what stems from effects of the field and from the logic of internal opposition.

Those who dominate the party, and who have a close interest in the existence and persistence of this institution and in the specific profits it secures for them, find, in the freedom they gain through their monopoly of the production and imposition of *instituted political interests*, the possibility of imposing their own interests as the interests of those whom they represent. And yet nothing demonstrates unambiguously that the interests of the representatives, thus universalized and ratified by plebiscite, do not coincide with the unexpressed interests of the individuals represented, since the former hold a monopoly of the instruments of production of the political (that is, politically expressed and recognized) interests of the latter – nothing except that form of active abstention that is rooted in revolt against a twofold impotence: an impotence with regard to politics and all the purely serial actions it proposes, and an impotence with regard to the political apparatuses. Apoliticism, which sometimes takes the form of anti-parliamentarianism and which can be channelled into various forms of Bonapartism, Boulangism and Gaullism, is fundamentally a protest against the monopoly of the politicians, and represents the political equivalent of what was in previous periods the religious revolt against the monopoly of the clerics.

COMPETENCE, STAKES AND SPECIFIC INTERESTS

In politics as in art, the dispossession of the majority of the people is a correlate, or even a consequence, of the concentration of the specifically political means of production in the hands of professionals, who can enter into the distinctive political game with some chance of success only on condition that they possess a specific competence. Indeed, nothing is less natural than the mode of thought and action demanded by participation in the political field: like the religious, artistic or scientific habitus, the habitus of the politician depends on a special training. This includes in the first instance, of course, the entire apprenticeship necessary to acquire the corpus of specific kinds of knowledge (theories, problematics, concepts, historical traditions, economic data, etc.) produced and accumulated by the political work of the professionals of the present or the past, or to acquire the more general skills such as the mastery of a certain kind of language and of a certain political rhetoric – that of the *popular orator*, indispensable when it comes to cultivating one's relations with non-professionals, or that of the *debater*, which is necessary in relations between fellow professionals. But it is also and above all that sort of *initiation*, with its ordeals and its rites of passage, which tends to inculcate the *practical mastery* of the immanent logic of the political field and to impose a *de facto submission* to the values, hierarchies and censorship mechanisms inherent in this field, or in the specific form that the constraints and control mechanisms of the field assume within each political party. This means that, to gain a complete understanding of the political discourses that are on offer in the market at a given moment and which, when considered together, define the universe of what can be said and thought politically, as opposed to what is rejected as unsayable and unthinkable, we would have to analyse the entire process of production of the professionals of ideological production, starting with the way they are marked out, according to the frequently implicit definition of the desired competence, which designates them for these functions, then considering the general or specific education which prepares them to assume these functions, and finally examining the action of continuous normalization imposed on them, with their own complicity, by the older members of their group, in particular when, newly elected, they gain access to a political organization into which they might bring a certain outspokenness and an independence of manners which might be prejudicial to the rules of the game.

The dispossession that goes together with the concentration of the means of production of the instruments of production of discourse or actions socially recognized as political has continued to increase as the field of ideological production has increased its autonomy with the appearance of the great political bureaucracies of full-time professionals and with the appearance of institutions (such as, in France, the *Institut des sciences politiques* and the *Ecole nationale d'administration*) whose function is to select and educate the professional producers of the schemes of thought and expression of the social world – politicians, political journalists, high-ranking civil servants, etc. – at the same time as they codify the *rules* according to which the field of ideological production functions and the corpus of knowledge and practical skills indispensable for them to conform to these rules. The 'political science' taught in the institutions specially designed to fulfil this purpose is the *rationalization* of the competence demanded by the universe of politics and possessed in a practical form by professionals: it aims at increasing the efficiency of this practical mastery by putting at its service rational techniques, such as opinion polls, public relations and political marketing, at the same time as it tends to legitimate it by giving it the appearance of scientificity and by treating political questions as matters for specialists which it is the specialists' responsibility to answer in the name of knowledge and not of class interests.[11]

The process whereby the field of ideological production becomes more autonomous is doubtless accompanied by an increase in the standards expected of anyone seeking right of entry to the field and, in particular, by a reinforcement of the demands on their general or even specific competence. (This helps to explain the increase in the influence of professionals educated in the universities and even the specialized higher-education institutions – the *Institut des sciences politiques* and the *Ecole nationale d'administration* – to the detriment of ordinary militants.)[12] It is also doubtless accompanied by a strengthening of the effect of the internal laws of the political field – and in particular of competition between professionals – when compared with the effect of direct or indirect transactions between professionals and non-professionals.[13] This means that, in order to understand a political stance, programme, intervention, electioneering speech, etc., it is at least as important to know the universe of stances currently offered by the field as it is to know the demands made by non-professionals of whom the leaders, in adopting these stances, are the declared representatives (the 'base'): adopting a stance, a *prise de position*, is, as the phrase clearly suggests, an act which has meaning only relationally, in and through difference, the *distinctive deviation*. The well informed politician is the one who manages to master practically the objective meaning and social effect of his stances by virtue of having mastered the space of actual and

A SELF-INTERESTED BLUNDER

Coluche's decision to stand for President in France was immediately condemned by almost all political professionals, who
called it *Poujadism*. However, you would seek in vain among the
themes proposed by the Paris comedian the most typical topics
of the bookseller from Saint-Céré, Poujade, as the classic study
by Stanley Hoffman has listed them: nationalism, anti-
intellectualism, anti-Parisianism, racist and quasi-fascist xenopho-
bia, exaltation of the middle classes, moralism, and so on. And it is
difficult to understand how 'well-informed observers' were able to
confuse the 'candidate of all minorities', of all those 'who are
never represented by political parties', 'gays, apprentices, Blacks,
Arabs, etc.', with the defender of small shopkeepers struggling
against 'wogs' and 'the stateless mafia of drug-traffickers and
queers'.*

Although the social bases of the Poujadist movement are poorly
understood, it is clear that it found its first troops and its most
faithful supporters in the petite bourgeoisie of provincial craftsmen and small traders, most of them getting on in years and
threatened by economic and social transformations. Two inquiries, by the two French opinion poll organizations IFRES and
IFOP, produced similar results, showing that those who sym-
pathized with Coluche's *candidature* displayed completely different characteristics. The tendency to approve of Coluche's candidature varied in inverse proportion to age: it reached its maximum
among the youngest (and among these, especially the men), and
only a fraction (about a third) of people aged over 65 found it
scandalous. In the same way, support tended to increase with the
size of the town where one lived: it was very small in rural districts
and small towns, and reached a maximum in cities and in Paris and
its suburbs. Although the categories employed in the two polling
institutes are both imprecise and difficult to compare directly,
everything seems to suggest that it was workers and employees,
and also intellectuals and artists, who declared themselves most
clearly in favour of this anomic candidate, whereas he was most
vigorously rejected by captains of industry and commerce. This is
easily understood if we realize that the votes thus diverted came
principally from the left (more from the Socialist Party than from
the Communist Party) and also from ecologists and abstainers.
The proportion of people questioned who, had Coluche not been
standing, would have voted for right-wing parties was small, and

these votes would have tended to go back to the Socialist Party in particular (the proportion of those who would have chosen abstention is of course very high in all categories). The fact that the proportion of Coluche supporters was clearly higher among men than among women allows us to suppose that this choice was the expression of an active abstentionism, something very different from the simple indifference linked to the incompetence due to low status.

Thus the professionals, politicians and journalists, tried to refuse to this 'troublemaker' a right of entry which the non-professionals granted him overwhelmingly (two thirds of them were favourable to the *principle* of his standing). This is doubtless because, by entering the game without taking it seriously and without taking himself seriously, this extra-ordinary player threatened the very foundation of the game, in other words, both the belief and the credibility of the ordinary players. The authorized representatives of power were caught in the very act of abusing power: whereas, in the normal course of events, they present themselves as spokespersons of 'public opinion', and as guarantors of all authorized words, they give us, not the truth about the social world, but the truth about their relation to that world, forcing us to ask whether the same is not equally the case on other occasions.

* S. Hoffman, *Le mouvement Poujade*, Cahiers de la fondation nationale des sciences politiques (Paris: A. Colin, 1956), pp. 209–60, 246.

especially potential stances or, better, of the principle underlying these stances, namely, the space of objective positions in the field and the dispositions of those who occupy them. This 'practical sense' of the possible and impossible, probable and improbable stances for the different occupants of different positions is what enables the politician to 'choose' suitable and agreed stances, and to avoid 'compromising' stances, which would mean being of the same mind as the occupants of opposite positions in the space of the political field. This feel for the political game, which enables politicians to predict the stances of other politicians, is also what makes them predictable for other politicians: predictable and thus responsible, in other words, competent, serious, trustworthy – in short, ready to play, with consistency and without arousing surprise or disappointing people's expectations, the role assigned to them by the structure of the space of the game.

Nothing is demanded more absolutely by the political game than this fundamental adherence to the game itself, *illusio, involvement, commitment*, investment in the game which is the product of the game at the same time as it is the condition of the game being played. So as to avoid excluding themselves from the game and the profits that can be derived from it, whether we are talking about the simple *pleasure* of playing, or of all the material and symbolic advantages associated with the possession of symbolic capital, all those who have the *privilege* of investing in the game (instead of being reduced to the indifference and apathy of apoliticism) accept the tacit contract, implied in the fact of participating in the game, of recognizing thereby that it is indeed *worth playing*. This contract unites them to all the other participants by a sort of *initial collusion*, one far more powerful than all open or secret agreements. This solidarity between all the initiates, linked together by the same fundamental commitment to the game and its stakes, by the same respect (*obsequium*) for the game itself and the unwritten laws which define it, by the same fundamental investment in the game of which they have a monopoly and which they have to perpetuate in order that their own investments are profitable, is never demonstrated so clearly as when the game itself is threatened.

> For groups united by some form of collusion (such as sets of *colleagues*), it is a fundamental imperative to maintain *discretion* about, to keep *secret*, everything which concerns the intimate beliefs of the group. They fiercely condemn manifestations of cynicism displayed to the outside world, even though such manifestations are quite acceptable among *initiates* because they cannot by definition affect the fundamental belief in the value of the group – a certain free-and-easy attitude to values is often experienced as a supplementary proof of their value. (It is well known that politicians and political journalists, normally so zealous to peddle world-weary rumours and anecdotes about politicians, are parti-cularly indignant about those who, even for a single moment, make a show of 'wrecking the game' by bringing into political existence the apoliticism of the working class and petite bourgeoisie which is at once the condition and the product of the monopoly of the politicians.) But groups are hardly less mistrustful of those who, taking proclaimed values too seriously, refuse the compromises and shady deals which are the condition of the real existence of the group.

THE DOUBLE GAME

The struggle which sets professionals against each other is no doubt the form *par excellence* of the symbolic struggle for the conservation or transformation of the social world through the conservation or transformation of the vision of the social world and of the principles of di-vision of this world; or, more precisely, for the conservation or transformation of the divisions established between classes by the conservation or transformation of the systems of classification which are its incorporated form and of the institutions which contribute to perpetuating the current classification by legitimating it.[14] The social conditions of possibility of this struggle may be found in the specific logic by which, in each social formation, the distinctively political game is organized. What is at stake in this game is, on the one hand, the monopoly of the elaboration and diffusion of the legitimate principle of di-vision of the social world and, thereby, of the mobilization of groups, and, on the other hand, the monopoly of the use of objectified instruments of power (objectified political capital). It thus takes the form of a struggle over the specifically symbolic power of making people see and believe, of predicting and prescribing, of making known and recognized, which is at the same time a struggle for power over the 'public powers' (state administrations). In parliamentary democracies, the struggle to win the support of the citizens (their votes, their party subscriptions, etc.) is also a struggle to maintain or subvert *the distribution of power over public powers* (or, in other words, a struggle for the monopoly of the legitimate use of objectified political resources – law, the army, police, public finances, etc.). The most important agents of this struggle are the political parties, combative organizations specially adapted so as to engage in this *sublimated form of civil war* by *mobilizing in an enduring way*, through prescriptive predictions, the greatest possible number of agents endowed with the same vision of the social world and its future. So as to ensure that this enduring mobilization comes about, political parties must on the one hand develop and impose a representation of the social world capable of obtaining the support of the greatest possible number of citizens, and on the other hand win positions (whether of power or not) capable of ensuring that they can wield power over those who grant that power to them.

Thus, the production of ideas about the social world is always in fact subordinated to the logic of the conquest of power, which is the logic of the mobilization of the greatest number. This explains, no doubt, the privilege granted, in the way the legitimate representation is built up, to the *ecclesial* mode of production, in which the proposals (motions, platforms, programmes, etc.) are immediately subjected to the approval of a group and thus can be imposed only by professionals capable of manipulating ideas and groups at one and the same time, of producing ideas capable of producing groups by manipulating ideas in such a way as to ensure that they gain the support of a group (through, for example, the rhetoric of the political meeting or the mastery of the whole set of techniques of public speaking, of wording one's proposals or of manipulating the gathering, techniques which allow you to 'get your motion carried', not to mention the mastery of the procedures and tactics which, like the manipulation of the number of *mandates*, directly control the very production of the group).

It would be wrong to underestimate the autonomy and the specific effectiveness of all that happens in the political field and to reduce political history properly speaking to a sort of epiphenomenal manifestation of economic and social forces of which political actors would be, so to speak, the puppets. This would mean not only ignoring the specifically symbolic effectiveness of representation, and of the mobilizing belief that it elicits by virtue of objectification; it would also mean forgetting the proper political power of *government* which, however dependent it may be on economic and social forces, can have a real impact on these forces via its control over the instruments of the administration of things and persons.

We can compare political life to a theatre only on the condition that we envisage the relation between party and class, between the struggle of political organizations and class struggle, as a truly symbolic relation between a signifier and a signified, or, better, between *representatives* providing a *representation* and the agents, actions and situations that are represented. The congruence between signifier and signified, between the representative and the represented, doubtless results less from the conscious quest to meet the demands of the clientele, or from the mechanical constraint exerted by external pressures, than from the homology between the structure of the political field and the structure of the world represented, between the class struggle and the sublimated form of this struggle which is played out in the political field.[15] It is this homology which means that, by pursuing the satisfaction of the specific interests imposed on them by competition within the field, professionals satisfy in addition the interests of those who delegate them: the struggles of the representatives can be described as a political *mimesis* of the struggles of the groups or classes whose champions they claim to be. But, on the other hand, this homology also means that, in adopting stances that are most in conformity with the interests of those whom they represent, the professionals are still pursuing – without necessarily admitting it to themselves – the satisfaction of their own interests, as these are assigned to them by the structure of positions and oppositions constitutive of the internal space of the political field.

The obligatory devotion to the interests of those who are represented leads one to forget about the interests of the representatives. In other words, the (apparent) relation between representatives and represented, the latter being imagined as a determining cause ('pressure groups', etc.) or final cause ('causes' to be defended, interests to be 'served', etc.), conceals the relation of competition between the representatives and, thereby, the relation of orchestration (or of pre-established harmony) between the representatives and the represented. Max Weber is doubtless right to note, with a healthy materialist bluntness, that there are two kinds of professional politicians, those who live 'off' politics and those who live 'for' politics.[16] To be competely rigorous, we would have to say, rather, that one can live off politics only by living for politics. For it is the relation between professionals which defines the particular kind of interest in politics that determines each category of representatives to devote themselves to politics and, thereby, to those they represent. More precisely, the relation that the professional sellers of political services (politicians, political journalists, etc.) maintain with their clients is always mediated, and more or less completely determined, by the relation they maintain with their competitors.[17] They serve the interests of their clients in so far (and only in so far) as they *also* serve themselves while serving others, that is, *all the more precisely when their position in the structure of the political field coincides more precisely with the position of those they represent in the structure of the social field*. (The closeness of the correspondence between the two spaces doubtless depends to a great extent on the intensity of the competition, that is, first and foremost on the *number* of parties or tendencies, a number which determines the diversity and renewal of products on offer by forcing, for instance, the different political parties to modify their programmes to win new clienteles.) As a consequence, the political discourses produced by professionals are always doubly determined, and affected by a duplicity which is not in the least intentional since it results from the duality of fields of reference and from the necessity of serving at one and the same time the esoteric aims of internal struggles and the exoteric aims of external struggles.[18]

A SYSTEM OF DEVIATIONS

Thus, it is the structure of the political field which, being subjectively inseparable from the direct – and always declared – relation to those who are represented, determines the stances taken, through the intermediary of the constraints and interests associated with a given position in this field. In concrete terms, the production of stances adopted depends on the system of stances that are conjointly proposed by the set of antagonistic political parties, in other words on the *political problematic* as a field of strategic possibilities objectively offered to the choice of agents in the form of positions that are actually occupied and stances that are actually proposed in the field. Political parties, like tendencies within these parties, have only a relational existence and it would be futile to try to define what they are and what they profess independently of what their competitors in the same field are and profess.[19]

There is no clearer demonstration of this effect of the field than that sort of *esoteric culture*, comprised of problems that are completely alien or inaccessible to ordinary people, of concepts and discourses that are without referents in the experience of ordinary citizens and, especially, of distinctions, nuances, subtleties and niceties that pass unnoticed by the uninitiated and which have no *raison d'être* other than the relations of conflict or competition between the different organizations or between the 'tendencies' and 'trends' of one and the same organization. We can here cite, once again, the testimony of Gramsci: 'We are becoming separated from the masses. Between us and these masses a cloud of ambiguity, misunderstanding and obscure squabbles is being formed. At a certain point, we will appear like men who want to hold their positions at any price.'[20] In reality, the fact that this properly political culture remains inaccessible to the majority of people is no doubt due less to the complexity of the language in which it is expressed than to the complexity of the social relations that are constitutive of the political field and expressed within it. This artificial creation of Byzantine power struggles appears less as something unintelligible than as something which appears pointless in the eyes of those who, not being players in the game, 'can't see the interest in it' and who cannot understand how this or that distinction between two words or two turns of phrase in a crucial debate, programme, platform, motion or resolution can have given rise to such arguments, because they do not adhere to the principle of the oppositions which produced the arguments that generated these distinctions.[21]

The fact that every political field tends to be organized around the opposition between two poles (which, like political parties in the American system, may themselves be constituted by real fields, organized in accordance with analogous distinctions) should not lead us to forget that the recurrent properties of doctrines or groups situated in positions that are polar opposites, 'the party in favour of change' and the 'party of law and order', 'progressives' and 'conservatives', 'left' and 'right', are *invariants* which can be realized only in and through the relation to a given field. In this way the properties of political parties recorded by realist typologies can be immediately understood if they are related to the relative power of the two poles, to the distance which separates them and which determines the properties of their occupants, parties or politicians (and, in particular, their tendency to diverge towards the extremes or converge on the centre), and which therefore also determines the probability of the central, intermediary position – the neutral zone – being occupied. The field as a whole is defined as a system of deviations on different levels and nothing, either in the institutions or in the agents, the acts or the discourses they produce, has meaning except relationally, by virtue of the interplay of oppositions and distinctions. It is in this way, for instance, that the opposition between the 'right' and the 'left' can be maintained in a structure transformed at the cost of a partial exchange of roles between those who occupy those positions at two different moments (or in two different places): rationalism and the belief in progress and science which, between the wars, in France as well as in Germany, were a characteristic of the left (whereas the nationalist and conservative right succumbed instead to irrationalism and to the cult of nature), have become today, in these two countries, the heart of the new conservative creed, based on confidence in progress, technical knowledge and technocracy, while the left finds itself falling back on ideological themes or on practices which used to belong to the opposite pole, such as the (ecological) cult of nature, regionalism and a certain nationalism, the denunciation of the myth of absolute progress, the defence of the 'person', all of which are steeped in irrationalism.

The acts of theatricalization through which groups exhibit themselves (and, above all, to themselves) in ceremonies, festivals (like the Panathenaea), processions, parades, etc. constitute the elementary form of objectification and, at the same time, the conscious realization of the principles of division according to which these groups are objectively organized and through which the perception that they have of themselves is organized.

It is in this respect that representative institutions (parliaments, general assemblies, councils, *cortes*, etc.) no doubt underlie the most fundamental representations, mental or objective, of the nation and its structure. As a ceremonial which makes *visible* the *ranks* and *numbers* (and which can, for this reason, become a topic of discussion, as was the case with the opening of the General Assembly in France), the spatial projection realized by the two-dimensional schema highlights the *hierarchy* of the groups represented (expressed by their ranking from the top down, or from right to left) and, in some cases, their numerical weight; and, more importantly, it highlights the very *existence* of the groups that are represented and *named*. (In fact, it seems that the idea of representing the *numerical weight* of groups – as exemplified by some engravings representing the 'election table' for the General Assembly, with double representation accorded to the Third Estate, on 27 December 1788 – presupposes that the idea of number and numerical *representativeness* (cf. head counts) has begun to compete with the idea of rank.)

Representative assemblies are a kind of spatial projection of the political field and, through this, of the field of class relations of which the political scene is a theatricalized representation. In other words, the structure according to which these assemblies are organized – and, in particular, the opposition between left and right – tends to impose itself as a paradigmatic manifestation of the social structure and to function in people's heads as a principle of di-vision of the social world and, in particular, of the division into classes. (The tradition in France which prescribes that, in all parliaments, the conservatives sit on the right and the liberals on the left of the President goes back to the Constituent Assembly: after the reunion of the three orders, one began to distinguish the members of the assembly who, having abandoned distinction by dress, grouped themselves according to their ideas, with the partisans of the monarchy on the right and the partisans of the Revolution on the left or, more simply, on the *right-side* and the *left-side*, then *right* and *left*.)

The same dyadic or triadic structure which organizes the field as a whole can be reproduced in each of its points – that is, within the political party or splinter group – according to the same double logic, both internal and external, which relates the specific interests of professionals to the real or presumed interests of their real or presumed supporters. It is probably within the political parties whose supporters are the most deprived, and thus most inclined to depend on the party, that the logic of internal oppositions can most clearly be demonstrated. Hence nothing can explain better the stances adopted than a *topology* of the positions from which they are expressed. 'So far as Russia is concerned, I have always known that in the *topography* of the factions and tendencies, Radek, Trotsky and Bukharin occupied a left position, Zinoviev, Kamenev and Stalin a right position, while Lenin was in the *centre* and acted as *arbiter* in the whole situation. This, of course, in current political language. The so-called Leninist nucleus, as is well known, maintains that these "topographic" positions are absolutely illusory and fallacious.'[22] It is just as if the distribution of positions in the field implied a distribution of roles; as if each of the protagonists were brought to or forced to assume his position as much through *competition* with the occupants of both the most distant and the closest positions, which threaten his existence in very different ways, as through the *logical contradiction* between the stances adopted.[23]

Thus, certain recurrent oppositions, such as the one established between the libertarian tradition and the authoritarian tradition, are merely the transcription, on the level of ideological struggles, of the fundamental contradiction within the revolutionary movement, which is forced to resort to discipline and authority, even violence, in order to combat authority and violence. As a heretical protest against the heretical church, as a revolution against 'established revolutionary power', the 'leftist' critique in its 'spontaneist' form seeks to exploit, against those who dominate the party, the contradiction between 'authoritarian' strategies within the party and the 'anti-authoritarian' strategies of the party within the political field as a whole. And even within the anarchist movement, which reproaches Marxism with being too authoritarian,[24] one finds a similar opposition between, on the one hand, the kind of demagoguery associated with the political platform which, aiming above all at laying the foundations for a powerful anarchist organization, treats as secondary the demands made by individuals and small groups for unlimited freedom and, on the other hand, a more 'synthesizing' tendency which aims at ensuring that individuals maintain their full independence.[25]

But even in this case, internal conflicts are superimposed on external conflicts. It is thus in so far as (and only in so far as) each tendency is inclined to appeal to the corresponding fraction of its clientele, thanks to the homologies between the positions occupied by the leaders in the political field and the positions occupied in the field of the lower classes by their real or presumed supporters, that the real divisions and contradictions of the working class can find a corresponding expression in the contradictions and divisions of the working-class parties. The interests of the unorganized sub-proletariat have no chance of gaining access to political representation (especially when that sub-proletariat is made up of foreigners without the right to vote or of stigmatized racial minorities) unless those interests become a weapon and a stake in the struggle which, in certain states of the political field, sets two things against each other: on the one hand, spontaneism or, up to a point, ultra-revolutionary voluntarism, both of which are always inclined to favour the least organized fractions of the proletariat, whose spontaneous action precedes or goes beyond the organization; and, on the other hand, centralism (which its adversaries label 'bureaucratic–mechanistic'), for which the organization, that is, the party, precedes and conditions the class and its struggle.[26]

SLOGANS AND MOBILIZING IDEAS

The tendency towards greater autonomy and towards the indefinite partition into minuscule antagonistic sects which is, as an objective potentiality, built into the constitution of a body of specialists possessing specific interests and set up against each other in competition for power in the political field (or in one or other sector of this field – for instance, a party apparatus) is counterbalanced to varying degrees by the fact that the outcome of internal struggles depends on the power that the agents and institutions involved in this struggle can mobilize from outside the field. In other words, the tendency towards fission is limited by the fact that the power of a discourse depends less on its intrinsic properties than on the mobilizing power it exercises – that is, at least to some extent, on the degree to which it is *recognized* by a numerous and powerful group that can recognize itself in it and whose interests it expresses (in a more or less transfigured and unrecognizable form).

A mere 'current of ideas' becomes a political movement only when the ideas being put forward are recognized outside the circle of professionals. The strategies which the logic of the internal struggle imposes on professionals, and whose objective foundation may be, over and above the differences explicitly professed, differences of habitus and interests (or, more precisely, of economic and educational capital, and of social trajectory), differences which are associated with different positions in the field, can succeed only if they converge with the (sometimes unconscious) strategies of groups

outside the field. (The entire difference between utopianism and
realism is to be found here.) In this way, the tendencies to sectarian
splits are continually being counterbalanced by the necessities of
competition which mean that, in order to triumph in their internal
struggles, professionals have to appeal to forces which are not all,
and not totally, internal (unlike the situation in the scientific or
artistic field, in which appealing to non-professionals discredits you).
Avant-garde splinter groups can bring into the political field the logic
characteristic of the intellectual field only because they have no base;
they thus have no constraints upon them, but they also have no real
power. Functioning as *sects* that have come into being as breakaway
groups, they are dedicated to scissiparity and founded on a
renunciation of any claim to universality; a loss of power and
effectiveness is the price they have to pay for being able to affirm the
full technical and ethical qualification that defines the *ecclesia pura*
(the Puritans), the universe of the 'pure' and the 'purists', capable of
demonstrating their excellence as political virtuosi in their adherence
to the purest and most radical traditions ('permanent revolution',
'the dictatorship of the proletariat', etc.). However, if the party is to
avoid the risk of excluding itself from the political game and from the
ambition of participating, if not in power, at least in the power of
influencing the way power is distributed, it cannot sacrifice itself to
such exclusive virtues; and, just as the Church takes on as its mission
the diffusion of its institutional grace to all the faithful, be they just
or unjust, and the submission of sinners without distinction to the
discipline of God's commands, the party aims at winning over to its
cause the greatest number of those who resist it (this is the case when
the Communist Party addresses itself, in an electoral period, to 'all
progressive republicans'). And the party does not hesitate, so as to
broaden its base and attract the clientele of the competing parties, to
compromise with the 'purity' of its party line and to play more or less
consciously on the ambiguities of its programme. A result of this is
that, among the struggles which beset every party, one of the most
constant is that between two groups of people: on the one hand,
those who denounce the compromises necessary to increase the
strength of the party (and thus of those who dominate it), but to the
detriment of its *originality*, in other words, at the cost of abandoning
its distinctive and original (in both senses of the word: new and
fundamental) positions – those people, that is, who thus advocate a
return to basics, to a restoration of the original purity; and, on the
other hand, those people who are inclined to seek a strengthening of
the party, in other words, a broadening of its clientele, even if this is

at the cost of compromises and concessions or even of a methodical interference with everything that is too 'exclusive' in the original stances adopted by the party. The former group draws the party towards the logic of the intellectual field which, when pushed to the limit, can deprive it of all temporal power; the latter group has on its side the logic of *Realpolitik* which is the condition of entry to political reality.[27]

The political field is thus the site of a competition for power which is carried out by means of a competition for the control of non-professionals or, more precisely, for the monopoly of the right to speak and act in the name of some or all of the non-professionals. The spokesperson appropriates not only the words of the group of non-professionals, that is, most of the time, its silence, but also the very power of that group, which he helps to produce by lending it a voice recognized as legitimate in the political field. The power of the ideas that he proposes is measured not, as in the domain of science, by their truth-value (even if they owe part of their power to his capacity to convince people that he is in possession of the truth), but by the power of mobilization that they contain, in other words, by the power of the group that recognizes them, even if only by its silence or the absence of any refutation – a power that the group can demonstrate by registering its different voices or assembling them all together in the same space. It is for this reason that the field of politics – in which one would seek in vain for any authority capable of legitimating the chances of legitimacy and any basis of competence other than class interests, properly understood – always swings between two criteria of validation: science and the plebiscite.[28]

In politics, 'to say is to do', that is, it is to get people to believe that you can do what you say and, in particular, to get them to know and recognize the principles of di-vision of the social world, the *slogans*, which produce their own verification by producing groups and, thereby, a social order. Political speech – and this is what defines its specificity – commits its author completely because it constitutes a commitment to action which is truly political only if it is the commitment of an agent or group of agents who are *politically responsible*, that is, capable of committing a group, and a group, moreover, capable of carrying out the action: it is only on this condition that it is equivalent to an act. The truth of a promise or a prognosis depends not only on the truthfulness but also on the authority of the person who utters it – that is, on his capacity to make people believe in his truthfulness and his authority. When it is acknowledged that the future under discussion depends on collective will and action, the mobilizing ideas of the spokesperson who is capable of giving rise to this action are unfalsifiable because they have the power to ensure that the future they are announcing will come about. (This is probably what lies behind the fact that, for the entire revolutionary tradition, the question of truth is inseparable from the question of freedom or historical necessity. If it is acknowledged that the future, that is, political truth, depends on the action of political leaders and the masses – though we would have to specify to what degree –, Rosa Luxemburg was right in her quarrel with Kautsky, who contributed to bringing about what was probable, and which he predicted, by not doing what, according to Rosa Luxemburg, needed to be done; in the opposite case, Rosa Luxemburg was wrong because she did not foretell the most probable future.)

What would be an 'irresponsible discourse' in the mouth of one person is a reasonable forecast when made by someone else. Political propositions, programmes, promises, predictions or prognostications ('We will win the elections') are never logically verifiable or falsifiable. They are true only in so far as the person who utters them (on his own behalf or in the name of a group) is capable of making them historically true, by making them come about in history; and this is inextricably bound up with his aptitude for judging realistically the chances of success of the action whose aim it is to make them come about in reality, and with his capacities for mobilizing the forces necessary to achieve that end, by managing to inspire confidence in his own truthfulness, and thus in his chances of success. In other words, the speech of the *spokesperson* owes part of its 'illocutionary force' to the force (the number) of the group that he helps to produce as such by the act of symbolization or representation; it is based on the metaphorical *coup d'état* by which the speaker invests his utterance with all the power his utterance helps to produce by mobilizing the group to which it is addressed. This can be clearly seen in the logic, so typically political, of the promise or, even better, of the prediction: a veritable self-fulfilling prophecy, the words through which the spokesperson endows a group with a will, a plan, a hope or, quite simply, a future, *does what it says* in so far as the addressees recognize themselves in it, conferring on it the symbolic and also material power (in the form of votes, but also of subsidies, subscriptions, or the power of their labour or their capacity to struggle, etc.) which enables the words to come true. It is because it is enough for ideas to be professed by *political leaders* in order to become mobilizing ideas capable of making themselves believed, or even slogans capable of mobilizing or demobilizing, that mistakes are *misdeeds* or, in the native language of politics, 'betrayals'.[29]

CREDIT AND CREDENCE

Political capital is a form of symbolic capital, *credit* founded on *credence* or belief and *recognition* or, more precisely, on the innumerable operations of credit by which agents confer on a person (or on an object) the very powers that they recognize in him (or it). This is the ambiguity of the *fides*, analysed by Benveniste:[30] an objective power which can be objectified in things (and in particular in everything that constitutes the symbolic nature of power – thrones, sceptres and crowns), it is the product of subjective acts of recognition and, in so far as it is credit and credibility, exists only in and through representation, in and through trust, belief and obedience. Symbolic power is a power which the person submitting to it *grants* to the person who exercises it, a credit with which he credits him, a *fides*, an *auctoritas*, with which he entrusts him by placing his trust in him. It is a power which exists because the person who submits to it believes that it exists. *Credo*, says Benveniste, 'is *literally* "to place one's *kred*", that is "magical powers", in a person from whom one expects protection thanks to "believing" in him'.[31] The *kred*, the credit, the charisma, that *'je ne sais quoi'* with which one keeps hold over those from whom one holds it, is this product of the *credo*, of belief, of obedience, which seems to produce the *credo*, the belief, the obedience.

Like the divine or human champion who, according to Benveniste, 'needs people to believe in him, to entrust their *kred* to him, on condition that he lavishes his benefits on those who have thus supported him',[32] the politician derives his political power from the trust that a group places in him. He derives his truly magical power over the group from faith in the representation that he gives to the group and which is a representation of the group itself and of its relation to other groups. As a representative linked to those he represents by a sort of rational contract (the programme), he is also a champion, united by a magical relation of identification with those who, as the saying goes, 'pin all their hopes on him'. And it is because his specific capital is a pure *fiduciary value* which depends on representation, opinion, belief, *fides*, that the man of politics, like the man of honour, is especially vulnerable to suspicions, malicious misrepresentations and scandal, in short, to everything that threatens belief and trust, by bringing to light the hidden and secret acts and remarks of the present or the past which can undermine present acts and remarks and discredit their author (and this takes place all the more completely, as we shall see, the less his capital depends on delegation).[33] This supremely *free-flowing* capital can be conserved only at the cost of unceasing work which is necessary both to accumulate credit and to avoid discredit: hence all the precautions, the silences and the disguises, imposed on public personalities, who are forever forced to stand before the tribunal of public opinion, their constant need to ensure that they neither say nor do anything which might contradict their present or past professions of faith, or might show up their inconsistency over the course of time. And the special attention that politicians must give to everything which helps to produce the representation of their *sincerity* or of their disinterestedness can be explained by remembering that these dispositions appear to be the final guarantor of the representation of the social world that they are seeking to impose, of the 'ideals' and 'ideas' which they are striving to get people to accept.[34]

'In Homer this *skeptron* is the attribute of the king, of heralds, messengers, judges, and all persons who, whether of their own nature or because of a particular occasion, are invested with authority. The *skeptron* is passed to the orator before he begins his speech so that he may speak with authority.'[35] The abundance of microphones, cameras, journalists and photographers, is, like the Homeric *skeptron* described by Benveniste, the visible manifestation of the hearing granted to the orator, of his credit, of the social importance of his acts and his words. Photography – which, by recording, eternalizes – has the effect, here as elsewhere, of *solemnizing* the exemplary acts of the political ritual. It follows that the intervention of this instrument of perception and objectification *designates* the situations (official openings, laying the first stone, processions, etc.) in which politicians are *being represented*, are acting in order to be *seen* acting, and are representing themselves as good representatives. Thus a number of actions which seem to be an end in themselves and whose voluntarist gratuity might seem out of place on the political terrain (as with so many demonstrations or petitions that have no effect) do not, for all that, lack all function: by demonstrating the demonstrators and, above all, the leaders of the demonstration, the demonstration demonstrates the existence of the group capable of demonstrating its existence and of leaders who can demonstrate its existence – thereby justifying *their* existence.

The Kinds of Political Capital

'A banker of men in a monopoly system',[36] as Gramsci says of trade union officials, the politician owes his specific authority in the political field – what ordinary language calls his 'political clout' – to the power of mobilization that he has at his disposal, either personally or else by delegation, as the representative of an organization (a party or trade union) which itself holds political capital accumulated in the course of previous struggles, first and foremost in the form of jobs – inside or outside the apparatus – and of militants *attached* to those jobs.[37] The personal capital of 'fame' and 'popularity' based on the fact of *being known and recognized* in person (of having a 'name', 'renown', etc.), and also on the possession of a certain number of specific qualifications which are the condition of the acquisition and conservation of a 'good reputation', is often the product of the reconversion of the capital of fame accumulated in other domains: in particular, in professions which, like the liberal professions, ensure that you have some free time and which presuppose a certain cultural capital and, in the case of lawyers, a professional mastery of eloquence. While the professional capital of the *notable* is the product of a slow and continuous accumulation which in general takes a whole life time, the personal capital which can be called heroic or prophetic, and which Max Weber has in mind when he talks of 'charisma', is the product of an inaugural action, performed in a crisis situation, in the vacuum and silence left by institutions and apparatuses: the prophetic action of giving meaning, which founds and legitimates itself, retrospectively, by the confirmation that its own success confers on the language of crisis and on the initial accumulation of the power of mobilization which its success has brought about.[38]

At the other end of the scale from the personal capital which disappears with the person of its bearer (although it may give rise to quarrels over the inheritance), the delegated capital of political authority is, like that of the priest, the teacher and, more generally, the *official*, the product of a limited and provisional transfer (but one that is renewable, sometimes for life) of a capital held and controlled by the institution and by it alone:[39] it is the party which, through the action of its officers and its militants, has, in the course of history, accumulated a symbolic capital of *recognition* and *loyalties* and which has given itself, for and through political struggle, a permanent organization of party officials (*permanents*) capable of mobilizing militants, supporters and sympathizers, and of organizing the work of propaganda necessary to obtain votes and thus jobs, enabling party officials to be maintained and retained on a long-term basis. This apparatus of mobilization, which distinguishes the party or the trade union both from the aristocratic club and from the intellectual group, depends *at one and the same time* on two things: first, on objective structures such as the bureaucracy of the organization properly speaking, the jobs it offers, with all the correlative profits, in itself or in the different branches of public administration, the traditions of recruitment, education and selection which characterize it, etc.; and second, on dispositions, whether this is a matter of loyalty to the party or of the incorporated principles of di-vision of the social world which the leaders, party officials or militants implement in their daily practice and in their properly political action.

The acquisition of a delegated capital obeys a very specific logic: *investiture*, the veritably magical act of *institution* by which the party officially *consecrates* the official candidate at an election and which marks the transmission of political capital, just as the medieval investiture solemnized the transfer of a fief or of a piece of landed property, can only be the counterpart of a long *investment* of time, work, dedication and devotion to the institution. It is no coincidence that churches, like political parties, so often appoint oblates to lead them.[40] The law which governs the exchanges between agents and institutions can be expressed in this way: the institution gives everything, starting with power over the institution, to those who have given everything to the institution, but this is because they were nothing outside the institution or without the institution and because they cannot deny the institution without purely and simply denying themselves by depriving themselves of everything that they have become through and for the institution to which they owe everything.[41] In short, the institution invests those who have *invested* in the institution: investment consists not only in services rendered, which are frequently more rare and precious when they are more costly psychologically (such as all initiatory 'ordeals'), or even in obedience to orders or in conformity to the demands of the institution, but also in psychological investments, which mean that exclusion, as a withdrawal of the capital of institutional authority, so often takes the form of financial *failure*, of *bankruptcy*, both social and psychological. (This is all the truer when, as in the case of excommunication and exclusion from the divine sacrifice, it is accompanied by 'the strictest social boycott' which takes the form of a refusal to have anything to do with the excluded person.)[42] The person invested with a *functional capital*, equivalent to the 'institutional grace' or the 'functional charisma' of the priest, may possess no other 'qualification' than that granted to him by the institution in the act of investiture. And it is still the institution which controls access to *personal fame* by controlling, for example, access to the most *conspicuous* positions (that of general secretary or spokesperson) or to the places of publicity (such as, today, television and press conferences) – though the person endowed with delegated capital can still obtain personal capital through a subtle strategy consisting of distancing himself from the institution as far as is compatible with still belonging to it and keeping the correlative advantages.

It follows that the elected member of a party apparatus depends at least as much on the apparatus as on his electors – whom he owes to the apparatus and whom he loses if he breaks away from the apparatus. It also follows that, as politics becomes more professionalized and parties more bureaucratic, the struggle for the political power of mobilization tends to become more and more a two-stage competition: the choice of those who will be able to enter the struggle for the conquest of the non-professionals depends on the outcome of the competition for power over the apparatus that takes place, within the apparatus, *between professionals alone*. What this means, in short, is that the struggle for the monopoly of the development and circulation of the principles of di-vision of the social world is more and more strictly reserved for professionals and for the large units of production and circulation, thus excluding *de facto* the small independent producers (starting with the 'free intellectuals').

THE INSTITUTIONALIZATION OF POLITICAL CAPITAL

The delegation of political capital presupposes the objectification of this kind of capital in permanent institutions, its materialization in political 'machines', in jobs and instruments of mobilization, and its continual reproduction by mechanisms and strategies. It is thus the result of already established political enterprises which have accumulated a significant amount of objectified political capital, in the form of jobs within the party itself, in all the organizations that are more or less subordinate to the party, and also in the organs of local or central power and in the whole network of industrial or commercial enterprises which live in a state of symbiosis with these organs. The objectification of political capital secures a relative independence from the electoral sanction by replacing the direct domination of people and personal investment strategies ('self-sacrifice') by the mediated domination which enables one to keep a lasting hold over those who hold jobs by holding those jobs open for them in the first place.[43] And it is easy to see that this new definition of positions brings with it new characteristics in the dispositions of those who occupy them: political capital is increasingly institutional-ized in the form of available jobs, and it becomes more profitable to enter the apparatus – quite the opposite of what happens in the initial phases or in times of crisis (in a revolutionary period, for example) when the risks are great and profits reduced.

The process often designated by the vague word 'bureaucratiza-tion' can be understood if one sees that, as one advances in the life cycle of the political enterprise, the effects on recruitment produced by the supply of stable party jobs begin to exacerbate the frequently observed effects[44] produced by access to such jobs (and to the – relative – privileges that they make available to militants from the working class). The more advanced the process of institutionaliza-tion of political capital is, the more the winning of 'hearts and minds' tends to become subordinated to the winning of jobs; and the more militants, linked by their 'devotion' to the 'cause' and by nothing else, have to make way for the 'prebendaries', as Weber calls them, lastingly linked to the apparatus by the benefits and advantages that it grants them, and holding on to the apparatus as long as the apparatus keeps them in its grasp by redistributing to them part of the material or symbolic booty that it wins with their help (as in the case of the spoils of American parties).[45] In other words, as the process of institutionalization advances and as the apparatus of mobilization grows, so the weight of the imperatives linked to the reproduction of the apparatus and the jobs it offers, tying to itself those who fill those jobs by all sorts of material or symbolic interests, continues to grow, both in reality and in people's heads; and this grows faster than the weight of imperatives that would be imposed by the realization of the declared aims of the apparatus. It is thus easy to understand how political parties can be brought in this way to sacrifice their programmes so as to keep themselves in power or simply in existence.

'AS FAR AS I'M CONCERNED, YOU'RE EITHER A COMMUNIST
OR YOU'RE NOT.'

'When someone says to me: "We can't understand you communists: you don't have different tendencies – there aren't any
right-wing communists, there aren't any left-wing communists,
there aren't any moderates. So there's no freedom!", I reply:
"What do you call a right-wing communist, what do you call a
left-wing communist, what do you call a moderate? As far as I'm
concerned, you're either a communist or you're not, and in the
communist organization, when we're discussing things, everyone
gives his point of view about the day's agenda, and when it's
something important, we take a vote. It's the majority that
decides." What do you call democracy? In my view, democracy is
50% of the vote plus one – that's easy to understand! It's the
majority that decides. If you join the communist party in order to
combat the directives that have been freely discussed and debated
in a session of congress, in order to have your point of view carried
– reformist without reforms, since that's what naturally suits your
state of mind (you have a sensitive backside, you need a nicely-
padded armchair so as not to get it overheated) – well, then you'll
sit back in your armchair and say: "Aha! I don't agree with the
party leadership – I'm a right-wing communist, I'm . . . a moderate." If you're an electioneering sort, I'll tell you right away: "Go
somewhere else; we don't need you here, because you may
perhaps have brains, you may perhaps be very clever, but your
arguments are very poor and above all your facts are all wrong. So
despite all your cleverness and your gift of the gab, workers in
your section may well never choose you to carry the flag of the
organization. They naturally prefer a worker who has proved
himself and they prefer a communist, even if he is an intellectual,
since there are good ones and bad ones . . . just as there are good
ones and bad ones in the working class – that's a fact!"'

(Blacksmith's mate, miner, then chainmaker, born in 1892 in
Saint-Amand-des-Eaux; he was secretary of the Saint-Nazaire
section of the French Communist Party in 1928, and the CGTU
union representative for the Saint-Nazaire region.)

Source: 'Autobiographies de militants CGTU–CGT', edited and introduced by
Jean Peneff, *Les Cahiers du LERSCO*, 1 (December 1979), pp. 28–9.

FIELD AND APPARATUS

While it is true to say that there is no political enterprise which, however monolithic it may appear, is not the site of confrontation between divergent tendencies and interests,[46] the fact remains that parties are more likely to function in accordance with the logic of the apparatus capable of responding instantaneously to the strategic demands that are part and parcel of the logic of the political field when the people they represent are more deprived culturally and more attached to the values of loyalty, and thus more inclined to unconditional and lasting delegation. The same is true when the parties are older and richer in objectified political capital, and thus more powerfully determined, in their strategies, by the need to 'defend their gains'; when, likewise, they are more deliberately arranged for the purposes of the struggle, and thus organized in accordance with the military model of the apparatus of mobilization; and when their officers and party officials are more deprived of economic and cultural capital, and thus more totally dependent on the party.

The combination of inter- and intragenerational loyalty, which ensures that parties will always have a relatively stable clientele, thus depriving the electoral sanction of a large part of its effectiveness, with the *fides implicita*, which shelters political leaders from the control of non-professionals, implies that, paradoxically, there are no political enterprises more independent of the constraints and controls of demand and freer to obey exclusively the logic of competition between professionals (sometimes at the cost of the most sudden and paradoxical U-turns) than the parties that most loudly claim to be defending the working masses.[47] This is all the more true when they tend to accept the Bolshevik dogma according to which the fact of bringing non-professionals into the internal struggles of the party, and of appealing to them or, quite simply, of allowing internal disagreements to filter through to the outside world, is perceived as verging on the illegitimate.

In the same way, the party officials never depend on the party so much as when their profession allows them to participate in political life only at the cost of sacrificing time and money. They can then expect to receive only from the party the *free time* that notables owe to their revenue or to the manner in which they acquire it, that is, without working or by working only intermittently.[48] And their dependence is all the more total if the economic and cultural capital that they possessed before joining the party was slight. This explains the fact that party officials from the working class feel that they owe the party everything – not just their position, which frees them from the servitudes of their former condition, but also their culture, in short, everything that constitutes their present way of life: 'The fact is that the person who lives the life of a party like ours can only rise in status. I started out with the baggage of a primary-school pupil and the party forced me to educate myself. You have to work, slave over your books, you have to read, you have to put yourself in the picture . . . It's a real obligation! If not . . . I'd have stayed the same donkey as I was fifty years ago! What I say is: "a militant owes his party everything." '[49] It also explains the fact that, as Denis Lacorne has demonstrated, 'the party spirit' and 'partisan pride' are significantly clearer among the party officials of the Communist Party than among those of the Socialist Party, since the latter are more frequently from the middle and upper classes, especially from the teaching profession, and thus depend far less completely on the party.

Discipline and training, so often overestimated by analysts, would remain completely powerless without the complicity that they find in the dispositions to forced or chosen submission which agents bring to the apparatus, and which are themselves continually reinforced by the confrontation with similar dispositions and by the interests that are part and parcel of the jobs in the party apparatus. One can thus say both that certain kinds of habitus find the conditions of their realization, indeed of their blossoming, in the logic of the apparatus; and, conversely, that the logic of the apparatus 'exploits' for its own profit tendencies that are inscribed in the different kinds of habitus. One could mention, on the one hand, all the procedures, common to all total institutions, by which the apparatus, or those who dominate it, impose discipline and bring into line heretics and dissidents, or the mechanisms which, with the complicity of those whose interests they serve, tend to ensure the reproduction of institutions and of their hierarchies. On the other hand, there would be no end to an enumeration and analysis of the dispositions which provide militarist mechanization with its cogs and wheels: this is true whether we are talking about the dominated relation to culture which inclines party officials from the working class to a form of anti-intellectualism which is bound to serve as a justification or alibi for a sort of spontaneous Zhdanovism and workerist corporatism; or about the resentment which draws on the Stalinist (in the historical sense of the word) vision of 'fractions' – in other words, the policeman's vision –

and on the propensity to think of history as ruled by the logic of the conspiracy; or even about the sense of guilt which, as an essential part of the precarious position of the intellectual, reaches its maximum intensity in the intellectual from the dominated classes, a renegade and often the son of a renegade, as Sartre has magnificently shown in his preface to *Aden Arabie*. And it would be impossible to understand certain extreme 'successes' in the way the apparatus can be manipulated if one did not take into account the extent to which these dispositions are objectively orchestrated, the different forms of preoccupation with the poor and sordid, which predispose intellectuals to *ouvriérisme*, adjusting themselves for instance to spontaneous Zhdanovism in order to favour the establishment of social relations in which the persecuted makes himself the accomplice of the persecutor.

The fact remains that the Bolshevik-type organizational model that was imposed on most communist parties enables the tendencies inscribed in the relation between the working classes and the parties to be taken to their ultimate consequences. As an apparatus (or total institution) designed for the purpose of the (real or represented) struggle, and based on the *discipline* which allows a group of agents (in this case, militants) to act 'as one man' for a common cause, the communist party finds the conditions of its functioning in the permanent struggle that takes place in the political field and that can be re-activated or intensified at will. Indeed, since discipline, which, as Weber observes, ensures 'that the obedience of a plurality of men is rationally uniform',[50] finds its justification, if not its basis, in struggle, one need only mention the real or potential struggle, or even re-kindle it more or less artificially, in order to restore the legitimacy of discipline.[51] It follows that, more or less as Weber says, the situation of struggle reinforces the position occupied by the dominant members within the apparatus of struggle and relegates militants from the role of popular orators responsible for expressing the will of the base (a role that they can sometimes claim by virtue of the official definition of their function) to the function of mere 'executives' responsible for *executing* the orders and commands coming from the central leadership and forced by 'competent comrades' to devote their energies to a 'democracy of ratification'.[52] And there is no better expression of the logic of this organization designed for combat than the 'who is against?' procedure as described by Bukharin; and as they are all more or less afraid of being against, the individual designated is appointed secretary, the resolution proposed is adopted, and always unanimously.[53] The process

called 'militarization' consists in assuming authority on the basis of
the 'war' situation which confronts the organization – a situation
which can be produced by working on the way the situation is
represented, so as to produce and reproduce, continuously, the *fear
of being against*, the ultimate basis of all militant or military
disciplines. If anti-communism did not exist, 'war communism'
would not fail to invent it. Since all opposition from within is bound
to appear as collusion with the enemy, it reinforces the militarization
it combats by reinforcing the unanimity of the besieged 'us' which
predisposes people to military obedience. The historical dynamic of
the field of struggles between the orthodox and heretics, those for
and those against, gives way to the mechanism of the apparatus
which annuls all practical possibility of being against, by a semi-
rational exploitation of the psychosomatic effects of the euphoria
caused by the unanimity of adherence and aversion, or, on the
contrary, of the anguish caused by exclusion and excommunication,
turning the 'party spirit' into a real *esprit de corps*.

In this way, the very ambiguity of the political struggle, this
combat for 'ideas' and 'ideals' which is inseparably a combat for
powers and, whether one likes it or not, for privileges, is the source
of the contradiction which haunts all political organizations designed
to subvert the established order: all the necessities which weigh
down on the social world work together to ensure that the function
of mobilization, which calls for the mechanical logic of the apparatus, tends to supplant the function of expression and representation
claimed by all the professional ideologies of those who occupy the
apparatus (the ideology of the 'organic intellectual' as much as that
of the party which 'acts as midwife' to the class) and which cannot be
really ensured other than by the dialectical logic of the field.
'Revolution from above', a plan hatched by the apparatus, and one
which presupposes and produces the apparatus, has the effect of
interrupting this dialectic, which is history itself: initially in the
political field, that field of struggles about a field of struggles and
about the legitimate representation of those struggles, and then
within the political enterprise, party, trade union or association,
which can function as a single individual only by sacrificing the
interests of a part, if not all, of those whom it represents.

9

Delegation and Political Fetishism

The aristocrats of intelligence find that there are truths which should not be told to the people. As a revolutionary socialist, and a sworn enemy of all aristocracies and all tutelage, I believe on the contrary that the people must be told everything. There is no other way to restore to them their full liberty.

Mikhail Bakunin

The delegation through which one person gives power, as the saying goes, to another, the transference of power through which a mandator authorizes a mandatary to sign on his behalf, to act on his behalf, to speak on his behalf, and gives him the power of a proxy, in other words the *plena potentia agendi*, full power to act for him, is a complex act which deserves some reflection. The plenipotentiary, minister, mandatary, delegate, spokesperson, deputy or member of parliament is a person who has a mandate, a commission or a power of proxy, to represent – an extraordinarily polysemic word – in other words, to show and throw into relief the interests of a person or a group. But if it is true that to delegate is to entrust a function or a mission to someone, by transmitting one's power to him, the question arises as to how the delegate can have power over the person who gives him power. When the act of delegation is performed by a single person in favour of a single person, things are relatively clear. But when a single person is entrusted with the powers of a whole crowd of people, that person can be invested with a power which transcends each of the individuals who delegate him. And, thereby, he can be as it were an incarnation of that sort of transcendence of the social that the Durkheimians have frequently pointed out.

But that is not the whole truth, and the relation of delegation risks concealing the truth of the relation of representation and the paradox of the situations in which a group can exist only by delegation to an individual person – the general secretary, the Pope, etc. – who can act as a moral person, that is, as a substitute for the group. In all these cases (following the formula established by canon lawyers, 'the Church is the Pope'), *in appearance* the group creates the man who speaks in its place and in its name – to put it that way is to think in terms of delegation – whereas *in reality* it is more or less just as true to say that it is the spokesperson who creates the group. It is because the representative exists, because he *represents* (symbolic action), that the group that is represented and symbolized exists and that in return it gives existence to its representative as the representative of a group. One can see in this circular relation the root of the illusion which results in the fact that, ultimately, the spokesperson may appear, even in his own eyes, as *causa sui*, since he is the cause of that which produces his power, since the group which makes of him someone invested with powers would not exist – or at least, would not exist fully, as a represented group – if he were not there to incarnate it.

This sort of original circle of representation has been concealed: it has been replaced by hundreds of questions, the commonest of them being the question of the 'awakening of consciousness'. The question of political fetishism has been concealed, as has the process through which individuals constitute themselves (or are constituted) as a group but at the same time lose control over the group in and through which they are constituted. There is a sort of antinomy inherent in the political sphere which stems from the fact that individuals – and this is all the more true the more they are deprived – cannot constitute themselves (or be constituted) as a group, that is, as a force capable of making itself heard, of speaking and being heard, unless they dispossess themselves in favour of a spokesperson. One must always risk political alienation in order to escape from political alienation. (In reality, this antinomy really exists only for the dominated. One might say, for the sake of simplicity, that the dominant always exist, whereas the dominated exist only if they mobilize or avail themselves of instruments of representation. Except perhaps in the times of restoration which follow great crises, it is in the interests of the dominant to leave things alone, to allow agents, who need merely to be responsible in order to be rational and reproduce the established order, to pursue their independent and isolated strategies.)

It is the process of delegation which, because it is forgotten and ignored, becomes the source of political alienation. Delegates and ministers, in the sense of ministers of religion or ministers of state, are, according to Marx's formula about fetishism, among those 'products of the human brain [which] appear as autonomous figures endowed with a life of their own'. Political fetishes are people, things, beings, which seem to owe to themselves alone an existence that social agents have given to them; those who create the delegate adore their own creature. Political idolatry consists precisely in the fact that the value which resides in the political personality, that product of men's brains, appears as a mysterious objective property of the person, a charm, charisma: the *ministerium* appears as a *mysterium*. Here again I could quote Marx, *cum grano salis*, of course, since his analyses of fetishism were clearly – and quite justifiably – not meant to explain political fetishism. Marx said, in the same famous passage: 'Value does not wear a statement of what it is written on its own brow.' That is the very definition of charisma, that sort of power which seems to be its own source. Charisma, in Weber's definition, is that *'je ne sais quoi'* which is its own foundation – gift, grace, mana, etc.

Thus, delegation is the act by which a group undertakes to constitute itself by endowing itself with that set of things which create groups, in other words, a permanent office and party officials, a bureau in all senses of the word, and first of all in the sense of a bureaucratic mode of organization, with its own seal, acronym, signature, delegation of signature, official rubber-stamp, etc. (as in the case of the Politburo). The group exists when it has provided itself with a permanent organ of representation endowed with the *plena potentia agendi* and the *sigillum authenticum*, and is thus capable of *substituting itself* (to speak for somebody is to speak in their place) for the serial group, made up of separated and isolated individuals, in a state of constant renewal, being able to act and speak only for themselves. The second act of delegation, which is far better concealed and to which I will have to return, is the act by which the social reality thus constituted, the Party, the Church, etc., mandates an individual. I use the term 'bureaucratic mandate' on purpose, to refer to the secretary (bureau or office goes together well with secretary), the minister, the general secretary, etc. It is no longer the mandator who chooses his delegate, but the bureau which mandates a plenipotentiary. I will be exploring this sort of black box: first, the transition from atomistic subjects to the bureau, and second, the transition from the bureau to the secretary. To analyse these two mechanisms, we have a paradigm: that of the Church. The Church, and through it each of its members, possesses the 'monopoly of the legitimate manipulation of the goods of salvation'. Delegation in this case is the act by which the Church (and not mere believers) delegates to the minister the power to act in its place.

In what does the mystery of the ministry consist? The delegate becomes, through unconscious delegation (I have been speaking as if it were conscious, for reasons of clarity, by an artefact analogous to the idea of the social contract), capable of acting as a substitute for the group which gives him a mandate. In other words, the delegate is, so to speak, in a *metonymic* relation with the group; he is a part of the group and can function as a sign in place of the totality of the group. He can function as a passive, objective sign, who signifies or manifests the existence of his mandators, as a representative, as a group *in effigy*. (To say that the communist-affiliated CGT trade union was received at the Elysée is equivalent to saying that the sign was received in place of the thing signified.) But in addition, it is a sign which speaks, which, as a spokesperson, can say what he is, what he does, what he represents, what he imagines himself to be representing. And when someone says that 'the CGT was received at the Elysée', they mean that the set of members of the organization were expressed in two ways: in the fact of demonstration, of the presence of the representative, and, possibly, in the discourse of the representative. By this token, it is easy to see how the possibility of a sort of embezzlement is part and parcel of the very act of delegation. To the extent to which, in most cases of delegation, the mandators write a blank cheque for their delegate, if only because they are frequently unaware of the questions to which their delegate will have to respond, they put themselves in his hands. In the medieval tradition, the faith shared by delegates who put themselves in the hands of the institution was called *fides implicita* – a magnificent expression which can easily be transferred to politics. The more people are dispossessed, especially culturally, the more constrained and inclined they are to rely on delegates in order to acquire a political voice. In fact, isolated, silent, voiceless individuals, without either the capacity or the power of making themselves heard and understood, are faced with the alternative of keeping quiet or of being spoken for by someone else.

In the limiting case of dominated groups, the act of symbolization by which the spokesperson is constituted, the constitution of the 'movement', happens at the same time as the constituting of the group; the sign creates the thing signified, the signifier is identified with the thing signified, which would not exist without it, and which can be reduced to it. The signifier is not only that which expresses and represents the signified group: it is that which *signifies* to it that it exists, that which has the power to call into visible existence, by mobilizing it, the group that it signifies. The signifier is the only one which, under certain conditions, by using the power conferred on it by delegation, can mobilize the group: that is, in a demonstration or display of the group's existence. When the signifier, the representative, says: 'I am going to show you that I am representative, by introducing you to the people that I represent' (here we have the eternal debate over the exact number of demonstrators), the spokesperson demonstrates his legitimacy by demonstrating or displaying those who have delegated him. But he has this power to demonstrate the demonstrators because he is, in a certain sense, the very group whose existence he is demonstrating.

In other words, as can be shown in the case of managers (*cadres*), as Luc Boltanski has done, as well as that of the proletariat, or of teachers, in many cases, in order to escape from the type of existence Sartre called serial, in order to gain access to collective existence, there is no other route than by way of a spokesperson. It is objectification in a 'movement', an 'organization', which by a *fictio juris* typical of social magic allows a simple *collectio personarum plurium* to exist as a 'moral person', as a *social agent*.

I am going to take an example from the most humdrum and ordinary sphere of politics, that which we see in front of us every day. I am doing this so as to make myself understood but also at the risk of being understood too easily, with that sort of common half-understanding which is the principal obstacle to true understanding. The difficulty, in sociology, is to manage to think in a completely astonished and disconcerted way about things you thought you had always understood. That is why you sometimes have to begin with the most difficult things in order to understand the easier things properly. That brings me to my example: during the events of May 1968, we saw the emergence of a certain M. Bayet who, throughout those famous 'days', continued to speak on behalf of *agrégés* in his capacity as president of the *Société des agrégés*, a society which, at least at that time, had practically no base. There we have a typical case of usurpation with a person who makes other people believe (but who? the press, at least, which *recognizes* and knows only spokespersons, condemning everyone else to their 'personal opinions') that he has 'behind him' a group by virtue of the fact that he can speak in their name, in his capacity as a 'moral person', without being contradicted by anyone. (Here we reach the limits: the fewer supporters he has, the more protected he may be from contradiction, the absence of any contradiction demonstrating in fact the absence of supporters.) What can be done against someone like that? You can protest publicly, or you can draw up a petition. When members of the Communist Party want to get rid of their Politburo, they are relegated to the serial, to recurrence, to the status of isolated individuals who have to find a spokesperson for themselves, then an office, then a group in order to get rid of the spokesperson, the office and the group. (This is what most movements, and in particular socialist movements, have always denounced as the capital sin – namely, 'factionalism'.) In other words, what can one do to combat the usurpation of authorized spokespersons? There are, of course, individual solutions against all the ways of being crushed by the collective: 'exit and voice', as Albert Hirschman says, in other words, leaving or protesting. But one may also establish another organization. If you look at newspapers of the period, you will see that, around 20 May 1968, another *Société des agrégés* appeared, with a general secretary, a seal, an office, etc. There's no escaping it.

So delegation – this sort of originary act of constitution in both the philosophical and political senses of the word – is an act of magic which enables what was merely a collection of several persons, a series of juxtaposed individuals, to exist in the form of a fictitious person, a *corporatio*, a body, a mystical body incarnated in a social body, which itself transcends the biological bodies which compose it ('*corpus corporatum in corpore corporato*').

> 'The only way [for men] to erect such a Common Power ... is, to conferre all their power and strength upon one Man, or upon one Assembly of men, that may reduce all their Wills, by plurality of voices, unto one Will: which is as much as to say, to appoint one man, or Assembly of men, to beare their Person; and every one to owne, and acknowledge himselfe to be Author of whatsoever he that so beareth their Person, shall Act, or cause to be Acted, in those things which concerne the Common Peace and Safetie.'[1] In this passage from *Leviathan*, in which Hobbes describes the 'Generation of a Commonwealth', one can read one of the clearest and most concise formulations of the theory of *unifying representation*: the multitude of isolated individuals accedes to the status of a moral person when it finds, in the unified representation of its diversity given to it by its representative, the constitutive image of its unity; in other words, the multitude constitutes itself as a unity by recognizing itself in its unique representative.[2] Hobbes

is repeating or developing the doctrine of 'corporation' elaborated by thirteenth-century canonists, especially with regard to the Church, insisting only on the unifying effect which results from the uniqueness of the representative, being understood both as a plenipotentiary and as a symbol of the group, *corpus unum* of which he is the visible *incarnation* or, better, the manifestation in effigy.[3]

THE SELF-CONSECRATION OF THE DELEGATE

Now that I have shown how usurpation already exists potentially in delegation, and how the fact of speaking for someone, that is, on behalf of and in the name of someone, implies the propensity to speak in that person's place, I would like to discuss the universal strategies through which the delegate tends to concentrate himself. In order to identify himself with the group and say 'I am the group,' 'I am, therefore the group is,' the delegate must, as it were, abolish himself in the group, make a gift of his person to the group, declare and proclaim: 'I exist only through the group.' The usurpation of the delegate is necessarily modest and presupposes a certain modesty. This is no doubt the reason why all apparatchiks have a family resemblance. There is a sort of structural bad faith attached to the delegate who, in order to appropriate for himself the authority of the group, must identify himself with the group, reduce himself to the group which authorizes him. But I would like to cite Kant who, in *Religion within the Limits of Reason Alone*, notes that a church founded on unconditional faith, and not on rational faith, would not have any 'servants' (*ministri*) but 'commanding high officials' (*officiales*) who give the orders and who, even when they 'do not appear in hierarchical splendour', as in the Protestant Church, and even when they 'protest verbally against all this . . . actually wish to feel themselves regarded as the only chosen interpreters of a Holy Scripture', and thus transform 'the *service* of the Church [*minister-ium*] into a domination of its members [*imperium*] although, in order to conceal this usurpation, they make use of the modest title of the former'.[4] The mystery of ministry works only if the minister conceals his usurpation, and the *imperium* it confers on him, by asserting that he is just an ordinary minister. It is possible for such a person to confiscate the properties associated with his position only in so far as he conceals himself – that is the very definition of symbolic power. A symbolic power is a power which presupposes recognition, that is, misrecognition of the violence that is exercised through it. So the symbolic violence of the minister can be exercised only with that sort of complicity granted to him, via the effect of misrecognition encouraged by denial, by those on whom that violence is exercised.

Nietzsche puts this very well in *The Antichrist*, which is less a critique of Christianity than a critique of the delegate, since the minister of the Catholic faith is the incarnation of the delegate: that is why in this book he obsessively attacks the priest and priestly hypocrisy and the strategies through which the delegate absolutizes himself and consecrates himself. The first procedure the minister may employ is the one which consists in making himself appear necessary. Kant had already referred to the way exegesis, as a form of legitimate reading, was invoked as necessary. Nietzsche spells it out in full: 'One cannot read these Gospels too warily: there are difficulties behind every word.'[5] What Nietzsche is suggesting is that in order to consecrate himself as a necessary interpreter, the intermediary must produce the need for his own product. And in order to do that, he must produce the difficulty that he alone will be able to solve. The delegate thus performs – to quote Nietzsche again – a 'transformation of himself into something holy'. To enable his necessity to be fully felt, the delegate thus resorts to the strategy of 'impersonal duty'. 'Nothing works more profound ruin than any "impersonal" duty, any sacrifice to the Moloch of abstraction.'[6] The delegate is the one who assigns sacred tasks to himself. 'If one considers that the philosopher is, in virtually all nations, only the further development of the priestly type, one is no longer surprised to discover this heirloom of the priest, *self-deceptive fraudulence*. If one has sacred tasks, for example that of improving, saving, redeeming mankind . . . one *is* already sanctified by such a task.'[7]

These priestly strategies are all based on bad faith, in the Sartrean sense of the term: lying to oneself, that 'sacred lie' by which the priest decides the value of things by declaring that things are good absolutely when they are good for him: the priest, says Nietzsche, is the one who 'calls his own will God'.[8] (The same could be said of the politician when he calls his own will 'people', 'opinion' or 'nation'.) To quote Nietzsche again: 'The "law", the "will of God", the "sacred book", "inspiration" – all merely words for the conditions *under* which the priest comes to power, by which he maintains his power – these concepts are to be found at the basis of all priestly organizations, all priestly or priestly–philosophical power-structures.'[9] What Nietzsche means is that delegates *base universal values on themselves*, appropriate values, 'requisition morality', and thus monopolize the notions of God, Truth, Wisdom, People,

Message, Freedom, etc. They make them synonyms. What of? Of themselves. 'I am the Truth.' They turn themselves into the sacred, they consecrate themselves and thereby draw a boundary between themselves and ordinary people. They thus become, as Nietzsche says, 'the measure of all things'.

It is in what I would call the *oracle effect*, thanks to which the spokesperson gives voice to the group in whose name he speaks, thereby speaking with all the authority of that elusive, absent phenomenon, that the function of priestly humility can best be seen: it is in abolishing himself completely in favour of God or the People that the priest turns himself into God or the People. It is when I become Nothing – and because I am capable of becoming Nothing, of abolishing myself, of forgetting myself, of sacrificing myself, of dedicating myself – that I become Everything. I am nothing but the delegate of God or the People, but that in whose name I speak is everything, and on this account I am everything. The oracle effect is a veritable *splitting of personality*: the individual personality, the ego, abolishes itself in favour of a transcendent moral person ('I give myself to France'). The condition of access to the priesthood is a veritable *metanoia*, a conversion. The ordinary individual must die in order for the *moral person* to come into being; die and become an *institution* (that is the effect of the rites of institution). Paradoxically, those who have made themselves nothing in order to become everything can invert the terms of the relation and reproach those who are merely themselves, *who speak only for themselves*, with being nothing either *de facto* or *de jure* (because they are incapable of dedication, etc.). The right of reprimanding other people and making them feel guilty is one of the advantages enjoyed by the militant.

In short, the oracle effect is one of those phenomena that we delude ourselves too quickly into thinking that we have understood (we have all heard of Delphi, of the priests who interpret oracular discourse), and hence we cannot recognize this effect in the set of situations in which someone speaks in the name of something which he brings into existence by his very discourse. A whole series of symbolic effects that are exercised every day in politics rest on this sort of usurpatory ventriloquism, which consists in giving voice to those in whose name one is authorized to speak. It happens very rarely that, when a politician says 'the people, the working classes, the working masses, etc.', he does not thereby produce the oracle effect, in other words, the trick which consists in producing both the message and the interpretation of the message, in creating the belief that '*je est un autre*', that the spokesperson, a simple symbolic substitute of the people, is really the people in the sense that everything he says is the truth and life of the people.

The usurpation which consists in the fact of asserting that one is capable of speaking *in the name of* is what authorizes a move from the indicative to the *imperative*. If I, Pierre Bourdieu, a single and isolated individual, speak only for myself, say 'you must do this or that, overthrow the government or refuse Pershing missiles', who will follow me? But if I am placed in statutory conditions such that I may appear as speaking 'in the name of the masses', or, *a fortiori*, 'in the name of the masses and of Science, of scientific socialism', that changes everything. The move from the indicative to the imperative – Durkheim's followers had sensed this very clearly when they tried to ground a morality on the science of mores – presupposes a move from the individual to the collective, the principle of all recognized or recognizable constraint. The oracle effect, a limiting form of performativity, is what enables the authorized spokesperson to take his authority from the group which authorizes him in order to exercise recognized constraint, symbolic violence, on each of the isolated members of the group. If I am an incarnation of the collective, of the group, and if this group is the group to which you belong, which defines you, which gives you an identity, which means you are *really* a teacher, *really* a Protestant, *really* a Catholic, etc., you *really* have no choice but to obey. The oracle effect is the exploitation of the transcendence of the group in relation to the single individual, a transcendence that comes about through an individual who in effect is to some extent the group, if only because nobody can stand up and say 'you are not the group' unless they establish another group and get themselves recognized as delegate of that new group.

This paradox of the monopolization of collective truth is the source of every effect of symbolic imposition: I am the group, in other words, collective constraint, the constraint of the collective over each of its members. I am an incarnation of the collective and, by virtue of that fact, I am the one who manipulates the group in the very name of the group. I take my authority from the group, and that group authorizes me to impose constraints on the group. (The violence that is part and parcel of the oracle effect can never be felt more strongly than in *assembly situations*, typically *ecclesial* situations, in which the normally authorized spokespersons and, in a crisis situation, the professional spokespersons who are authorized, can speak in the name of the entire group assembled. This violence makes its presence felt in the quasi-physical impossibility of producing a divergent, dissident speech against the *enforced* unanimity which is produced by the monopoly of speech and the techniques for creating unanimity, such as votes taken by a show of hands or by the acclamation of manipulated motions.)

We would have to carry out a linguistic analysis of that double-dealing (or dealing with the ego and its double) and of the rhetorical strategies through which the structural bad faith of the spokesperson is expressed, which includes, for instance, the permanent shift from *I* to *we*. In the symbolic domain, takeovers by force appear as *takeovers of form* – and it is only when this is realized that one can turn linguistic analysis into an instrument of political critique, and rhetoric into a science of symbolic powers. When an apparatchik wants to make a symbolic takeover by force, he shifts from saying 'I' to saying 'we'. He does not say: 'I think that you sociologists should study the workers,' he says: 'We think that you should . . .' or 'the needs of society require that . . . ' So the 'I' of the delegate, the particular interest of the delegate, must conceal itself behind the professed interest of the group, and the delegate must 'universalize his particular interest', as Marx said, so as to get it passed off as the interests of the group. More generally, the use of an *abstract* language, of the big abstract words of political rhetoric, the verbalism of abstract virtue which, as Hegel clearly saw, engenders fanaticism and Jacobin terrorism (try reading the dreadful phraseology of Robespierre's correspondence), all of that participates in the logic of double-dealing, of the ego and its double which underlies the subjectively and objectively legitimate usurpation of the delegate.

I would like to consider the example of the debate on popular art. (I am somewhat worried by the communicability of what I have to say and that must be evident in the difficulty I have in saying it.) You are aware of the recurring debate on popular art, proletarian art, socialist realism, popular culture, etc., a typically theological debate into which sociology cannot enter without getting caught in a trap. Why? Because it is the terrain *par excellence* of the oracle effect I have just been describing. For example, what is called socialist realism is in fact the typical product of that substitution of the individual 'I' of the political delegates, of the Zhdanovian 'I' to call it by its real name, in other words, the second-rate petit-bourgeois intellectual who wants to impose order, especially on first-rate intellectuals, and who universalizes himself by setting himself up as the people. And an elementary analysis of socialist realism would show that there is nothing popular in what is in reality a formalism or even an academicism, based on a highly abstract *allegorical ico-nography*, 'the Worker', etc. (even if this art seems to satisfy, very superficially, the popular demand for realism). What is expressed in this formalist and petit-bourgeois art – which, far from expressing the people, involves rather a *negation of the people*, in the form of that naked-torsoed, muscular, sun-tanned, optimistic people turned towards the future, etc. – is the social philosophy and the uncon-scious ideal of a petite bourgeoisie of party men who betray their real fear of the real people by identifying themselves with an idealized people, torches aloft, the living flame of Humanity . . . The same could be demonstrated of popular culture, etc. What we are dealing with are typical cases of *subject substitution*. The priesthood – and this is what Nietzsche was getting at – the priest, the Church, the apparatchik of every country substitutes his own vision of the world (a vision deformed by his own *libido dominandi*) for that of the group of which he is supposedly the expression. The 'people' is used these days just as in other times God was used – to settle accounts between clerics.

HOMOLOGY AND THE EFFECTS OF MISRECOGNITION

But we must now ask how all these double-dealing strategies, these strategies of the ego and its double, manage to work in spite of everything: how is it that the delegate's double-dealing doesn't betray itself? What has to be understood is what comprises the heart of the mystery of the ministry, namely, 'legitimate imposture'. It is not, in fact, a question of getting away from the naïve representation of the dedicated delegate, the disinterested militant, the self-abnegating leader, in order to fall back into the cynical view of the delegate as a conscious and organized usurper – that is the eight-eenth-century view, as found in Helvetius and d'Holbach, of the priest, and a very naïve view, for all its apparent lucidity. Legitimate imposture succeeds only because the usurper is not a cynical calculator who consciously deceives the people, but someone who in all good faith *takes himself to be* something that he is not.

One of the mechanisms that allow usurpation and double-dealing to work (if I may put it like this) in all innocence, with the most perfect sincerity, consists in the fact that, in many cases, the interests of the delegate and the interests of the mandators, of those he represents, coincide to a large extent, so that the delegate can believe and get others to believe that he has no interests outside those of his mandators. In order to explain this, I have to make a detour through a rather more complicated analysis. There is a political space, there is a religious space, etc.: I call each of these a *field*, that is, an autonomous universe, a kind of arena in which people play a game which has certain rules, rules which are different from those of the game that is played in the adjacent space. The people who are involved in the game have, as such, specific interests, interests which are not defined by their mandators. The political space has a left and a right, it has its dominant and its dominated agents; the social space also has its dominant and its dominated, the rich and the poor; and these two spaces correspond. There is a homology between them. This means that, *grosso modo*, the person who in this game occupies a position on the left, *a*, is related to the person occupying a position on the right, *b*, in the same way that the person occupying a position on the left *A* is related to the person occupying a position on the right *B* in the other game. When *a* wants to attack *b* to settle certain specific scores, he helps himself, but in helping himself he also helps *A*. This structural coincidence of the specific interests of the delegates and the interests of the mandators is the basis of the miracle of a sincere and successful ministry. The people who serve the interests of their mandators well are those who serve their own interests well by serving the others; it is to their advantage and it is important that it should be so for the system to work.

If we are obliged to talk of interests, it is because this notion has a radically disruptive function: it destroys the ideology of disinterest, which is the professional ideology of clerics of every kind. People who are in the religious, intellectual or political game have specific interests which, however different they may be from the interests of the managing director who is playing in the economic field, are none the less *vital*. All these symbolic interests – not losing face, not losing your constituency, shutting up your opponent, triumphing over an adverse trend, being made chairperson, etc. – are such that, by serving them and obeying them, it often happens that agents serve their mandators. (There are, of course, cases of discrepancy, in which the interests of the delegates come into conflict with the interests of the mandators.) In any case, what happens far more frequently than one might expect if everything happened randomly, or in accordance with the logic of the purely statistical aggregation of individual interests, is that, because of homology, agents who are content to carry out the duties imposed by their position in the game serve, *eo ipso* and in addition, the people they use to serve themselves and whom they are supposedly serving. The effect of metonymy makes possible a universalization of the particular interests of the apparatchik, the attribution of the interests of the delegate to the mandators he is supposed to be representing. The principal merit of this model is that it explains the fact that the delegates are not cynical (or far less and far less often than one might believe), that they are absorbed in the game and that they really believe in what they are doing.

There are many cases like that, in which the mandators and the delegates, customers and producers, are in a relation of structural homology. It is true of the intellectual field and of the field of journalism: the journalist from the left-wing *Nouvel Observateur* is to the journalist of the right-wing *Figaro* what the reader of the *Nouvel Observateur* is to the reader of the *Figaro*; and so when he enjoys settling accounts with the *Figaro* journalist, he also gives pleasure to the reader of the *Nouvel Observateur* even without trying to please that reader directly. It is a very simple mechanism, but one which contradicts the ordinary way that we represent ideological action as self-interested service or servility, as self-interested subservience to a function. The *Figaro* journalist is not a boot-licking hack writer for the bishops or the lapdog of capitalism, etc.: he is first and foremost a journalist who, from time to time, is obsessed by left-wing journals such as the *Nouvel Observateur* or *Libération*.

THE DELEGATES OF THE APPARATUS

Up to now I have been emphasizing the relation between mandators and delegates. I must now examine the relation between the body of delegates, the apparatus, which has its own interests and, as Weber says, its 'own tendencies', such as the tendency to reproduction, and particular delegates. When the body of delegates, the priestly body, the Party, etc., asserts its own tendencies, the interests of the apparatus take precedence over the interests of individual delegates who, therefore, cease to be the delegates of their mandators, and become responsible to the apparatus: from then on, the properties and practices of the delegates cannot be understood without an understanding of the apparatus.

The fundamental law of bureaucratic apparatuses is that the apparatus gives everything (including power over the apparatus) to those who give it everything and expect everything from it because they themselves have nothing or are nothing outside it; to put it more bluntly, the apparatus depends most on those who most depend on it because they are the ones it holds most tightly in its clutches. Zinoviev, who understood all this very cleverly, and for good reason, but who remained trapped in value judgements, said in *The Yawning Heights*: 'The source of Stalin's success resides in the fact that he is an extraordinarily mediocre person.' Here he comes very close to stating the law that operates in such cases. Still talking about the apparatchik, he also talks about 'an extraordinarily insignificant and thus invincible force'. These are very fine formulae, but they are somewhat false, since the polemical intention, which gives them their charm, prevents one from grasping the facts as they are (which is not the same as accepting them). Moral indignation cannot understand the fact that the ones who succeed in the apparatus are those whom charismatic intuition perceives as the most stupid, the most ordinary, those who have no value in themselves. In fact, they succeed not because they are the most ordinary but because they have nothing outside the apparatus, nothing which would authorize them to take liberties with regard to the apparatus, to try to be smart.

There is thus a sort of structural and non-accidental correspondence between the different kinds of apparatus and certain categories of people, defined above all negatively, as having none of the properties that it is advantageous to possess at the moment under consideration in the field concerned. In more neutral terms, one might say that the apparatus will consecrate people who are reliable. But *why* are they reliable? Because they have nothing they might use to oppose the apparatus. This is why in the French Communist Party of the 1950s, as in the China of the Cultural Revolution, the young frequently served as symbolic warders and watchdogs. Young people, after all, do not just represent enthusiasm, naïvety, conviction, everything which one associates somewhat unthinkingly with youth; from the point of view of my model, they are also the people who have nothing. They are the new entrants, those who are arriving in the field without any capital. And from the point of view of the apparatus, they are cannon-fodder against their elders who, now starting to have capital, either through the Party or through themselves, use this capital to take issue with the Party. The person who has nothing is an unconditional supporter; he has all the less to oppose in that the apparatus gives him a great deal, befitting the unconditional nature of his support and his own nothingness. This is why in the 1950s this or that 25-year-old intellectual could have, *ex officio*, by delegation from the apparatus, the kind of audience which only the most established intellectuals could enjoy, though in the latter case this was, so to speak, because of their status as authors.

This sort of iron law of the apparatus is coupled with another process which I will mention very briefly and which I will call the 'organization effect'. I refer you to Marc Ferro's analysis of the process of Bolshevization. In the district soviets, the factory committees and other spontaneous groups of the beginning of the Russian Revolution, everyone was present, people talked, etc. And then, as soon as a party worker was chosen, people started to come less. With the institutionalization incarnated in the party worker and the organization, everything is inverted: the organization tends to monopolize power, the number of participants in the assemblies diminishes. It is the organization which *calls* meetings and the participants serve, on the one hand, to demonstrate the representativeness of their representatives and, on the other, to *ratify* their decisions. Party workers start to reproach ordinary members for not coming often enough to meetings which reduce them to these functions.

This process of concentration of power in the hands of delegates is a sort of historical realization of what is described by the theoretical model of the process of delegation. People are there and speak. Then comes the party official, and people come less often. And then there is an organization, which starts to develop a specific competence, a language all of its own. (Mention might be made here of the way the bureaucracy of research develops: there are researchers, and there are scientific administrators who are supposed to serve the researchers. Researchers do not understand the administrators' language, which may be bureaucratic – 'research budget', 'priority', etc. – and, nowadays, technocratic–democratic – 'social need'. They immediately stop coming and their absenteeism is denounced. But certain researchers, those who have time, do stay. The rest of the story is easy to predict.) The party official (*permanent*) is, as the term suggests, the person who devotes all his time to what is, for others, a secondary or, at least, part-time activity. He has time, and he has time on his side. He is in a position to dissolve all the prophetic, that is, discontinuous struggles for power into the tempo of the bureaucracy, into that repetition that swallows up time and energy. It is in this way that delegates secure a certain concentration of power and develop a specific ideology, based on the paradoxical reversal of their relation with their mandators – whose absenteeism, incompetence and indifference to collective interests are denounced, without it being seen that this indifference is the result of the concentration of power in the hands of the party officials. The dream of all party officials is an apparatus without a base, without faithful followers, without militants . . . They have their permanent status to protect them from discontinuity; they have their specific competence, their own language, a culture which belongs to them, apparatchik culture, based on its own history, that of their own petty affairs (Gramsci says this somewhere: we have debates of Byzantine complexity, conflicts between tendencies, trends which nobody understands the slightest thing about). Then, a specific social technology emerges: people become professionals of the manipulation of the only situation which could create problems for them, namely, confrontation with their mandators. They know how to manipulate general assemblies, transform votes into acclamations, etc. And in addition, they have social logic on their side because, although I do not have time to demonstrate this here, they need do absolutely nothing and yet things will tend to go the way that suits their interests, and their power often resides in the – entropic – choice not to do, not to choose.

It is thus easy to understand that the central phenomenon is that sort of reversal of the table of values which ultimately enables opportunism to be converted into militant dedication. There are jobs, privileges, and people who take them; far from feeling guilty about having served their interests, they will claim that they are not taking these jobs for their own benefit, but for that of the Party or the Cause, just as they will invoke, so as to hang on to those jobs, the rule that says you do not give up a position you have won. And they will even go as far as to describe as abstentionism or culpable dissidence any ethical reservations that might be expressed concerning the concentration of power.

There is a sort of self-consecration of the apparatus, a theodicy of the apparatus. The apparatus is always right (and the self-critique of individuals provides it with a final defence against any questioning of the apparatus as such). The reversal of the table of values, together with the Jacobin exaltation of the political and of the political priesthood, has meant that the political alienation to which I was referring at the beginning has ceased to be noticed; it has also meant that, on the contrary, it is the priestly vision of politics which has imposed itself, to the point of viewing as guilty all those who do not play the political games. In other words, the view which decreed that the fact of not being a militant, of not being involved in politics, was a kind of sin for which one had eternally to make amends has been so strongly internalized that the final political revolution, the revolution against the political clericature and against the usurpation which is always potentially present in delegation, is yet to be carried out.

10

Identity and Representation

Elements for a Critical Reflection on the Idea of Region

The confusion surrounding debates concerning the notion of region and, more generally, of 'ethnic group' or 'ethnicity' (scientific euphemisms that have been substituted for the notion of 'race', which is none the less still present in actual practice) stems in part from the fact that the desire to submit to logical criticism the categories of common sense – emblems or stigmata – and to substitute for the practical principles of everyday judgement the logically controlled and empirically based criteria of science, leads one to forget that practical classifications are always subordinated to practical functions and oriented towards the production of *social effects*. One also tends to forget that the practical representations that are the most exposed to scientific criticism (for example, the statements made by regionalist militants about the unity of the Occitan language) may *contribute to producing* what they apparently describe or designate, in other words, the *objective reality* to which the objectivist critique refers them in order to show their delusions or incoherence.

But on a deeper level, the quest for the 'objective' criteria of 'regional' or 'ethnic' identity should not make one forget that, in social practice, these criteria (for example, language, dialect and accent) are the object of *mental representations*, that is, of acts of perception and appreciation, of cognition and recognition, in which agents invest their interests and their presuppositions, and of *objectified representations*, in things (emblems, flags, badges, etc.) or acts, self-interested strategies of symbolic manipulation which aim at determining the (mental) representation that other people may form

of these properties and their bearers. In other words, the characteristics and criteria noted by objectivist sociologists and anthropologists, once they are perceived and evaluated as they are in practice,
function as signs, emblems or stigmata, and also as powers. Since
this is the case, and since there is no social subject who can in
practical terms be unaware of the fact, it follows that (objectively)
symbolic properties, even the most negative, can be used strategical-
ly according to the material but also the symbolic interests of their
bearer.[1]

One can understand the particular form of struggle over classifications that is constituted by the struggle over the definition of
'regional' or 'ethnic' identity only if one transcends the opposition
that science, in order to break away from the preconceptions of
spontaneous sociology, must first establish between representation
and reality, and only if one includes in reality the representation of
reality, or, more precisely, the struggle over representations, in the
sense of mental images, but also of social demonstrations whose aim
it is to manipulate mental images (and even in the sense of
delegations responsible for organizing the demonstrations that are
necessary to modify mental representations).

Struggles over ethnic or regional identity – in other words, over
the properties (stigmata or emblems) linked with the *origin* through
the *place* of origin and its associated durable marks, such as accent –
are a particular case of the different struggles over classifications,
struggles over the monopoly of the power to make people see and
believe, to get them to know and recognize, to impose the legitimate
definition of the divisions of the social world and, thereby, to *make
and unmake groups*. What is at stake here is the power of imposing a
vision of the social world through principles of di-vision which, when
they are imposed on a whole group, establish meaning and a
consensus about meaning, and in particular about the identity and
unity of the group, which creates the reality of the unity and the
identity of the group. The etymology of the word region (*regio*), as
described by Emile Benveniste, leads to the source of the di-vision: a
magical and thus essentially social act of *diacrisis* which introduces
by *decree* a decisive discontinuity in natural continuity (between the
regions of space but also between ages, sexes, etc.). *Regere fines*, the
act which consists in 'tracing out the limits by straight lines', in
delimiting 'the interior and the exterior, the realm of the sacred and
the realm of the profane, the national territory and foreign territory',
is a *religious* act performed by the person invested with the highest
authority, the *rex*, whose responsibility it is to *regere sacra*, to fix the

rules which bring into existence what they decree, to speak with authority, to pre-dict in the sense of calling into being, by an enforceable saying, what one says, of making the future that one utters come into being.[2] The *regio* and its frontiers (*fines*) are merely the dead trace of the act of authority which consists in circumscribing the country, the territory (which is also called *fines*), in imposing the legitimate, known and recognized definition (another sense of *finis*) of frontiers and territory – in short, the source of legitimate di-vision of the social world. This rightful act, consisting in asserting with authority a truth which has the force of law, is an act of cognition which, being based, like all symbolic power, on recognition, brings into existence what it asserts (*auctoritas*, as Benveniste again re-minds us, is the capacity to produce which is granted to the *auctor*).[3] Even when he merely states with authority what is already the case, even when he contents himself with asserting what is, the *auctor* produces a change in what is: by virtue of the fact that he states things with authority, that is, in front of and in the name of everyone, publicly and officially, he saves them from their arbitrary nature, he sanctions them, sanctifies them, consecrates them, mak-ing them worthy of existing, in conformity with the nature of things, and thus 'natural'.

Nobody would want to claim today that there exist criteria capable of founding 'natural' classifications on 'natural' regions, separated by 'natural' frontiers. The frontier is never anything other than the product of a division which can be said to be more or less based on 'reality', depending on whether the elements it assembles show more or less numerous and more or less striking resemblances among themselves (given that it will always be possible to argue over the limits of variations between non-identical elements that taxonomy treats as similar). Everyone agrees that 'regions' divided up accord-ing to the different conceivable criteria (language, habitat, cultural forms, etc.) never coincide perfectly. But that is not all: 'reality', in this case, is social through and through and the most 'natural' classifications are based on characteristics which are not in the slightest respect natural and which are to a great extent the product of an arbitrary imposition, in other words, of a previous state of the relations of power in the field of struggle over legitimate delimita-tion. The frontier, that product of a legal act of delimitation, produces cultural difference as much as it is produced by it: one need only consider the role of the educational system in the development of language to see that political will can undo what history had done.[4] Thus the science which claims to put forward the criteria that are the most well founded in reality would be well advised to remember that it is merely recording a *state* of the struggle over classifications, in other words, a state of the relation of material or symbolic forces between those who have a stake in one or other mode of classification, and who, just as science does, often invoke scientific authority to ground in reality and in reason the *arbitrary* division they seek to impose.

Regionalist discourse is a *performative discourse* which aims to impose as legitimate a new definition of the frontiers and to get people to know and recognize the *region* that is thus delimited in opposition to the dominant definition, which is misrecognized as such and thus recognized and legitimate, and which does not acknowledge that new region. The act of categorization, when it manages to achieve recognition or when it is exercised by a recognized authority, exercises by itself a certain power: 'ethnic' or 'regional' categories, like categories of kinship, institute a reality by using the power of *revelation* and *construction* exercised by *objectification in discourse*. The fact of calling 'Occitan'[5] the language spoken by those who are called 'Occitans' because they speak that language (a language that nobody speaks, properly speaking, because it is merely the sum of a very great number of different dialects), and of calling the region (in the sense of physical space) in which this language is spoken 'Occitanie', thus claiming to make it exist as a 'region' or as a 'nation' (with the historically constituted implications that these notions have at the moment under consideration), is no ineffectual fiction.[6] The act of social magic which consists in trying to bring into existence the thing named may succeed if the person who performs it is capable of gaining recognition through his speech for the power which that speech is appropriating for itself by a provisional or definitive usurpation, that of imposing a new vision and a new division of the social world: *regere fines, regere sacra*, to consecrate a new limit. The effectiveness of the performative discourse which claims to bring about what it asserts in the very act of asserting it is directly proportional to the authority of the person doing the asserting: the formula 'I authorize you to go' is *eo ipso* an authorization only if the person uttering it is authorized to authorize, has the authority to authorize. But the cognition effect brought about by the fact of objectification in discourse does not depend only on the recognition granted to the person who utters that discourse: it also depends on the degree to which the discourse which announces to the group its identity is grounded in the objectivity of the group to which it is addressed, that is, in the recognition and the belief granted to it by the members of this group, as well as in the economic or cultural properties they share in common, since it is only in accordance with a given principle of pertinence that the relation between these properties can appear. The power over the group that is to be brought into existence as a group is, inseparably, a power of creating the group by imposing on it common principles of vision and division, and thus a unique vision of its identity and an identical vision of its unity.[7]

The fact that struggles over identity – that being-perceived which exists fundamentally through recognition by other people – concern the imposition of perceptions and categories of perception helps to explain the decisive place which, like the strategy of the *manifesto* in artistic movements, the *dialectic of manifestation or demonstration* holds in all regionalist or nationalist movements.[8] The almost magical power of words comes from the fact that the objectification and *de facto* officialization brought about by the public act of naming, in front of everyone, has the effect of freeing the particularity (which lies at the source of all sense of identity) from the unthought, and even unthinkable. (This is what happens when an unnameable 'patois' is asserted as a language capable of being spoken publicly.) And officialization finds its fulfilment in *demonstration*, the typically magical (which does not mean ineffectual) act through which the practical group – virtual, ignored, denied, or repressed – makes itself visible and manifest, for other groups and *for itself*, and attests to its existence as a group that is known and recognized, laying a claim to institutionalization. The social world is also will and representation, and to exist socially means also to be perceived, and perceived as distinct.

In fact, it is not a question of a choice between, on the one hand, objectivist arbitration, which measures *representations* (in all senses of the term) by 'reality', forgetting that they can give rise in reality, by the specific effectiveness of evocation, to the very thing they represent, and, on the other hand, the subjectivist commitment which, privileging representation, ratifies in the domain of science that falsehood in sociological writing by which militants pass from the representation of reality to the reality of the representation. One can avoid the alternative by taking it as an object or, more precisely, by taking into account, in the science of the object, the objective foundations of the alternative of objectivism and subjectivism which divides science, preventing it from apprehending the specific logic of the social world, that 'reality' which is the site of a permanent struggle to *define* 'reality'. To grasp at one and the same time *what is instituted* (without forgetting that it is only a question of the outcome, at a given point in time, of the struggle to bring something into existence or to force out of existence something that already exists) and *representations*, performative statements which seek to bring about what they state, to restore at one and the same time the objective structures and the subjective relation to those structures, starting with the claim to transform them: this is to give oneself the means of explaining 'reality' more completely, and thus of understanding and foreseeing more exactly the potentialities it contains or, more precisely, the chances it objectively offers to different subjective demands.

When scientific discourse is dragged into the very struggles over classification that it is attempting to objectify (and, unless the disclosure of scientific discourse is forbidden, it is difficult to see how this usage could be prevented), it begins once again to function in the reality of struggles over classification. It is thus bound to appear as either *critical* or *complicitous*, depending on the critical or complicitous relation that the reader himself has with the reality being described. Thus the mere fact of *showing* can function as a way of pointing the finger, of accusing (*kategorein*) or, on the other hand, as a way of showing and throwing into relief. This is as true of classification into social classes as it is of classification into 'regions' or 'ethnic groups'. Hence the necessity of making completely explicit the relation between the struggles over the source of legitimate di-vision which occur in the scientific field and those which take place in the social field (and which, because of their specific logic, grant a preponderant role to intellectuals). Any position claiming 'objectivity' about the actual or potential, real or foreseeable existence, of a region, an ethnic group or a social class, and thereby about the *claim to institution* which is asserted in 'partisan' *representations*, constitutes a certificate of *realism* or a verdict of *utopianism* which helps to determine the objective chances that this social entity has of coming into existence.[9] The symbolic effect to which scientific discourse gives rise by consecrating a state of the divisions and of the vision of the divisions is all the more inevitable because, in symbolic struggles over cognition and recognition, so-called 'objective' criteria, the very ones which are well known to scientists, are used as weapons: they designate the characteristics on which a symbolic action of mobilization can be based in order to produce real unity or the belief in unity (both in the group itself and in others) which ultimately, and in particular via the actions of the imposition and inculcation of legitimate identity (such as those actions performed by the school or the army), tends to generate real unity. In short, the most 'neutral' verdicts of science contribute to modifying the object of science. Once the regional or national question is objectively raised in social reality, even if only by an active minority (which may exploit its very weakness by playing on the properly symbolic strategy of *provocation* and *testimony* in order to draw out ripostes, whether symbolic or not, which imply a certain recognition), any utterance about the region functions as an *argument* which helps to favour or penalize the chances of the region's acquiring recognition and thereby existence.

Nothing is less innocent than the question, which divides the scientific world, of knowing whether one has to include in the system of pertinent criteria not only the so-called 'objective' categories (such as ancestry, territory, language, religion, economic activity, etc.), but also the so-called 'subjective' properties (such as the feeling of belonging), i.e. the *representations* through which social agents imagine the divisions of reality and which contribute to the reality of the divisions.[10] When, as their education and their specific interests incline them, researchers try to set themselves up as judges of all judgements and as critics of all criteria, they prevent themselves from grasping the specific logic of a struggle in which the social force of representations is not necessarily proportional to their truth-value (measured by the degree to which they express the state of the relation of material forces at the moment under consideration). Indeed, as pre-dictions, these 'scientific' mythologies can produce their own verification, if they manage to impose themselves on collective belief and to create, by their mobilizing capacity, the conditions of their own realization. But they do no better when, giving up the distance of the observer, they adopt the representation of the agents and participants, in a discourse which, by failing to provide itself with the means of describing the game in which this representation is produced and the belief which underlies it, is nothing more than one contribution among many to the production of the belief whose foundations and social effects should be described.

It can be seen that, as long as they do not submit their practice to sociological criticism, sociologists are determined, in their orientation towards the objectivist or subjectivist pole of the universe of possible relations to the object, by social factors such as their position in the social hierarchy of their discipline (in other words, their level of certified competence which, in a socially hierarchized geographical space, often coincides with their central or local position, a particularly important factor when the matter at hand is that of regionalism) and also their position in the technical hierarchy: 'epistemological' strategies which are at such opposite ends of the spectrum as the dogmatism of the guardians of theoretical orthodoxy and the spontaneism of the apostles of participation in the movement may have in common a way of avoiding the demands of scientific work without giving up their claims to *auctoritas* when they either will not or cannot satisfy these demands, or when they satisfy only the most superficial of them. But they may also swing, following their directly experienced relation to the object, between objectivism and subjectivism, blame and praise, mystified and mystificatory complicity and reductionist demystification, because they accept the objective problematic, in other words, the very structure of the field of struggle in which the region and regionalism are at stake, instead of objectifying it; because they enter into the debate on the criteria enabling one to state the meaning of the regionalist movement or to predict its future without asking themselves about the logic of a struggle which bears precisely on the determination of the meaning of the movement (is it regional or national, progressive or regressive, right-wing or left-wing, etc.) and on the criteria capable of determining this meaning.

Here as elsewhere, in sum, one must escape the alternative of the 'demystifying' recording of objective criteria and the mystified and mystificatory ratification of wills and representations in order to keep together what go together in reality: on the one hand, the objective classifications, whether incorporated or objectified, sometimes in institutional form (like legal boundaries), and, on the other hand, the practical relation to those classifications, whether acted out or represented, and in particular the individual and collective strategies (such as regionalist demands) by which agents seek to put these classifications at the service of their material or symbolic interests, or to conserve and transform them; or, in other words, the objective relations of material and symbolic power, and the practical schemes (implicit, confused and more or less contradictory) through which agents classify other agents and evaluate their position in these objective relations as well as the symbolic strategies of presentation and self-representation with which they oppose the classifications and representations (of themselves) that others impose on them.[11]

In short, it is by exorcizing the dream of the 'royal science' invested with the regal right of *regere fines* and *regere sacra*, with the nomothetic or law-giving power of decreeing union and separation, that science can take as its object the very game whose stake is the power of governing the sacred frontiers, that is, the quasi-divine power over the vision of the world, and in which one has no choice, if one seeks to exercise it (rather than submit to it), other than to mystify or demystify.

11

Social Space and the Genesis of 'Classes'

The construction of a theory of the social space presupposes a series of breaks with Marxist theory. It presupposes a break with the tendency to emphasize substances – here, real groups whose number, limits, members, etc. one claims to be able to define – at the expense of *relations* and with the intellectualist illusion which leads one to consider the theoretical class, constructed by the social scientist, as a real class, an effectively mobilized group; a break with economics, which leads one to reduce the social field, a multi-dimensional space, to the economic field alone, to the relations of economic production, which are thus established as the co-ordinates of social position; and a break, finally, with objectivism, which goes hand in hand with intellectualism, and which leads one to overlook the symbolic struggles that take place in different fields, and where what is at stake is the very representation of the social world, and in particular the hierarchy within each of the fields and between the different fields.

THE SOCIAL SPACE

To begin with, sociology presents itself as a *social topology*. Accordingly, the social world can be represented in the form of a (multi-dimensional) space constructed on the basis of principles of differentiation or distribution constituted by the set of properties active in the social universe under consideration, that is, able to confer force or power on their possessor in that universe. Agents and groups of agents are thus defined by their *relative positions* in this space. Each of them is confined to a position or a precise class of neighbouring positions (i.e. to a given region of this space), and one cannot in fact occupy – even if one can do so in thought – two opposite regions of the space. In so far as the properties chosen to construct this space are active properties, the space can also be described as a field of forces: in other words, as a set of objective power relations imposed on all those who enter this field, relations which are not reducible to the intentions of individual agents or even to direct *interactions* between agents.[1]

The active properties that are chosen as principles of construction of the social space are the different kinds of power or capital that are current in the different fields. Capital, which can exist in objectified form – in the form of material properties – or, in the case of cultural capital, in an incorporated form, one which can be legally guaranteed, represents power over a field (at a given moment) and, more precisely, over the accumulated product of past labour (and in particular over the set of instruments of production) and thereby over the mechanisms which tend to ensure the production of a particular category of goods and thus over a set of revenues and profits. The kinds of capital, like trumps in a game of cards, are powers which define the chances of profit in a given field (in fact, to every field or sub-field there corresponds a particular kind of capital, which is current, as a power or stake, in that field). For example, the volume of cultural capital (the same would be true, *mutatis mutandis*, of economic capital) determines the aggregate chances of profit in all games in which cultural capital is effective, thereby helping to determine position in the social space (in so far as this position is determined by success in the cultural field).

The position of a given agent in the social space can thus be defined by the position he occupies in the different fields, that is, in the distribution of the powers that are active in each of them. These are, principally, economic capital (in its different kinds), cultural capital and social capital, as well as symbolic capital, commonly called prestige, reputation, fame, etc., which is the form assumed by these different kinds of capital when they are perceived and recognized as legitimate. One can thus construct a simplified model of the social field as a whole, a model which allows one to plot each agent's position in all possible spaces of the game (it being understood that, while each field has its own logic and its own hierarchy, the hierarchy which is established between the kinds of capital and the statistical relation between different assets mean that the economic field tends to impose its structure on other fields).

The social field can be described as a multi-dimensional space of positions such that each actual position can be defined in terms of a multi-dimensional system of co-ordinates whose values correspond to the values of the different pertinent variables. Agents are thus distributed, in the first dimension, according to the overall volume of the capital they possess and, in the second dimension, according to the composition of their capital – in other words, according to the relative weight of the different kinds of capital in the total set of their assets.[2]

> The form assumed, at each moment, in each social field, by the set of the distributions of the different kinds of capital (whether incorporated or materialized), as instruments for the appropriation of the objectified product of accumulated social labour, defines the state of the relations of power, institutionalized in durable social statuses that are socially recognized or legally guaranteed, between agents who are objectively defined by their position within these relations; this form determines the actual or potential powers in different fields and the chances of access to the specific profits they procure.[3]
>
> Knowledge of the position occupied in this space contains information on the intrinsic properties (i.e. condition) and the relational properties (i.e. position) of agents. This is particularly clear in the case of those who occupy intermediate or middle positions – those which, apart from the middle or median values of their properties, owe a certain number of their most typical characteristics to the fact that they are situated *between* the two poles of the field, in the *neutral* point of the space, and are balanced between the two extreme positions.

CLASSES ON PAPER

On the basis of knowledge of the space of positions, one can carve out *classes* in the logical sense of the word, i.e. sets of agents who occupy similar positions and who, being placed in similar conditions and submitted to similar types of conditioning, have every chance of having similar dispositions and interests, and thus of producing similar practices and adopting similar stances. This 'class on paper' has the *theoretical* existence which belongs to all theories: as the product of an explanatory classification, one which is altogether similar to that of zoologists or botanists, it allows one to *explain* and predict the practices and properties of the things classified – including their propensity to constitute groups. It is not really a class, an actual class, in the sense of being a group, a group mobilized for struggle; at most one could say that it is a *probable class*, in so far as it is a set of agents which will place fewer objective obstacles in the way of efforts of mobilization than any other set of agents.

Thus, contrary to the *nominalist relativism* which cancels out social differences by reducing them to pure theoretical artefacts, we have to affirm the existence of an objective space determining compatibilities and incompatibilities, proximities and distances. Contrary to the *realism of the intelligible* (or the reification of concepts), we have to affirm that the classes which can be carved out of the social space (for instance, for the purposes of statistical analysis, which is the sole means of demonstrating the structure of the social space) do not exist as real groups, although they explain the probability of individuals constituting themselves as practical groups, families (homogamy), clubs, associations and even trade-union or political 'movements'. What exists is a *space of relations* which is just as real as a geographical space, in which movements have to be paid for by labour, by effort and especially by time (to move upwards is to raise oneself, to climb and to bear the traces or the stigmata of that effort). Distances can also be measures in time (the time of ascent or of the reconversion of capital, for example). And the probability of mobilization into organized movements, endowed with an apparatus and a spokesperson, etc. (the very thing which leads us to talk of a 'class'), will be inversely proportional to distance in this space. While the probability of bringing together, really or nominally, a set of agents – by virtue of the delegate – is greater when they are closer together in the social space and belong to a more restricted and thus more homogeneous constructed class, nevertheless the alliance of the closest agents is never *necessary* or inevitable (because the effects of immediate competition may get in the way), and the alliance of the agents that are most separated from one another is never *impossible*. Although there is more chance of mobilizing in the same real group the set of workers than the set of bosses and workers, it is possible, in the context, for example, of an international crisis, to provoke a grouping on the basis of links of national identity. (This is in part because, due to its specific history, each of the national social spaces has its own structure – for instance, as regards hierarchical divergences in the economic field.)

Like 'being' according to Aristotle, the social world can be uttered and constructed in different ways: it can be practically perceived, uttered, constructed, in accordance with different principles of vision and division (for instance, ethnic divisions), it being understood that groupings founded in the struggle of the space constructed on the basis of the distribution of capital have a greater chance of being stable and durable and that other forms of grouping will always be threatened by splits and oppositions linked to distances in the social space. To speak of a social space means that one cannot group together just anyone with anyone else while ignoring the fundamental differences, particularly economic and cultural differences, between them. But this never completely excludes a possible organization of agents in accordance with other principles of division – ethnic, national, etc. – though it should be remembered that these are generally linked to the fundamental principles, since ethnic groups are themselves at least roughly hierarchized in the social space, for instance, in the USA (by the criterion of how long it has been since one's family first immigrated – blacks excepted).[4]

This marks a first break with the Marxist tradition: this tradition either identifies, without further ado, the constructed class with the real class (i.e., as Marx himself reproached Hegel with doing, it confuses the things of logic with the logic of things); or else, when the tradition does draw the distinction, opposing the 'class-in-itself', defined on the basis of a set of objective conditions, to the 'class-for-itself', based on subjective factors, it describes the movement from the one to the other, a movement which is always celebrated as a real ontological advance, in accordance with a logic which is either totally determinist or on the contrary fully voluntarist. In the former case, the transition appears as a logical, mechanical or organic necessity (the transformation of the proletariat from a class-in-itself to a class-for-itself being presented as an inevitable effect of time, of the 'maturing of the objective conditions'); in the latter case, it is presented as the effect of an 'awakening of consciousness', conceived as a 'taking cognizance' of the theory which occurs under the enlightened leadership of the party. In both cases nothing is said about the mysterious alchemy by which a 'group in struggle', as a personalized collective, a historical agent setting its own aims, arises from the objective economic conditions.

By a sort of sleight of hand, the most essential questions are spirited away: first, the very question of the political, of the specific action of agents who, in the name of a theoretical definition of 'class', assign to the members of that class the aims which officially conform most closely to their 'objective' (i.e. theoretical) interests, and of the labour through which they succeed in producing, if not the mobilized class, a belief in the existence of the class, which is the basis of the authority of its spokespersons; and second, the question of the relations between the supposedly objective classifications produced by the social scientist, similar in that respect to the zoologist, and the classifications which agents themselves continually produce in their ordinary existence, and through which they seek to modify their position in the objective classifications or to modify the very principles in accordance with which these classifications are produced.

THE PERCEPTION OF THE SOCIAL WORLD AND POLITICAL STRUGGLE

The most resolutely objectivist theory must take account of agents' representation of the social world and, more precisely, of the contribution they make to the construction of the vision of this world, and, thereby to the very construction of this world, via the *labour of representation* (in all senses of the term) that they continually perform in order to impose their own vision of the world or the vision of their own position in this world, that is, their social identity. The perception of the social world is the product of a double social structuring: on the 'objective' side, this perception is socially structured because the properties attached to agents or institutions do not make themselves available to perception independently, but in combinations whose probability varies widely (and just as feathered animals have a greater chance of having wings than furry animals, so the possessors of a substantial cultural capital are more likely to be museum visitors than those who lack such capital); on the 'subjective' side, it is structured because the schemes of perception and evaluation susceptible of being brought into operation at a given moment, including all those which are laid down in language, are the product of previous symbolic struggles and express, in a more or less transformed form, the state of symbolic relations of power. The fact remains, none the less, that the objects of the social world can be perceived and expressed in different ways because, like the objects of the natural world, they always include a certain indeterminacy and vagueness – because, for example, the most constant combinations of properties are never founded on anything other than statistical connections between interchangeable features; and also because, as historical objects, they are subject to variations in time and their meaning, in so far as it depends on the future, is itself in suspense, in a pending and deferred state, and is thus relatively indeterminate. This element of risk, of uncertainty, is what provides a basis for the plurality of world views, a plurality which is itself linked to the plurality of points of view, and to all the

symbolic struggles for the production and imposition of the legitimate vision of the world and, more precisely, to all the cognitive
strategies of *fulfilment* which produce the meaning of the objects of
the social world by going beyond the directly visible attributes by
reference to the future or the past. This reference may be implicit
and tacit, through what Husserl calls protension and retention,
practical forms of prospection or retrospection excluding the posi-
tioning of past and future as such; or it may be explicit, as in political
struggles in which the past, with the retrospective reconstruction of a
past adjusted to the needs of the present ('La Fayette, here we
are!'[5]), and especially the future, with the creative foresight associated with it, are continually invoked, in order to determine, delimit,
and define the ever-open meaning of the present.

To point out that perception of the social world implies an act of
construction is not in the least to accept an intellectualist theory of
knowledge: the essential part of one's experience of the social world
and of the labour of construction it implies takes place in practice,
without reaching the level of explicit representation and verbal
expression. Closer to a class unconscious than to a 'class consciousness' in the Marxist sense, the sense of the position one occupies in
the social space (what Goffman calls the 'sense of one's place') is the
practical mastery of the social structure as a whole which reveals
itself through the sense of the position occupied in that structure.
The categories of perception of the social world are essentially the
product of the incorporation of the objective structures of the social
space. Consequently, they incline agents to accept the social world
as it is, to take it for granted, rather than to rebel against it, to put
forward opposed and even antagonistic possibilities. The sense of
one's place, as the sense of what one can or cannot 'allow oneself',
implies a tacit acceptance of one's position, a sense of limits ('that's
not meant for us') or – what amounts to the same thing – a sense of
distances, to be marked and maintained, respected, and expected of
others. And this is doubtless all the more true when the conditions of
existence are more rigorous and the reality principle is more
rigorously imposed. (Hence the profound realism which most often
characterizes the world view of the dominated and which, functioning as a sort of socially constituted instinct of conservation, can
appear conservative only with reference to an external and thus
normative representation of the 'objective interest' of those whom it
helps to live or to survive.[6])

If the objective relations of power tend to reproduce themselves in
visions of the social world which contribute to the permanence of

those relations, this is therefore because the structuring principles of
the world view are rooted in the objective structures of the social
world and because the relations of power are also present in people's
minds in the form of the categories of perception of those relations.
But the degree of indeterminacy and vagueness characteristic of the
objects of the social world is, together with the practical, pre-
reflexive and implicit character of the patterns of perception and
evaluation which are applied to them, the Archimedean point which
is objectively made available to truly political action. Knowledge of
the social world and, more precisely, the categories which make it
possible, are the stakes *par excellence* of the political struggle, a
struggle which is inseparably theoretical and practical, over the
power of preserving or transforming the social world by preserving
or transforming the categories of perception of that world.

The capacity for bringing into existence in an explicit state, of
publishing, of making public (i.e. objectified, visible, sayable, and
even official) that which, not yet having attained objective and
collective existence, remained in a state of individual or serial
existence – people's disquiet, anxiety, expectation, worry – represents a formidable social power, that of bringing into existence
groups by establishing the *common sense*, the explicit consensus, of
the whole group. In fact, this labour of categorization, of making
things explicit and classifying them, is continually being performed,
at every moment of ordinary existence, in the struggles in which
agents clash over the meaning of the social world and their position
in it, the meaning of their social identity, through all the forms of
speaking well or badly of someone or something, of blessing or
cursing and of malicious gossip, eulogy, congratulations, praise,
compliments, or insults, rebukes, criticism, accusations, slanders,
etc.

It is easy to understand why one of the elementary forms of
political power should have consisted, in many archaic societies, in
the almost magical power of *naming* and bringing into existence by
virtue of naming. Thus in traditional Kabylia, the function of making
things explicit and the labour of symbolic production that poets
performed, particularly in crisis situations, when the meaning of the
world is no longer clear, conferred on them major political functions,
those of the war-lord or ambassador.[7] But with the growing differentiation of the social world and the constitution of relatively
autonomous fields, the labour of the production and imposition of
meaning is performed in and through struggles in the field of cultural
production (and especially in the political sub-field); it becomes the

particular concern, the specific interest, of the professional producers of objectified representations of the social world, or, more
precisely, of the methods of objectification.

If the legitimate mode of perception is such an important stake in
different struggles, this is because on the one hand the movement
from the implicit to the explicit is in no way automatic, the same
experience of the social being recognizable in very different expressions, and on the other hand, the most marked objective differences
may be hidden behind more immediately visible differences (such as,
for example, those which separate ethnic groups). It is true that
perceptual configurations, social *Gestalten*, exist objectively, and
that the proximity of conditions and thus of dispositions tends to be
re-translated into durable links and groupings, immediately percepti-
ble social units such as socially distinct regions or districts (with
spatial segregation), or sets of agents possessing altogether similar
visible properties, such as Weber's *Stände*. But the fact remains that
socially known and recognized differences exist only for a subject
capable not only of perceiving the differences, but of recognizing
them as significant and interesting, i.e., exists only for a subject
endowed with the aptitude and the inclination to *establish* the
differences which are held to be significant in the social world under
consideration.

In this way, the social world, particularly through properties and
their distribution, attains, in the objective world itself, the status of a
symbolic system which, like a system of phonemes, is organized in
accordance with the logic of difference, of differential deviation,
which is thus constituted as significant *distinction*. The social space,
and the differences that 'spontaneously' emerge within it, tend to
function symbolically as *a space of life-styles* or as a set of *Stände*, of
groups characterized by different life-styles.

Distinction does not necessarily imply, as is often supposed, following
Veblen and his theory of conspicuous consumption, a quest for distinction. All consumption and, more generally, all practice, is *conspicuous*,
visible, whether or not it was performed *in order to be seen*: it is
distinctive, whether or not it was inspired by the desire to get oneself
noticed, to make oneself conspicuous, to distinguish oneself or to act
with distinction. Hence, every practice is bound to function as a
distinctive sign and, when the difference is recognized, legitimate and
approved, as a *sign of distinction* (in all senses of the term). The fact
remains that social agents, being capable of perceiving as significant
distinctions the 'spontaneous' differences that their categories of perception lead them to consider as pertinent, are also capable of intentionally

underscoring these spontaneous differences in life-style by what Weber calls 'the stylization of life' (*Stilisierung des Lebens*). The pursuit of distinction – which may be expressed in ways of speaking or in a refusal to countenance marrying beneath one's station – produces separations which are meant to be perceived or, more precisely, known and recognized as legitimate differences – most frequently as differences of nature (in French we speak of 'natural distinction').

Distinction – in the ordinary sense of the word – is the difference written into the very structure of the social space when it is perceived in accordance with the categories adapted to that structure; and the Weberian *Stand*, which people so often like to contrast with the Marxist class, is the class adequately constructed when it is perceived through the categories of perception derived from the structure of that space. Symbolic capital – another name for distinction – is nothing other than capital, of whatever kind, when it is perceived by an agent endowed with categories of perception arising from the incorporation of the structure of its distribution, i.e. when it is known and recognized as self-evident. Distinctions, as symbolic transformations of *de facto* differences, and, more generally, the ranks, orders, grades and all the other symbolic hierarchies, are the product of the application of schemes of construction which – as in the case, for instance, of the pairs of adjectives used to express most social judgements – are the product of the incorporation of the very structures to which they are applied; and recognition of the most absolute legitimacy is nothing other than an apprehension of the everyday social world as taken for granted, an apprehension which results from the almost perfect coincidence of objective structures and incorporated structures.

It follows, among other consequences, that symbolic capital is attracted to symbolic capital and that the – real – autonomy of the field of symbolic production does not prevent this field from remaining dominated, in its functioning, by the constraints which dominate the social field as a whole. It also follows that objective relations of power tend to reproduce themselves in symbolic relations of power, in visions of the social world which contribute to ensuring the permanence of those relations of power. In the struggle for the imposition of the legitimate vision of the social world, in which science itself is inevitably involved, agents wield a power which is proportional to their symbolic capital, that is, to the recognition they receive from a group. The authority which underlies the performative effectiveness of discourse about the social world, the symbolic force of visions and pre-visions aimed at imposing the principles of vision and division of this world, is a *percipi*, a being known and recognized (*nobilis*), which allows a *percipere* to be imposed. It is the most *visible* agents, from the point of view of the prevailing categories of perception, who are the best placed to change the vision by changing the categories of perception. But they are also, with a few exceptions, the least inclined to do so.

THE SYMBOLIC ORDER AND THE POWER OF NAMING

In the symbolic struggle for the production of common sense or, more precisely, for the monopoly of legitimate *naming* as the official – i.e. explicit and public – imposition of the legitimate vision of the social world, agents bring into play the symbolic capital that they have acquired in previous struggles, in particular all the power that they possess over the instituted taxonomies, those inscribed in people's minds or in the objective world, such as qualifications. Thus all the symbolic strategies through which agents aim to impose their vision of the divisions of the social world and of their position in that world can be located between two extremes: the insult, that *idios logos* through which an ordinary individual attempts to impose his point of view by taking the risk that a reciprocal insult may ensue, and the *official naming*, a symbolic act of imposition which has on its side all the strength of the collective, of the consensus, of common sense, because it is performed by a delegated agent of the state, that is, the holder of the *monopoly of legitimate symbolic violence*. On the one hand, there is the world of particular perspectives, of individual agents who, on the basis of their particular point of view, their particular position, produce namings – of themselves and others – that are particular and self-interested (nicknames, insults, or even accusations, indictments, slanders, etc.), and all the more powerless to gain recognition, and thus to exert a truly symbolic effect, the less their authors are *authorized*, either personally (*auctoritas*) or institutionally (by delegation), and the more directly they are concerned to gain recognition for the point of view that they are seeking to impose.[8] On the other hand, there is the authorized point of view of an agent who is personally authorized, such as a great critic or prestigious preface-writer or established author (Zola's '*J'accuse*'), and above all the legitimate point of view of the authorized spokesperson, the delegate of the state, the official naming, or the *title* or qualification which, like an educational qualification, is valid on all markets and which, as an official definition of one's official identity, saves its bearers from the symbolic struggle of all against all, by establishing the authorized perspective, the one recognized by all and thus universal, from which social agents are viewed. The state, which produces official classifications, is to some extent the supreme tribunal to which Kafka was referring when he made Block say, speaking of the advocate and his claim to be among the 'great advocates': 'any man can call himself "great", of course, if he pleases, but in this matter the Court tradition must decide.'[9] The truth is that scientific analysis does not have to choose between perspectivism and what has to be called absolutism: indeed, the truth of the social world is the stake in a struggle between agents who are very unequally equipped to attain absolute, that is, self-verifying, vision and pre-vision.

One could analyse from this point of view the functioning of an institution such as the French national statistics office, INSEE, a state institute which, by producing the official taxonomies that are invested with a quasi-legal authority, and, particularly in the relations between employers and employees, that of a qualification capable of conferring rights independent of actually performed productive activity, tends to fix hierarchies and thereby to sanction and consecrate a relation of power between agents with respect to the names of professions and occupations, an essential component of social identity.[10] The management of names is one of the instruments of the management of material scarcity, and the names of groups, especially of professional groups, record a particular state of struggles and negotiations over the official designations and the material and symbolic advantages associated with them. The professional name granted to agents, the title they are given, is one of the positive or negative retributions (for the same reason as one's salary), in so far as it is a *distinctive mark* (emblem or stigma) which takes its *value* from its position in a hierarchically organized system of titles, and which thereby contributes to the determination of the relative positions between agents and groups. As a consequence of this, agents resort to practical or symbolic strategies aimed at maximizing the symbolic profit of naming: for example, they may give up the economic gratifications assured by a certain job so as to occupy a less well paid position, but one which is endowed with a more prestigious name; or they may orient themselves towards positions whose designations are less precise, and thus escape the effects of symbolic devaluation. In the same way, in the expression of their personal identity, they may give themselves a name which includes them in a class which is sufficiently broad to include agents occupying positions superior to their own, such as the 'instituteur' or primary-school teacher who calls himself an 'enseignant' or teacher, without specifying the level at which he teaches. More generally, agents always have a choice between several names and they may play on the uncertainties and the effects of vagueness linked to the plurality of perspectives so as to try to escape the verdict of the official taxonomy.

But the logic of official naming is most clearly demonstrated in the case of the *title* – whether titles of nobility, educational qualifications or professional titles. This is a symbolic capital that is socially and even legally guaranteed. The nobleman is not only someone who is known, famous, and even renowned for his good qualities, prestigious, in a word, *nobilis*: he is also someone who is recognized by an *official* authority, one that is 'universal', i.e. known and recognized by all. The professional or academic title is a sort of legal rule of social perception, a being-perceived that is guaranteed as a right. It is symbolic capital in an institutionalized, legal (and no longer merely legitimate) form. More and more inseparable from the educational qualification, by virtue of the fact that the educational system tends more and more to represent the ultimate and unique guarantor of all professional titles, it has a value in itself and, although we are dealing with a common noun, it functions like a great name (the name of some great family or a proper name), one which procures all sorts of symbolic profit (and goods that one cannot directly acquire with money).[11] It is the symbolic scarcity of the title in the space of the names of professions that tends to govern the rewards of the profession (and not the relation between the supply of and demand for a certain form of labour). It follows that the rewards associated with the title tend to become autonomous with regard to the rewards associated with the work. In this way, the same work can receive different remunerations depending on the titles and qualifications of the person doing it (e.g. a permanent, official post-holder as opposed to a part-timer or someone acting in that capacity, etc.). The qualification is in itself an *institution* (like language) that is more durable than the intrinsic characteristics of the work, and so the rewards associated with the qualification can be maintained despite changes in the work and its relative value: it is not the relative value of the work which determines the value of the name, but the institutionalized value of the title which acts as an instrument serving to defend and maintain the value of the work.[12]

This means that one cannot establish a science of classifications without establishing a science of the struggle over classifications and without taking into account the position occupied, in this struggle for the power of knowledge, for power through knowledge, for the monopoly of legitimate symbolic violence, by each of the agents or groups of agents involved in it, whether they be ordinary individuals, exposed to the vicissitudes of everyday symbolic struggle, or authorized (and full-time) professionals, which includes all those who speak or write about social classes, and who can be distinguished by the extent to which their classifications involve the authority of the state, as holder of the monopoly of *official naming*, of the right classification, of the right order.

While the structure of the social field is defined at each moment by the structure of the distribution of capital and the profits characteristic of the different particular fields, the fact remains that in each of these arenas, the very definition of the stakes and the trump cards can be called into question. Every field is the site of a more or less openly declared struggle for the definition of the legitimate principles of division of the field. The question of legitimacy arises from the very possibility of this questioning, from this break with the doxa which takes the ordinary order for granted. That being said, the symbolic force of the parties involved in this struggle is never completely independent of their positions in the game, even if the specifically symbolic power of naming constitutes a force which is relatively independent of the other forms of social power. The constraints of the necessity inscribed in the very structure of the different fields still weigh on the symbolic struggles which aim to preserve or transform that structure. The social world is, to a great extent, something which agents make at every moment; but they have no chance of unmaking and remaking it except on the basis of a realistic knowledge of what it is and of what they can do to it by virtue of the position they occupy in it.

In short, scientific work aims to establish an adequate knowledge both of the space of objective relations between the different positions which constitute the field and of the necessary relations that are set up, through the mediation of the habitus of those who occupy them, between these positions and the corresponding stances, i.e. between the points occupied in that space and the points of view on that very space, which play a part in the reality and development of that space. In other words, the objective delimitation of constructed classes, of *regions* of the constructed space of positions, enables one to understand the source and effectiveness of the classificatory strategies by means of which agents seek to preserve or modify this space, in the forefront of which we must place the constitution of groups organized with a view to defending the interests of their members.

Analysis of the struggle over classifications brings to light the political ambition which haunts the gnoseological ambition to produce the correct classification: an ambition which properly defines the *rex*, the one who has the task, according to Benveniste, of *regere fines* and *regere sacra*, of tracing in speech the frontiers between groups, and also between the sacred and the profane, good and evil, the vulgar and the distinguished. If social science is not to be merely a way of pursuing politics by other means, social scientists must take as their object the intention of assigning others to classes and of thereby telling them what they are and what they have to be (herein lies all the ambiguity of forecasting); they must analyse, in order to repudiate it, the ambition of the creative world vision, that sort of *intuitus originarius* which would make things exist in conformity with its vision (herein lies all the ambiguity of the Marxist conception of class, which is inseparably both a being and an ought-to-be). They must objectify the ambition of objectifying, of classifying from outside, objectively, agents who are struggling to classify others and themselves. If they do happen to classify – by carving up, for the purposes of statistical analysis, the continuous space of social positions – it is precisely so as to be able to objectify *all* forms of objectification, from the individual insult to the official naming, without forgetting the claim, characteristic of science in its positivist and bureaucratic definition, to arbitrate in these struggles in the name of 'axiological neutrality'. The symbolic power of agents, understood as a power of making people see – *theorein* – and believe, of producing and imposing the legitimate or legal classification, depends, as the case of *rex* reminds us, on the position they occupy in the space (and in the classifications that are potentially inscribed in it). But to objectify objectification means, above all, objectifying the field of production of the objectified representations of the social world, and in particular of the legislative taxonomies, in short, the field of cultural or ideological production, a game in which the social scientist is himself involved, as are all those who debate the nature of social classes.

THE POLITICAL FIELD AND THE EFFECT OF HOMOLOGIES

We must examine this field of symbolic struggles, in which the professionals of representation – in every sense of the term – confront one another in their debate over another field of symbolic struggles, if we are to understand, without succumbing to the mythology of the 'awakening of consciousness', the shift from the practical sense of the position occupied, *which is itself capable of being made explicit in different ways*, to properly political demonstrations. Those who occupy dominated positions in the social space are also situated in dominated positions in the field of symbolic production, and it is not clear whence they could obtain the instruments of symbolic production that are necessary in order for them to express their own point of view on the social space, were it not that the specific logic of the field of cultural production, and the specific interests that are generated within it, have the effect of inclining a fraction of the professionals engaged in this field to supply to the dominated, on the basis of a homology of position, the instruments that will enable them to break away from the representations generated in the immediate complicity of social structures and mental structures and which tend to ensure the continued reproduction of the distribution of symbolic capital. The phenomenon designated by the Marxist tradition as that of 'consciousness from outside', that is, the contribution made by certain intellectuals to the production and diffusion, especially among the dominated, of a vision of the social world that breaks with the dominant vision, cannot be understood sociologically without taking account of the homology between the dominated position of the producers of cultural goods within the field of power (or in the division of the labour of domination) and the position within the social space of the agents who are most completely dispossessed of the economic and cultural means of production. But the construction of the model of the social space which supports this analysis presupposes a definite break with the one-dimensional and one-directional representation of the social world underlying the dualist vision in which the universe of the oppositions constituting the social structure is reduced to the opposition between those who own the means of production and those who sell their labour-power.

The failings of the Marxist theory of class, above all its inability to explain the set of objectively observed differences, result from the fact that, by reducing the social world to the economic field alone, it is condemned to define social position with reference solely to the position within the relations of economic production. It thus ignores the positions occupied in the different fields and sub-fields, particularly in the relations of cultural production, as well as all those oppositions which structure the social field and which are not reducible to the opposition between the owners and non-owners of the means of economic production. Marxism imagines the social world as one-dimensional, as simply organized around the opposition between two blocs (one of the main questions thus becomes that of the *boundary* between these two blocs, with all the ensuing questions – which are endlessly debated – about the 'labour aristocracy', the 'embourgeoisement' of the working-class, etc.). In reality, the social space is a multi-dimensional space, an open set of relatively autonomous fields, fields which are more or less strongly and directly subordinate, in their functioning and their transformations, to the field of economic production. Within each of the sub-spaces, those who occupy dominant positions and those who occupy dominated positions are constantly involved in struggles of different kinds (without necessarily constituting themselves thereby as antagonistic groups).

But the most important fact, from the point of view of the problem of breaking out of the circle of symbolic reproduction, is that, on the basis of homologies between positions within different fields (and because, too, there is an invariant or even universal element in the relation between the dominant and the dominated), *alliances* can be set up which are more or less durable and which are always based on a more or less conscious misunderstanding. The homology of position between intellectuals and industrial workers – the former occupying within the field of power, that is, *vis-à-vis* the captains of industry and commerce, positions which are homologous to those occupied by industrial workers in the social space as a whole – is the source of an ambiguous alliance, in which cultural producers, the dominated among the dominant, supply to the dominated, by a sort of embezzlement of accumulated cultural capital, the means of constituting objectively their vision of the world and the representation of their interests in an explicit theory and in institutionalized instruments of representation – trade-union organizations, political parties, social technologies of mobilization and demonstration, etc.[13]

But one must be careful not to treat homology of position, a resemblance within difference, as an identity of condition (as happened, for instance, in the ideology of the 'three Ps', *patron*, *père*, *professeur* – 'boss', 'father', 'teacher' – developed by the ultra-left movement in France in the late 1960s). Doubtless, the same structure – understood as an invariant core of the forms of different distributions – recurs in different fields, and this explains why analogical thinking is so fertile in sociology. But the fact remains that the principle of differentiation is different each time, as are the stakes and the nature of the interest, and thus the *economy* of practices. It is after all important to establish a proper hierarchization of the principles of hierarchization, i.e. of the kinds of capital. Knowledge of the hierarchy of the principles of division enables us to define the limits within which the subordinate principles operate, and thus to define the limits of those similarities linked to homology. The relations of the other fields to the field of economic production are both relations of structural homology and relations of causal dependence, the form of causal determinations being defined by structural relations and the force of domination being greater when the relations in which it is exercised are closer to the relations of economic production.

We would have to analyse the specific interests which representatives owe to their position in the political field and in the sub-field of the party or the trade union, and show all the 'theoretical' effects that they produce. Numerous academic studies of 'social classes' – I have in mind, for instance, the problem of the 'labour aristocracy' or of the 'managerial class' (*cadres*) – merely elaborate the practical questions which are forced on those who hold political power. Political leaders are continually faced with the (often contradictory) practical imperatives which arise from the logic of the struggle within the political field, such as the need to prove their representativeness or the need to mobilize the greatest possible number of votes while at the same time asserting the irreducibility of their project to those of other leaders. Thus they are condemned to raise the problem of the social world in the typically substantialist logic of the boundaries between groups and the size of the mobilizable group; and they can try to solve the problem which forces itself on every group anxious to know and demonstrate its own strength – and thus its existence – and let other people know it too, by resorting to elastic concepts such as 'working class', 'the people' or 'the workers'. Moreover, as a result of the specific interests associated with the position they occupy in the competition to impose their particular visions of the social world, theoreticians and professional spokespersons, in other words, all 'party officials', are inclined to produce differentiated and distinctive products which, because of the homology between the field of professionals and the field of consumers of opinion, are as it were automatically adjusted to suit the different forms of demand. Demand is defined, in this case more than ever, as a demand for difference, for opposition, which these professionals themselves help to produce by enabling it to find expression. It is the structure of the political field, that is, the objective relation to the occupants of other positions, and the relation to the competing stances they offer which, just as much as any direct relation to those they represent, determines the stances they take, i.e. the supply of political products. By virtue of the fact that the interests directly involved in the struggle for the monopoly of the legitimate expression of the truth of the social world tend to be the specific equivalent of the interests of those who occupy homologous positions in the social field, political discourses are affected by a sort of structural duplicity: while they are in appearance directly aimed at the voters, they are in reality aimed at competitors within the field.

The political stances taken at any given moment (electoral results, for example) are thus the product of an encounter between a political supply of objectified political opinions (programmes, party platforms, declarations, etc.) linked to the entire previous history of the field of production, and a political demand, itself linked to the history of the relations between supply and demand. The correlation that can be observed at any given moment between stances on this or that political issue and positions in the social space can be understood completely only if one observes that the classifications which voters implement in order to make their choice (left/right, for instance) are the product of all previous struggles, and that the same is true of the classifications which the analyst implements in order to classify, not only opinions, but the agents who express them. The entire history of the social field is present, in each moment, both in a materialized form – in institutions such as the administrative organization of political parties or trade unions – and in an incorporated form – in the dispositions of agents who run these institutions or fight against them (with the effects of hysteresis linked to questions of loyalty). All forms of recognized collective identity – the 'working class' or the CGT trade union, 'independent craftsmen', 'managers', 'university graduates', etc. – are the product of a long and slow collective development. Without being completely artificial (if it were, the attempted establishment of these forms would not have succeeded), each of these representative bodies, which give existence to represented bodies endowed with a known and recognized social identity, exists through an entire set of institutions which are just so many historical inventions, a 'logo', *sigillum authenticum* as canon lawyers said, a seal or stamp, an office and a secretariat endowed with a monopoly over the corporate signature and the *plena potentia agendi et loquendi*, etc. As a product of the struggles which occurred within and outside the political field, especially concerning power over the state, this representation owes its specific characteristics to the particular history of a particular political field and state (which explains, *inter alia*, the differences between the representations of social divisions, and thus of groups represented, from one country to another). So as to avoid being misled by the effects of the labour of *naturalization* which every group tends to produce in order to legitimize itself and fully justify its existence, one must thus in each case reconstruct the *historical labour* which has produced social divisions and the social vision of these divisions. Social position, adequately defined, is what gives the best prediction of practices and representations; but, to avoid conferring on what was once called one's *station*, that is, on social identity (these days more and more completely identified with one's professional identity) the place that 'being' had in ancient metaphysics, namely, the function of an essence from which would spring all aspects of historical existence – as is expressed by the formula *operatio sequitur esse* – it must be clearly remembered that this *status*, like the habitus generated within it, are products of history, subject to being transformed, with more or less difficulty, by history.

CLASS AS WILL AND REPRESENTATION

But in order to establish how it is that the power of constituting and instituting held by the authorized spokesperson – party or union boss, for instance – is itself constituted and instituted, it is not enough to explain the specific interests of the theorists or spokespersons and the structural affinities which link them to those whom they represent. One must also analyse the logic of the process of institution, ordinarily perceived and described as a process of delegation, in which the representative receives from the group the power of creating the group. If we transpose their analyses, we can here follow the historians of law (Kantorowicz, Post, etc.) when they describe the mystery of ministry – a play on words dear to canon lawyers, who link *mysterium* with *ministerium*. The mystery of the process of transubstantiation, whereby the spokesperson becomes the group he expresses, can only be explained by a historical analysis of the genesis and functioning of *representation*, through which the representative creates the group which creates him. The spokesperson endowed with full power to speak and act in the name of the group, and first and foremost to act on the group through the magic of the slogan, is the substitute of the group which exists only through this proxy; as the personification of a fictitious person, of a social fiction, he raises those whom he represents out of their existence as separate individuals, enabling them to act and speak through him as a single person. In return, he receives the right to take himself for the group, to speak and act as if he were the group incarnate in a single person: '*Status est magistratus*', '*l'État, c'est moi*', 'the union thinks that . . .', etc.

The mystery of ministry is one of those cases of social magic in which a thing or a person becomes something other than what it/he is, a person (minister, bishop, delegate, member of parliament, general secretary, etc.) able to identify and be identified with a set of people (the People, the Workers) or with a social entity (the Nation, the State, the Church, the Party). The mystery of ministry is at its peak when the group can exist only by delegating power to a spokesperson who will bring it into existence by speaking for it, that is, on its behalf and in its place. The circle is then complete: the group is created by the person who speaks in its name, thus appearing as the source of the power that he exerts over those who are its real source. This circular relation is at the root of the charismatic illusion which means that, ultimately, the spokesperson may appear, to others as well as to himself, as *causa sui*. Political alienation results from the fact that isolated agents – and this is all the more true the more they are symbolically impoverished – cannot constitute themselves as a group, as a force capable of making itself heard in the political field, unless they dispossess themselves and hand over their power to a political apparatus: they must always risk political dispossession in order to escape from political dispossession. Fetishism, according to Marx, is what happens when 'the products of the human brain appear as autonomous figures endowed with a life of their own'; political fetishism lies precisely in the fact that the value of the hypostatized individual, that product of the human brain, appears as charisma, a mysterious objective property of the person, an elusive charm, an unnameable mystery. The minister – minister of religion or minister of state – is in a metonymic relation with the group; as part of the group, he functions as a sign replacing the group as a whole. It is the minister who, as an entirely real substitute for an entirely symbolic being, encourages one to make a 'category mistake', as Ryle would put it, rather similar to the one made by a child who, after having watched a procession of the soldiers composing the regiment, asks where the regiment is. By his mere visible existence, the minister constitutes the pure serial diversity of separate individuals into a moral person, transforms the *collectio personarum plurium* into a *corporatio*, a constituted body, and he may even, through mobilization and demonstration, make it appear as a social agent.

Politics is the site *par excellence* of symbolic effectiveness, an activity which works through signs capable of producing social entities and, above all, groups. By virtue of the oldest of the metaphysical effects linked to the existence of a certain symbolism – that which enables one to consider as existing everything which can be *signified* (God or non-being) – political representation produces and reproduces, at every moment, a derivative form of the argument of the bald King of France so dear to logicians: any predicative statement with 'the working class' as its subject conceals an existential statement (*there is* a working class). More generally, all statements which have as their subject a collective – People, Class, University, School, State, etc. – presuppose that the question of the existence of this group has been solved and conceal that sort of 'metaphysical fallacy' which has been criticized in the ontological argument. The spokesperson is the person who, speaking about a group, speaking on behalf of a group, surreptitiously posits the existence of the group in question, institutes the group, through that magical operation which is inherent in any act of naming. That is why we must proceed to a critique of political reason – a reason which is inclined to commit abuses of language which are abuses of power – if we want to raise the question with which all sociology ought to begin, that of the existence and mode of existence of collectives.

A class exists in so far as – and only in so far as – representatives with the *plena potentia agendi* may be and feel authorized to speak in its *name* – in accordance with the equation, 'the Party is the working class', or 'the working class is the Party', an equation which reproduces that of canon lawyers, 'the Church is the Pope (or the Bishops), the Pope (or the Bishops) is (or are) the Church'. In this way, a class can be given existence as a real force in the political field. The mode of existence of what is these days called, in a great number of societies (with variations, of course), the 'working class', is completely paradoxical: what we have is a sort of *existence in thought*, an existence in the minds of many of those who are designated by the different taxonomies as workers, but also in the minds of those who occupy the positions furthest removed from the workers in the social space. This almost universally recognized existence is itself based on the existence of a *working class in representation*, that is, on political and trade-union apparatuses and on party officials who have a vital interest in believing that this class exists and in spreading this belief among those who consider themselves part of it as well as those who are excluded from it; who are capable too of *giving voice* to the 'working class', and with a single voice to evoke it, as one evokes or summons up spirits, of invoking it, as one invokes gods or patron saints; who are capable, indeed, of manifesting it symbolically through *demonstration*, a sort of theatrical deployment of the class-in-representation, with on the one side the body of party officials and the entire symbolic system that constitutes its existence – slogans, emblems, symbols – and on the other side the most convinced fraction of the believers who, by their presence, enable their representatives to give a representation of their representativeness. This working class as 'will and repre-sentation' (as Schopenhauer's famous title puts it) has nothing in common with the class as action, a real and really mobilized group, imagined by the Marxist tradition; but it is no less real, with that magical reality which (with Durkheim and Mauss) defines institu-tions as social fictions. This is a true mystical body, created at the cost of an immense historical labour of theoretical and practical invention, starting with that of Marx himself, and endlessly re-created at the cost of innumerable and constantly renewed efforts and acts of commitment which are necessary in order to produce and reproduce belief and the institution designed to ensure the reproduc-tion of belief. The 'working class' exists in and through the body of representatives who give it an audible voice and a visible presence, and in and through the belief in its existence which this body of plenipotentiaries succeeds in imposing, by its mere existence and its representations, on the basis of affinities which objectively unite the members of the same 'class on paper' as a probable group.[14] The historical success of Marxist theory, the first social theory to claim scientific status that has so completely realized its potential in the social world, thus contributes to ensuring that the theory of the social world which is the least capable of integrating the *theory effect* – that it, more than any other, has created – is doubtless, today, the most powerful obstacle to the progress of the adequate theory of the social world to which it has, in times gone by, more than any other contributed.

Notes

Editor's Introduction

1 Born in 1930 in Béarn, a province in southern France, Bourdieu studied philosophy at the *École normale supérieure* in Paris in the late 1940s and early 1950s, before moving into anthropological and sociological research. His first studies of Algerian society, where he carried out his initial ethnographic research, were published in the late 1950s and early 1960s. The research in Algeria formed the basis of much of his subsequent theoretical writing, most notably *Outline of a Theory of Practice*, tr. R. Nice (Cambridge: Cambridge University Press, 1977) and *The Logic of Practice*, tr. R. Nice (Cambridge: Polity Press, 1990). In the early 1960s Bourdieu also initiated a series of collaborative research projects on French culture and education, from his institutional base at the *École des hautes études en sciences sociales* in Paris, where he founded the *Centre de Sociologie européenne*. These projects have resulted in numerous publications, among the most recent of which are *Distinction: A Social Critique of the Judgement of Taste*, tr. R. Nice (Cambridge, Mass.: Harvard University Press, 1984), *Homo Academicus*, tr. P. Collier (Cambridge: Polity Press, 1988), and *La noblesse d'état: grandes écoles et esprit de corps* (Paris: Minuit, 1989).

   Bourdieu is currently Professor of Sociology at the *Collège de France* and Director of the *Centre de sociologie européenne*. For a full bibliography of his writings, see Y. Delsaut, 'Bibliography of the works of Pierre Bourdieu, 1958–1988', in P. Bourdieu, *In Other Words: Essays toward a Reflexive Sociology*, tr. M. Adamson (Cambridge: Polity Press, 1990), pp. 199–218.

2 For helpful overviews and sympathetic criticism of Bourdieu's work, see R. Brubaker, 'Rethinking classical social theory: the sociological vision of Pierre Bourdieu', *Theory and Society*, 14 (1985), pp. 745–75; P. Dimaggio, 'Review essay on Pierre Bourdieu', *American Journal of*

Sociology, 84 (1979), pp. 1460–74; N. Garnham and R. Williams, 'Pierre Bourdieu and the sociology of culture: An introduction', *Media, Culture and Society*, 2 (1980), pp. 209–23; and A. Honneth, 'The fragmented world of symbolic forms: reflections on Pierre Bourdieu's sociology of culture', tr. T. Talbot, *Theory, Culture and Society*, 3/3 (1986), pp. 55–66. See also the volume of essays edited by C. Calhoun, E. LiPuma and M. Postone, *The Social Theory of Pierre Bourdieu* (Cambridge: Polity Press, forthcoming).

3 See P. Bourdieu, 'Célibat et condition paysanne', *Études rurales*, 5–6 (1962), pp. 32–136; 'Marriage strategies as strategies of social reproduction', tr. E. Forster, in R. Forster and O. Ranum (eds), *Family and Society: Selections from the* Annales (Baltimore, MD: Johns Hopkins University Press, 1976), pp. 117–44; and 'The Kabyle house or the world reversed', tr. R. Nice, published as the appendix in *The Logic of Practice*.

4 See Bourdieu's illuminating account of his own intellectual itinerary in the preface to *The Logic of Practice*.

5 F. de Saussure, *Course in General Linguistics*, tr. W. Baskin (Glasgow: Collins, 1974), pp. 9ff; N. Chomsky, *Aspects of the Theory of Syntax* (Cambridge, Mass.: MIT Press, 1965), pp. 3ff.

6 There is a growing literature on the development of languages in relation to the formation of modern nation-states and the history of colonialism. See, for instance, M. de Certeau, D. Julia and J. Revel, *Une politique de la langue. La revolution française et les patois* (Paris: Gallimard, 1975); A. Mazrui, *The Political Sociology of the English Language: An African Perspective* (The Hague: Mouton, 1975); R. L. Cooper (ed.), *Language Spread: Studies in Diffusion and Social Change* (Bloomington: Indiana University Press, 1982); and J. Steinberg, 'The historian and the *questione della lingua*', in P. Burke and R. Porter (eds), *The Social History of Language* (Cambridge: Cambridge University Press, 1987), pp. 198–209.

7 F. Brunot, *Histoire de la langue française des origines à nos jours* (Paris: Armand Colin, 1905–53).

8 P. Bourdieu, 'The production and reproduction of legitimate language', ch. 1 in this volume, p. 49.

9 Bourdieu's argument here is similar to that developed by the sociolinguist Dell Hymes, who maintains that Chomsky's notion of competence is too narrow and must be expanded to take account of social and circumstantial factors. See D. Hymes, *Foundations in Sociolinguistics: An Ethnographic Approach* (London: Tavistock, 1977), pp. 92–7 and *passim*.

10 Austin's classic text, *How to Do Things with Words* (English publication 1962), was not published in French until 1970, and the theory of speech acts was quite extensively discussed by French philosophers and linguists in the 1970s. See, for example, O. Ducrot, *Dire et ne pas dire* (Paris: Hermann, 1972) and *Le dire et le dit* (Paris: Minuit, 1984); and

A. Berrendonner, *Éléments de pragmatique linguistique* (Paris: Minuit, 1981).

11 J. L. Austin, *How to Do Things with Words*, second edition, ed. J. O. Urmson and Marina Sbisà (Oxford: Oxford University Press, 1975), Lecture II.

12 See J. Habermas, 'Toward a theory of communicative competence', in H. P. Dreitzel (ed.), *Recent Sociology*, no. 2 (New York: Macmillan, 1970), pp. 114–48; 'What is universal pragmatics?', in *Communication and the Evolution of Society*, tr. T. McCarthy (Cambridge: Polity Press, 1979), pp. 1–68; and *The Theory of Communicative Action*, vol. 1: *Reason and the Rationalization of Society*, tr. T. McCarthy (Cambridge: Polity Press, 1984), ch. 3.

13 For a discussion of this and related criticisms, see 'Symbolic violence: language and power in the writings of Pierre Bourdieu', in J. B. Thompson, *Studies in the Theory of Ideology* (Cambridge: Polity Press, 1984), pp. 42–72.

14 See A. Schutz, *The Phenomenology of the Social World*, tr. G. Walsh and F. Lehnert (London: Heinemann, 1972). In this context Bourdieu refers most frequently to phenomenology and its development by social philosophers such as Schutz and Sartre. But his argument could be developed *mutatis mutandis* with regard to the work of sociologists and anthropologists as diverse as Peter Berger, Harold Garfinkel, Aaron Cicourel and Clifford Geertz.

15 This point is developed at some length in P. Bourdieu, J-C. Chamboredon and J-C. Passeron, *Le métier de sociologue: préables épistémologiques* (Paris and The Hague: Mouton, 1968) and P. Bourdieu, *Homo Academicus*, ch. 1.

16 Bourdieu, *The Logic of Practice*, pp. 69–70.

17 See P. Bourdieu, 'Quelques propriétés des champs', in his *Questions de sociologie* (Paris: Minuit, 1980), pp. 113–20.

18 See P. Bourdieu and L. Boltanski, 'Formal qualifications and occupational hierarchies: the relationship between the production system and the reproduction system', tr. R. Nice, in E. J. King (ed.), *Reorganizing Education: Management and Participation for Change* (London and Beverly Hills: Sage, 1977), pp. 61–9.

19 Bourdieu, *The Logic of Practice*, p. 120.

20 Ibid., p. 122.

21 See P. Bourdieu, 'The field of cultural production, or: the economic world reversed', tr. R. Nice, *Poetics*, 12 (1983), pp. 311–56.

22 Bourdieu is sharply critical of the kind of rational action theory developed by Jon Elster; see *The Logic of Practice*, pp. 46ff.

23 See P. Guiraud, *Le Français populaire* (Paris: Presses Universitaires de France, 1965).

24 See W. Labov, *Sociolinguistic Patterns* (Philadelphia: University of Pennsylvania Press, 1972), pp. 301–4. See also R. Lakoff, *Language and Woman's Place* (New York: Harper & Row, 1975).

25   *La République des Pyrénées* (9 September 1974); relevant parts of the
     text are reproduced in P. Bourdieu and L. Boltanski, 'Le fétichisme de
     la langue', *Actes de la recherche en sciences sociales*, 4 (July 1975), pp.
     2–32. The example is also discussed in this volume, pp. 68–9.
26   Bourdieu offers a more extended analysis of Heidegger's work in his
     book *The Political Ontology of Martin Heidegger*, tr. P. Collier
     (Cambridge: Polity Press, 1991). The material which forms the basis of
     this book was originally published in French in 1975 in *Actes de la
     recherche en sciences sociales*, and hence predates by more than a
     decade the debates triggered off in France and elsewhere by the
     publication of Victor Farias's book *Heidegger et le nazisme* (Lagrasse:
     Verdier, 1987). Bourdieu's approach to Heidegger's work differs
     significantly from that of Farias and from the views expressed recently
     by philosophers such as Derrida, Lyotard and Lacoue-Labarthe.
27   The issues discussed by Bourdieu in this context, such as the opposition
     between distinguished and vulgar and the symbolic struggles waged by
     different classes in the social space, are examined in much greater
     detail in *Distinction*.
28   These points are brought out well in the work of Paul Willis, to which
     Bourdieu refers in this context. See P. E. Willis, *Profane Culture*
     (London: Routlege & Kegan Paul, 1978), and *Learning to Labour:
     How Working Class Kids Get Working Class Jobs* (Westmead, Farn-
     borough, Hants.: Saxon House, 1977).
29   See Bourdieu, *Outline of a Theory of Practice*, pp. 183ff; *The Logic of
     Practice*, pp. 122ff.
30   Bourdieu, *The Logic of Practice*, p. 127.
31   The role of the educational system as an institutional mechanism for
     creating and sustaining inequality is examined by Bourdieu and his
     associates in a variety of publications. See especially P. Bourdieu and
     J-C. Passeron, *Reproduction: In Education, Society and Culture*, tr. R.
     Nice (London and Beverly Hills: Sage, 1977); P. Bourdieu and J-C.
     Passeron, *The Inheritors: French Students and their Relation to Culture*,
     tr. R. Nice (Chicago: University of Chicago Press, 1979); and Bour-
     dieu, *La noblesse d'état*.
32   See, for example, P. Bourdieu 'Le marché des biens symboliques',
     L'année sociologique, 22 (1971), pp. 49–126; 'Genèse et structure du
     champ religieux', *Revue française de sociologie*, 12 (1971), pp. 295–334;
     and 'Legitimation and structured interests in Weber's sociology of
     religion', tr. C. Turner, in S. Whimster and S. Lash (eds), *Max Weber,
     Rationality and Modernity* (London: Allen & Unwin, 1987), pp. 119–
     36.
33   Bourdieu has developed this approach in more detail in other contexts.
     See especially Bourdieu, *Distinction*, ch. 8; Bourdieu, *La noblesse
     d'état*, part IV; and P. Bourdieu and L. Boltanski, 'La production de
     l'idéologie dominante', *Actes de la recherche en sciences sociales*, 2–3
     (June 1976), pp. 3–73.

34   In recent writings Bourdieu has given more attention to issues con-
     cerned with gender and relations of power between the sexes. See
     especially P. Bourdieu, 'La domination masculine', *Actes de la recher-
     che en sciences sociales*, 84 (September 1990), pp. 2–31.
35   See P. Bourdieu, 'Social space and the genesis of "classes" ', ch. 11 in
     this volume. See also 'A reply to some objections', tr. L. J. D.
     Wacquant and M. Lawson, in Bourdieu, *In Other Words*, pp. 106–19.
36   For a recent and well known example of this interpretation, see L.
     Ferry and A. Renaut, *La pensée 68. Essai sur l'anti-humanisme
     contemporain* (Paris: Gallimard, 1985), ch. 5.

Introduction to Part I

1   I have tried elsewhere to analyse the epistemological unconsciousness
    of structuralism, i.e. the presuppositions which Saussure very lucidly
    articulated in constructing the specific object of linguistics, but which
    have been forgotten or repressed by subsequent users of the Saussurian
    model (see P. Bourdieu, *The Logic of Practice*, tr. R. Nice (Cam-
    bridge: Polity Press, 1990), pp. 30ff.).
2   See G. Mounin, *La Communication Poétique, précédé de Avez-vous lu
    Char?* (Paris: Gallimard, 1969), pp. 21–61.
3   The ability to grasp simultaneously the different senses of one word
    (which is often measured by so-called intelligence tests) and, *a fortiori*,
    the ability to manipulate them practically (for example, by recovering
    the original sense of ordinary words, as philosophers like to do) are a
    good measure of the typically scholarly ability to remove oneself from a
    situation and to disrupt the practical relation which links a word to a
    practical context, restricting the word to one of its senses, in order to
    consider the word in itself and for itself, that is, as the focus for all the
    possible relations with situations thus treated as so many 'particular
    instances of the possible'. If this ability to play on different linguistic
    varieties, successively and especially simultaneously, is without doubt
    among the most unevenly distributed, it is because the mastery of
    different linguistic varieties – and especially the relation to language
    which it presupposes – can only be acquired in certain conditions of
    existence that are capable of authorizing a detached and free relation to
    language (see, in P. Bourdieu and J-C. Passeron, *Rapport pédagogique
    et communication* (Paris and The Hague: Mouton, 1965), the analysis
    of variations according to social origin of the *breadth of linguistic
    register*, i.e. the degree to which different linguistic varieties are
    mastered).
4   J. Vendryès, *Le langage. Introduction linguistique à l'Histoire* (Paris:
    Albin Michel, 1950), p. 208.
5   The imperatives of production, and even of domination, impose a
    minimum of communication between classes; hence the access of the

most deprived (immigrants, for example) to a kind of vital minimum of linguistic competence.

1 The Production and Reproduction of Legitimate Language

1 A. Comte, *System of Positive Polity*, 4 vols (London: Longmans Green and Co., 1875–77), vol. 2, p. 213.

2 N. Chomsky, *Aspects of the Theory of Syntax* (Cambridge, Mass.: MIT Press, 1965), p. 3 (my italics). See also N. Chomsky and M. Halle, *The Sound Pattern of English* (New York: Harper and Row, 1968), p. 3.

3 Chomsky himself makes this identification explicitly, at least in so far as competence is 'knowledge of grammar' (Chomsky and Halle, *The Sound Pattern of English*) or 'generative grammar internalized by someone' (N. Chomsky, *Current Issues in Linguistic Theory* (London and The Hague: Mouton, 1964), p. 10).

4 The fact that Habermas crowns his pure theory of 'communicative competence' – an essentialist analysis of the situation of communication – with a declaration of intentions regarding the degree of repression and the degree of development of the productive forces does not mean that he escapes from the ideological effect of absolutizing the relative which is inscribed in the silences of the Chomskyan theory of competence (J. Habermas, 'Toward a theory of communicative competence', in H. P. Dreitzel (ed.), *Recent Sociology*, no. 2 (New York: Macmillan, 1970), pp. 114–48). Even if it is purely methodological and provisional, and intended only to 'make possible' the study of 'the distortions of pure intersubjectivity', *idealization* (which is clearly seen in the use of notions such as 'mastery of the dialogue-constitutive universals' or 'speech situation determined by pure subjectivity') has the practical effect of removing from relations of communication the power relations which are implemented within them in a transfigured form. This is confirmed by the uncritical borrowing of concepts such as 'illocutionary force', which tends to locate the power of words in words themselves rather than in the institutional conditions of their use.

5 F. de Saussure, *Course in General Linguistics*, tr. W. Baskin (Glasgow: Collins, 1974), pp. 199–203.

6 L. Bloomfield, *Language* (London: George Allen, 1958), p. 29. Just as Saussure's theory of language forgets that a language does not impose itself by its own force but derives its geographical limits from a political act of institution, an arbitrary act misrecognized as such (and misrecognized by the science of language), so Bloomfield's theory of the 'linguistic community' ignores the political and institutional conditions of 'intercomprehension'.

7 The adjective 'formal', which can be used to describe a language that is guarded, polished and tense, as opposed to one that is familiar and relaxed, or a person that is starchy, stiff and formalist, can also mean

the same as the French adjective *officiel* (as in 'a formal dinner'), that is, conducted in full accordance with the rules, in due and proper order, by formal agreement.

8 Only by transposing the representation of the national language is one led to think that regional dialects exist, themselves divided into sub-dialects – an idea flatly contradicted by the study of dialectics (see F. Brunot, *Histoire de la langue française des origines à nos jours* (Paris: Colin, 1968), pp. 77–8). And it is no accident that nationalism almost always succumbs to this illusion since, once it triumphs, it inevitably reproduces the process of unification whose effects it denounced.

9 This is seen in the difficulties raised by the translation of decrees during the Revolutionary period in France. Because the practical language was devoid of political vocabulary and divided into dialects, it was necessary to forge an intermediate language. (The advocates of the *langues d'oc* do the same thing nowadays, fixing and standardizing orthography and thereby producing a language not readily accessible to ordinary speakers.)

10 G. Davy, *Éléments de sociologie* (Paris: Vrin, 1950), p. 233.

11 Humboldt's linguistic theory, which was generated from the celebration of the linguistic 'authenticity' of the Basque people and the exaltation of the language–nation couplet, has an intelligible relationship with the conception of the unifying mission of the university which Humboldt deployed in the creation of the University of Berlin.

12 Grammar is endowed with real legal effectiveness via the educational system, which places its power of certification at its disposal. If grammar and spelling are sometimes the object of ministerial decrees (such as that of 1900 on the agreement of the past participle conjugated with *avoir*), this is because, through examinations and the qualifications which they make it possible to obtain, they govern access to jobs and social positions.

13 Thus, in France, the numbers of schools and of pupils enrolled and, correlatively, the volume and spatial dispersion of the teaching profession increased steadily after 1816 – well before the official introduction of compulsory schooling.

14 This would probably explain the apparently paradoxical relationship between the linguistic remoteness of the different regions in the nineteenth century and their contribution to the ranks of the civil service in the twentieth century. The regions which, according to the survey carried out by Victor Duruy in 1864, had the highest proportion of adults who could not speak French, and of 7- to 13-year-olds unable to read or speak it, were providing a particularly high proportion of civil servants in the first half of the twentieth century, a phenomenon which is itself known to be linked to a high rate of secondary schooling.

15 This means that 'linguistic customs' cannot be changed by decree as the advocates of an interventionist policy of 'defence of the language' often seem to imagine.

16 The 'disintegrated' language which surveys record when dealing with speakers from the dominated classes is thus a product of the survey relationship.

17 Conversely, when a previously dominated language achieves the status of an official language, it undergoes a *revaluation* which profoundly changes its users' relationship with it. So-called linguistic conflicts are therefore not so unrealistic and irrational (which does not mean that they are directly inspired by self-interest) as is supposed by those who only consider the (narrowly defined) economic stakes. The reversal of the symbolic relations of power and of the hierarchy of the values placed on the competing languages has entirely real economic and political effects, such as the appropriation of positions and economic advantages reserved for holders of the legitimate competence, or the symbolic profits associated with possession of a prestigious, or at least unstigmatized, social identity.

18 Only the *optional* can give rise to effects of *distinction*. As Pierre Encrevé has shown, in the case of obligatory liaisons – those which are always observed by all speakers, including the lower classes – there is no room for manoeuvre. When the structural constraints of the language are suspended, as with optional liaisons, the leeway reappears, with the associated effects of distinction.

19 There is clearly no reason to take sides in the debate between the nativists (overt or not), for whom the acquisition of the capacity to speak presupposes the existence of an innate disposition, and the empiricists, who emphasize the learning process. So long as not everything is inscribed in nature and the acquisition process is something more than a simple maturation, there exist linguistic differences capable of functioning as signs of social distinction.

20 The hypothesis of equal chances of access to the conditions of acquisition of the legitimate linguistic competence is a simple *mental experiment* designed to bring to light one of the *structural effects* of inequality.

21 Situations in which linguistic productions are explicitly subjected to evaluation, such as examinations or job interviews, recall the evaluation which takes place in every linguistic exchange. Numerous surveys have shown that linguistic characteristics have a very strong influence on academic success, employment opportunities, career success, the attitude of doctors (who pay more attention to bourgeois patients and their discourse, e.g. giving them less pessimistic diagnoses), and more generally on the recipients' inclination to co-operate with the sender, to assist him or give credence to the information he provides.

22 Rather than rehearse innumerable quotations from writers or grammarians which would only take on their full meaning if accompanied by a thorough historical analysis of the state of the field in which they were produced in each case, I shall refer readers who would like to get a concrete idea of this permanent struggle to B. Quemada, *Les diction-*

naires du français moderne, 1539–1863 (Paris: Didier, 1968), pp. 193, 204, 207, 210, 216, 226, 228, 229, 230 n. 1, 231, 233, 237, 239, 241, 242, and Brunot, *Histoire de la langue française*, 11–13 and *passim*. A similar division of roles and strategies between writers and grammarians emerges from Haugen's account of the struggle for control over the linguistic planning of Norwegian: see E. Haugen, *Language Conflict and Language Planning: The Case of Norwegian* (Cambridge, Mass.: Harvard University Press, 1966), esp. pp. 296ff.

23 One might contrast a 'style-in-itself', the objective product of an unconscious or even forced 'choice' (like the objectively aesthetic 'choice' of a piece of furniture or a garment, which is imposed by economic necessity), with a 'style-for-itself', the product of a choice which, even when experienced as free and 'pure', is equally determined, but by the specific constraints of the economy of symbolic goods, such as explicit or implicit reference to the forced choices of those who have no choice, luxury itself having no sense except in relation to necessity.

24 Of the errors induced by the use of concepts like 'apparatus' or 'ideology' (whose naïve teleology is taken a degree further in the notion of 'ideological state apparatuses'), one of the most significant is neglect of the *economy* of the institutions of production of cultural goods. One only has to think, for example, of the *cultural industry*, oriented towards producing services and instruments of linguistic correction (e.g. manuals, grammars, dictionaries, guides to correspondence and public speaking, children's books, etc.), and of the thousands of agents in the public and private sectors whose most vital material and symbolic interests are invested in the competitive struggles which lead them to contribute, incidentally and often unwittingly, to the defence and exemplification of the legitimate language.

25 The social conditions of production and reproduction of the legitimate language are responsible for another of its properties: the autonomy with regard to practical functions, or, more precisely, the neutralized and neutralizing relation to the 'situation', the object of discourse or the interlocutor, which is implicitly required on all the occasions when solemnity calls for a controlled and tense use of language. The spoken use of 'written language' is only acquired in conditions in which it is objectively inscribed in the situation, in the form of freedoms, facilities and, above all, *leisure*, in the sense of the neutralization of practical urgencies; and it presupposes the disposition which is acquired in and through exercises in which language is manipulated without any other necessity than that arbitrarily imposed for pedagogic purposes.

26 It is therefore no accident that, as Troubetzkoy notes, 'casual articulation' is one of the most universally observed ways of marking distinction: see N. S. Troubetzkoy, *Principes de Phonologie* (Paris: Klincksieck, 1957), p. 22. In reality, as Pierre Encrevé has pointed out to me, the strategic relaxation of tension only exceptionally extends to the

phonetic level; spuriously denied distinction continues to be marked in pronunciation. And writers such as Raymond Queneau have, of course, been able to derive literary effects from systematic use of similar discrepancies in level between the different aspects of discourse.

2 Price Formation and the Anticipation of Profits

1 The *official* centenary celebration of the birth of the Béarnais-language poet, Simin Palay, whose entire work – language aside – is dominated in form as well as in content by French literature, created a linguistic situation that was totally unheard-of: not only the accredited guardians of Béarnais but also the administrative authorities themselves transgressed the unwritten rule which makes French *de rigueur* on all official occasions, especially in the mouths of *officials*. Whence the following journalistic observation (which is doubtless a faithful reflection of the impression generally received): 'The most notable speech was, however, made by the Prefect of Pyrénées-Atlantiques, Mr Monfraix, who addressed the audience in excellent Béarnais *patois* . . . Mr Labarrère [the mayor of Pau] replied to Miss Lamazou-Betbeder, head of the school, in good quality Béarnais. The audience was greatly moved by this thoughtful gesture and applauded at length' (*La République des Pyrénées*, 9 September 1974).

2 This is very clear in the case of regional languages whose use is reserved for private occasions – mainly in family life – and, in any case, for exchanges between socially homogeneous speakers (between peasants).

3 In the sphere of language, the only affirmation of authentic counter-legitimacy is slang; but this is a language of 'bosses'.

4 See P. Bourdieu, 'Le discours d'importance: quelques réflexions sociologiques sur "Quelques remarques critiques à propos de *Lire le Capital*"', in *Ce que parler veut dire* (Paris: Fayard, 1982), pp. 207–26.

5 Cf. B. de Cornulier, 'La notion d'auto-interprétation', *Études de linguistique appliquée*, 19 (1975), pp. 52–82.

6 F. Recanati, *Les énoncés performatifs* (Paris: Minuit, 1982), p. 192.

7 Ibid., p. 195.

8 E. Benveniste, *Problems in General Linguistics*, tr. M. Meek (Coral Gables, Fla: University of Miami Press, 1971), p. 236).

9 Of all linguists, Alain Berrendonner is the one who undoubtedly understands best the link between the performative and the social, or what he calls the 'institution', i.e. 'the existence of a normative power which, under threat of sanctions, ensures the mutual subjection of individuals to certain practices'; 'Substituting saying for doing will therefore only be practicable if there is some additional guarantee that the utterance-*ersatz* will have an effect after all' (A. Berrendonner, *Éléments de pragmatique linguistique* (Paris: Minuit, 1981), p. 95).

10   O. Ducrot, 'Illocutoire et performatif', *Linguistique et sémiologie*, 4 (1977), pp. 17–54.

11   Insults, blessings and curses are all acts of magical naming and, strictly speaking, prophecies which purport to be self-verifying. In so far as it always implies a more or less socially justified claim to perform a magical act of institution which can usher in a new reality, the performative utterance creates a future effect in words used in the present.

12   'Acts of authority are first and always utterances made by those to whom the right to utter them belongs' (Benveniste, *Problems in General Linguistics*, p. 236).

13   'The two words – *ministerium* and *mysterium* – were virtually inter-changeable since the time of primitive christianity and were constantly confused during the middle ages' (E. H. Kantorowicz, 'Mysteries of state: an absolutist concept and its late mediaeval origins', *Harvard Theological Review*, 48/1 (1955), pp. 65–91).

14   The two senses of competence come together if one sees that, according to Percy Ernst Schramm, just as the crown of the medieval king designates both the thing itself and the set of rights which constitute royal dignity (as in the term 'crown property'), so too linguistic competence is a symbolic attribute of the authority which *designates* a socially recognized status as a set of rights, beginning with the right to speak and the corresponding technical capacity.

15   This means giving a real meaning to the notion of 'acceptability', which linguists sometimes introduce to avoid the abstraction in the notion of 'grammaticality' without drawing *any of the consequences*.

16   This indicates that complete understanding of scholarly discourse (e.g. a literary text) presupposes, first, knowledge of the social conditions of production of the social competence (and not only linguistic compe-tence) of the producers, who employ the totality of their properties (those which define their position in the social structure and also in the structure of the field of specialized production) in each of their productions; and, second, a knowledge of the conditions which govern the *implementation* of this competence, of the specific laws of the market concerned which, in this particular case, coincide with the field of production itself (the fundamental characteristic of scholarly produc-tion consists in the fact that its clientele is the set of other producers, i.e. its rivals).

17   Given that the work of representation and of the imposition of form is the *sine qua non* for ascertaining the existence of the expressive intention, the very idea of grasping some sort of content in its raw state, which would remain invariant through different forms, is meaningless.

18   One can thus class as euphemisms all the kinds of *double meanings*, particularly frequent in religious discourse, which enable one to get round censorship by naming the unnamable in a form which avoids it being named (see 'Censorship and the imposition of form', ch. 6 in this

volume), and also all the forms of *irony* which, by denying the statement in the process of stating it, also produces double meaning – and twice the margin for manoeuvre – thereby enabling one to avoid the sanctions of a field. (On the defensive role of irony, see Berendonner, *Éléments de pragmatique linguistique*, esp. pp. 238–9).

19 C. Bally, *Le langage et la vie* (Geneva: Droz, 1965), p. 21.

20 This anticipation is guided by visible manifestations, like the attitude of the speaker, his expression (whether attentive or indifferent, haughty or engaging) and the encouragement in the voice or manner or the signs of disapproval. Different experiments in social psychology have shown that the speed of speech, the quantity of speech, the vocabulary, the complexity of syntax, etc., vary according to the attitude of the person conducting the experiment, i.e. according to the strategies of selective reinforcement that he applies.

21 Learning in language occurs through familiarization with persons playing very broad roles, of which the linguistic dimension is but one aspect and never isolated as such. This is probably what confers the power of practical evocation on certain words which, being linked with a whole bodily posture and an emotional atmosphere, resurrect a complete vision of the world, a whole world; no doubt it also produces the emotional attachment to the 'mother tongue', whose expressions, turns of phrase and words seem to imply a 'surplus of meaning'.

22 Different experiments in social psychology have shown that the petits bourgeois are more adept than members of the lower classes at picking out social class according to pronunciation.

23 One would need to take these analyses further: on the one hand, by a more complete examination of the properties of the petits bourgeois which are pertinent to understanding linguistic dispositions, like their trajectory (rising or falling) which, by providing them with an experience of different milieux, inclines them – especially when they have to function as intermediaries between classes – to a quasi-sociological form of awareness; and, on the other hand, by examining the variations in these properties according to secondary variables, such as the position in the space occupied by the middle classes and the previous trajectory (cf. P. Bourdieu, *Distinction: A Social Critique of the Judgement of Taste*, tr.R. Nice (Cambridge, Mass.: Harvard University Press, 1984), pt 3, ch. 6). Equally, one would need to distinguish, within the dominant class, between different relations to language.

24 Contrary to what Lakoff argues, the purely grammatical form of attenuation can be replaced by a whole series of substitutes, functioning as elements of a symbolic ritual. Anyone who has conducted an interview knows that the ground has to be laid well in advance for a 'difficult' question, and that the surest way of 'getting away with it' is not to surround it with circumlocutions and verbal attenuations which, on the contrary, would draw attention to it, but to create a climate of collusion and to give the interview an overall tone which has a euphoric

and euphemizing effect, through jokes, smiles and gestures, in short, by creating a symbolic whole in which the purely linguistic form is just an element.

25 G. Lakoff, 'Interview with Herman Parrett', University of California, mimeo, October 1973, p. 38; W. Labov, *Language in the Inner City* (Philadelphia: University of Pennsylvania Press, 1973), p. 219.

26 It is hardly necessary to recall that the primordial form of censorship, that concerning sexual matters, and bodily ones more generally, is applied with particular rigour to women (or – a fine example of the market effect – in the presence of women).

27 From the point of view of dominant individuals, the same opposition would seem to be apparent, by a simple inversion of the sign, in the logic of difficulty and 'ease', 'correctness' and negligence, culture and nature.

28 The intuitively perceived relationship between the 'articulatory style' and the life-style, which makes 'accent' such a powerful way of predicting social position, forces unequivocal value judgements from the few analysts who have devoted some space to it, like Pierre Guiraud: 'This carpet-slipper "accent", sloppy and limp'; 'the "lout's" accent is the one which belongs to the guy who spits his words out of the corner of his mouth, between the fag-end and where his lips meet'; 'this vague and soft consistency, in its most degraded forms, is limp and revolting' (P. Guiraud, *Le français populaire* (Paris: Presses Universitaires de France), pp. 111–16). Like all manifestations of the habitus, of the historical as natural, pronunciation, and more generally the relation to language, as commonly perceived, are revelations of a person in his true nature: class racism finds, in incorporated properties, the supreme justification for the propensity to naturalize social differences.

29 It is therefore no accident that a school system which, like the French *École républicaine*, was conceived during the Revolution and fully established during the Third Republic, tries to shape completely the habitus of the lower classes, and is organized around the inculcation of a certain relation to language (with the abolition of regional languages, etc.), a relation to the body (disciplines of hygiene, consumption – sobriety – etc.) and a relation to time (calculating – economical – saving, etc.).

Appendix to Part I

1 The fact that the costs of scientific objectification are particularly high for an especially low – or negative – profit has not entirely failed to influence the state of knowledge regarding these matters.

2 *Le Petit Robert* (Paris: Société du Nouveau Littré, 1979), p. xvii.

3 We know the role played by similar (conscious or unconscious) exclusions in the use that the National Socialist movement made of the word *völkisch*.

4 See H. Bauche, *Le langage populaire, grammaire, syntaxe et vocabu-laire du français tel qu'on le parle dans le peuple de Paris, avec tous les termes d'argot usuel* (Paris: Payot, 1920); P. Guiraud, *Le français populaire* (Paris: Presses Universitaires de France, 1965); also along the same lines, H. Frei, *La grammaire des fautes* (Paris and Geneva: 1929; Geneva: Slatkine Reprints, 1971).

5 For examples in French, see J. Cellard and A. Rey, *Dictionnaire du français non conventionnel* (Paris: Hachette, 1980), p. viii.

6 For example, in the discourse recorded on the market which is least tense – a conversation between women – slang vocabulary is more or less totally absent. In the case observed, it only appears when one of the female interlocutors quotes the utterances of a man ('bugger off right now'), of whom she says immediately: 'that's the way he talks, he used to know his way round Paris him, looks a bit down on his luck, wears his cap on one side, y'know what I mean.' A little further on, the same person employs the word 'stash' again just after having reported the utterances of a pub landlord in which it was used (cf. Y. Delsaut, 'L'économie du langage populaire', *Actes de la recherche en sciences sociales*, 4 (1975), pp. 33–40). Empirical studies ought to make an effort to determine the feeling speakers have with regard to whether a word is part of slang or part of the legitimate language (instead of imposing the definition of the observer); among other things, this would allow for an understanding of a number of features described as 'mistakes', which are the product of a misplaced sense of distinction.

7 This is why, while appearing to go around in circles or to be spinning in air, like so many circular and tautological definitions of vulgarity and of distinction, the legitimate language so often turns to the advantage of dominant speakers.

8 Given the role played in the preservation or transformation of language by spontaneous sociolinguists, and by the interventions expressly made by the family and the school which are elicited and oriented by it, a sociolinguistic analysis of linguistic change cannot ignore this kind of *right* or *linguistic custom* which governs, most notably, educational practices.

9 While accepting the division which is the basis of the very notion of 'popular speech', Henri Bauche observes that 'in familiar usage bourgeois talk shares numerous features in common with vulgar language' (*Le langage populaire*, p. 9). And further on he adds: 'The boundaries between slang – the different types of slang – and popular speech are sometimes difficult to determine. Equally vague are the limits, on the one hand, between popular speech and familiar speech, and, on the other, between specifically popular speech and the speech of vulgar people, i.e. people of modest means, of those who, without being exactly of the people, lack knowledge or education: those whom the "bourgeois" call common' (ibid., p. 26).

10 Although, for complex reasons which would have to be examined, the dominant vision does not give it a central place, the opposition between

masculine and feminine is one of the principles which give rise to the most typical contrasts, showing the 'people' as a 'female' populace, changeable and hungry for pleasure (according to the antithesis of head and gut).

11 This is what creates the ambiguity in the exaltation of the speech form of those regarded as 'dead straight': the vision of the world which it expresses and the virile virtues of the 'dead tough' find their natural extension in what has been called the 'popular Right' (see Z. Sternhell, *La droite révolutionnaire, 1885–1914. Les origines françaises du fascisme* (Paris: Seuil, 1978), a fascistic combination of racism, nationalism and authoritarianism. And this makes it easier to understand the apparent strangeness of Céline's case.

12 Everything seems to suggest that, due to the extension of schooling, the 'tough guy' character nowadays develops from his earliest schooldays, and against all the forms of submissiveness required by the school.

13 One of the effects of class racism, which, like the failure to distinguish among different yellow or black people, makes no distinction between the different types of 'poor', is the unwitting exclusion of even the possibility of difference (in fact, inventiveness, competence, etc.) and the pursuit of difference. The undiscriminating exaltation of the 'popular', which characterizes populism or radical chic, can thus lead to a kind of rapturous trust in what the 'natives' judge to be inept, stupid or coarse; or, what amounts to the same thing, it can lead one to retain only what appears out of the ordinary in the 'common' and to present it as representative of common speech.

14 By totally rejecting a 'French' society symbolized by school and also everyday racism, the young 'tough guys' who come from immigrant families undoubtedly represent the limit reached by the revolt of adolescents from the most economically and culturally deprived families, a revolt which often arises from educational failures, difficulties and disappointments.

15 P. E. Willis, *Profane Culture* (London: Routledge & Kegan Paul, 1978), esp. pp. 48–50.

16 As an exemplary manifestation of this principle of classification and of the breadth of its field of application, one only has to quote the case of the mason (a former miner) who, invited to classify the names of professions (in a test modelled on the techniques employed for the componential analysis of related terms) and to name the classes thus produced, wrote off the higher professions – of which he took the job of television presenter to be paradigmatic – with a wave of the hand and with the words: 'all a bunch of queers' (Enquête Yvette Delsaut, Denain, 1978).

17 In a more general way, since the more or less brutal evocation of sexual matters and the flattening projection of sentimental things on the physiological level often act as *euphemisms by hyperbole or antiphrasis* which, contrary to litotes, say more in order to say less, this vocabulary

changes meaning completely when it changes market, through romantic transcription or lexicological recollection.

18 Previously, the only equivalent situation was found in national military service, which was undoubtedly one of the principal sites for the production and inculcation of slang speech forms.

19 The small shopkeeper, and especially the pub landlord, particularly if he possesses the virtues of sociability which are part of his professional requisites, suffers no statutory hostility from the workers (contrary to what is usually supposed by intellectuals and the petite bourgeoisie with cultural capital, who are separated from them by a real cultural barrier). He often enjoys a certain symbolic authority – which may be exercised on the political level, although the subject is tacitly taboo in café conversations – because of the ease and self-confidence which he owes, among other things, to his comfortable economic circumstances.

20 One would have to check to see whether – apart from café owners – shopkeepers, and particularly those hawkers and travelling salesmen at fairs and markets specializing in patter and backchat, but also butchers and, in a different style and with correspondingly different structures of interaction, hairdressers, do not all contribute more than workers, mere *occasional* producers, to the production of verbal inventions.

21 This representation assigns a social nature to the masculine figure – that of the man 'who can take it' and who 'hangs in there', who gives nothing away and rejects feeling and sentimentality, who is solid and complete, 'all there', faithful and true, who 'you can count on', etc. – a nature which the harsh conditions of his existence would impose on him anyway, but which he feels duty bound to choose, because it is defined in opposition to the feminine 'nature', which is weak, gentle, docile, submissive, fragile, changeable, sensitive, sensual (effeminate and so 'contrary to nature'). This principle of di-vision operates not only in its specific field of application, i.e. in the domain of the relations between the sexes, but in a more general way, by imposing on men a strict, rigid and, in a word, essentialist vision of their identity and, more generally, of other social identities, and thus of the whole social order.

22 It goes without saying that these dealings tend to vary according to the wife's level of education and perhaps particularly according to the disparity in educational attainment between the spouses.

23 One can see that, according to this logic, women are always in the wrong, i.e. in their (misconceived) nature. One could quote examples *ad infinitum*: in the case of a woman delegated to carry out a task, if she succeeds, it is because it was easy, if she fails, it is because she did not know how to go about it.

24 The intention of inflicting a symbolic stain (for example, through insult, malicious gossip or erotic provocation) on what is perceived as inaccessible implies the most awful admission of the recognition of superiority. Thus, as Jean Starobinski aptly notes, 'coarse gossip, far from closing the gap between the social ranks, preserves and exacerbates it;

parading as irreverence and freedom, it abounds in the sense of degradation and is the self-confirmation of inferiority'. This refers to the gossip of the servants concerning Mademoiselle de Breil (cf. J. J. Rousseau, *Confessions*, III, in *Oeuvres complètes* (Paris: Gallimard, Plèiade, 1959), pp. 94–6) as analysed by J. Starobinski in *La Relation critique* (Paris: Gallimard, 1970), pp. 98–154.

Introduction to Part II

1 On the linguistic discussion of insults, see N. Ruwet, *Grammaire des insultes et autres études* (Paris: Seuil, 1982); J.-C. Milner, *Arguments linguistiques* (Paris: Mame, 1973).

3 Authorized Language: The Social Conditions for the Effectiveness of Ritual Discourse

1 See E. Benveniste, *Indo-European Language and Society*, tr. Elizabeth Palmer (London: Faber and Faber, 1973), pp. 323–6.
2 J. L. Austin, *How to Do Things with Words* (Oxford: Clarendon Press, 1962), p. 4.
3 The magical act extends to nature the action through words which, under certain conditions, is exercised on people. The equivalent, in the sphere of social action, is the attempt to act through words beyond the limits of delegated authority (speaking in the wilderness, outside one's parish).
4 Austin, *How to Do Things with Words*, p. 26.
5 R. P. Lelong, *Le dossier noir de la communion solennelle* (Paris: Mame, 1972), p. 183.
6 The specifically religious rite is simply a particular case of the social rituals whose magic does not reside in the discourses and convictions which accompany them (in this case, religious representations and beliefs) but in the system of social relations which constitute ritual itself, which make it possible and socially operative (among other things, in the representations of the beliefs it implies).

4 Rites of Institution

1 See P. Bourdieu, 'Épreuve scolaire et consécration sociale', *Actes de la recherche en sciences sociales*, 39 (September 1981), pp. 3–70.

5 Description and Prescription: The Conditions of Possibility and the Limits of Political Effectiveness

1 This is why conservatives throughout history, from Napoleon III to Pétain, have always condemned the 'political' behaviour which they identify with factional and party struggles (see M. Marcel, 'Inventaire des apolitismes en France', in Association française de science politique, *La dépolitisation, mythe ou réalité?* (Paris: Armand Colin, 1962), pp. 49–51.

2 The tension between sociological scientism and spontaneist voluntarism which always exists in the writings of Marxist theoreticians is doubtless due to the fact that they emphasize either class as condition or class as will, depending on their position in the division of labour of cultural production, and depending also on the state in which social classes find themselves.

3 This means that history (and particularly the history of categories of thought) constitutes one of the conditions under which political thought can become aware of itself.

4 G. Myrdal, *The Political Element in the Development of Economic Theory* (New York: Simon & Schuster, 1964), pp. 10–21.

6 Censorship and the Imposition of Form

1 It is only by perceiving the Freudian model as a particular example of a more general model, which makes any expression the product of a transaction between the expressive interest and the structural necessity of a field acting as a form of censorship, that one can return psychoanalytical concepts to the realm of *politics*, where they are often formed. The social repression that occurs in the domestic context, as the field for a particular type of relation of power (whose structure varies according to the social conditions), is very specific in its form (one of tacit injunction and suggestion) and applies to a very specific class of interests: sexual drives. But the Freudian analysis of the syntax of dreams and of all 'private' ideologies provides the instruments which are necessary for an understanding of the labour of euphemization and imposition of form which occurs each time a biological or social drive must come to terms with a social censorship.

2 Of course, nothing contributes quite as much to this as the status of 'philosopher' attributed to its author, and the signs and insignia – academic titles, publishing house, or quite simply his name – which identify his position in the philosophical hierarchy. To appreciate this effect we have only to imagine how we would read the page on the hydro-electric plant and the old wooden bridge (see M. Heidegger, 'The question concerning technology', in *Basic Writings*, ed. D. F.

Krell (London: Routledge & Kegan Paul, 1977), p. 297) which led to
the author being hailed as 'the first theorist of the ecological struggle'
by one of his commentators (R. Schérer, *Heidegger* (Paris: Sehers,
1973), p. 5), if it had borne the signature of a leader of an ecological
movement or a minister of the environment or the logo of a group of
leftist students. (It goes without saying that these different 'attributions' could not become truly plausible unless accompanied by some
modifications in *presentation*.)

3   'At bottom each system knows its own primitive expressions only, and
is incapable of discussing anything else' (J. Nicod, *Geometry and
Induction*, tr. J. Bell and M. Woods (London: Routledge & Kegan
Paul, 1969), p. 11). Bachelard notes, along the same lines, that
scientific language uses inverted commas to indicate when the words it
retains from an ordinary or formerly scientific language are completely
re-defined and derive their entire meaning from the system of theoretical relations in which they are integrated (G. Bachelard, *Le matérialisme rationnel* (Paris: Presses Universitaires de France, 1953),
pp. 216–17).

4   Language raises particular problems for the social sciences, at least if
one accepts that they must be oriented towards the broadest diffusion
of results, which is a condition for the 'defetishizing' of social relations
and the 're-appropriation' of the social world. The use of the vocabulary of ordinary language obviously implies the danger of a regression to
the ordinary sense which is correlative with the loss of the sense
imposed through integration in the system of scientific relations. The
resort to neologisms or to abstract symbols shows, better than straightforward 'inverted commas', the *break* with common-sense meaning,
but it also risks producing a break in the communication of the scientific
vision of the social world.

5   M. Heidegger, *Being and Time*, tr. J. Macquarrie and E. Robinson
(Oxford: Blackwell, 1967), p. 348. Heidegger was to go further down
this path as, with his growing authority, he felt authorized to engage in
the peremptory verbalism to which all discourses of authority ultimately give rise.

6   This is one of the spontaneous strategies of politeness which can really
neutralize the aggressive, arrogant or troublesome content of an order
or question only by integrating it in a set of symbolic expressions,
verbal or non-verbal, aimed at masking the raw meaning of the element
taken on its own.

7   Heidegger, *Being and Time*, pp. 163–4.

8   When writing this I could not recall exactly the passage in the essay on
the 'overcoming of metaphysics' (1939–1946) devoted to 'literary
dirigism' as an aspect of the reign of 'technology': 'The need for human
material underlies the same regulation of preparing for ordered mobilization as the need for entertaining books and poems, for whose
production the poet is no more important than the bookbinder's

apprentice, who helps bind the poems for the printer by, for example, bringing the covers for binding from the storage room.' M. Heidegger, *The End of Philosophy*, tr. J. Stambaugh (New York: Harper & Row, 1973), p. 106.

9 M. Heidegger, *An Introduction to Metaphysics* (New Haven: Yale University Press, 1987), p. 38. Another symptom of this aristocratism is the way all the adjectives which describe pre-philosophical existence are pejoratively coloured: 'inauthentic', 'vulgar', 'everyday', 'public', etc.

10 One would have to record systematically the entire system of symbols through which philosophical discourse declares its elevated nature as a dominant discourse.

11 One thinks, for example, of the developments regarding biologism (cf. M. Heidegger, *Nietzsche*, 4 vols, esp. 'Nietzsche's alleged biologism' in vol. 3, *The Will to Power as Knowledge and as Metaphysics*, tr. D. F. Krell (New York: Harper & Row, 1987), pp. 39–47.

12 Heidegger, *Being and Time*, pp. 83–4 (my emphasis). These cautionary strategies might have awakened the suspicions of non-German readers, if the latter had not been subject to conditions of reception which made it very unlikely that they would detect the hidden connotations, which are disowned in advance by Heidegger (all the more so since the translations 'suppress' them systematically in the name of the break between the ontical and the ontological). Indeed, in addition to the resistance to analysis offered by a work which is the product of such systematic strategies of euphemization, there is also in this case one of the most pernicious effects of the exportation of cultural products, the disappearance of all the subtle signs of social or political origins, of all the marks (often very discreet) of the social importance of discourse and the intellectual position of its author, in short, of all the infinitesimal features to which the native reader is obviously most vulnerable, but which he can apprehend better than others once he is equipped with techniques of objectification. One recalls, for example, all the 'administrative' connotations which Adorno discovered behind 'existential' terms like 'encounter' (*Begegnung*), or in words like 'concern' (*Anliegen*), and 'commission' (*Auftrag*), a pre-eminently ambiguous term, both 'the object of an administrative demand' and a 'heartfelt wish', which was already the object of a deviant usage in Rilke's poetry (T. W. Adorno, *The Jargon of Authenticity*, tr. K. Tarnowski and F. Will (London: Routledge & Kegan Paul, 1973), pp. 77–88).

13 We can see that the same logic applies in the use that other variants of priestly prophesying make nowadays of the 'epistemological break', a kind of rite of passage, accomplished once and for all, across the boundary laid down permanently between science and ideology.

14 Bachelard, *Le matérialisme rationnel*, p. 59.

15 M. Heidegger, 'The Anaximander Fragment', in *Early Greek Thinking*, tr. D. F. Krell and F. A. Capuzzi (San Francisco: Harper & Row, 1984), p. 33.

16   For another, particularly caricatural example of the omnipotence of
      'essential thought', one could refer to the text of the 1951 lecture
      'Building, dwelling, thinking', where the housing crisis is 'overcome' in
      favour of the ontological meaning of 'dwelling' (Heidegger, *Basic
      Writings*, p. 339).
17   This typically 'philosophical' effect is predisposed to being reproduced
      indefinitely, in all the encounters between 'philosophers' and 'laymen',
      and particularly the specialists in positive disciplines who are inclined to
      recognize the social hierarchy of legitimacies which confers on the
      philosopher the position of *last appeal*, which is both crowning and
      'founding' at the same time. This professorial 'coup' is obviously best
      employed in 'professional' usage: the philosophical text, the product of
      a process of *esoterization*, will be made *exoteric* at the cost of a process
      of commentary which its esoteric nature makes indispensable and
      whose best effects lie in the (artificial) concretizations which lead, in a
      process neatly reversing that of the (artificial) break, to the re-
      activation of the primary sense, initially euphemized to render them
      esoteric, but with a full accompaniment of *cautions* ('this is only an
      example') aimed at preserving the ritual distance.
18   Heidegger, *Being and Time*, p. 158.
19   J. Lacan, *Écrits*, tr. A. Sheridan (London: Tavistock, 1977), p. 173.
20   Heidegger, *Being and Time*, p. 165. Since the Heideggerian 'philo-
      sophical' style is the sum of a small number of effects that are repeated
      indefinitely, it was preferable to grasp them in the context of a single
      passage – the analysis of assistance – in which they are all concentrated
      and which should be re-read in one go in order to see how these effects
      are articulated in practice in a particular discourse.
21   Thus the innumerable binary oppositions imagined by anthropologists
      and sociologists to justify the *de facto* distinction that exists between the
      societies assigned to anthropology and the societies assigned to sociolo-
      gy – 'community'/'society', 'folk'/'urban', 'traditional'/'modern', 'warm
      societies'/'cold societies', etc. – constitute a prime example of the series
      of parallel oppositions which is by definition interminable, since each
      particular opposition seizes on part of the fundamental opposition,
      essentially multi-faceted and pluri-vocal, between classless societies
      and societies divided into classes, which it expresses in a way that is
      compatible with the properties and conventions which vary from one
      field to the next, and also from one state to another within the same
      field, i.e. more or less *ad infinitum*.
22   It is obvious that language offers other possibilities for ideological
      games than those exploited by Heidegger. Thus the dominant political
      jargon exploits principally the potential ambiguity and misunderstand-
      ing implied by the multiplicity of class usages or specialized usages
      (linked to specialist fields).
23   One could counter these analyses by arguing that to a certain extent
      they only elucidate those properties of the Heideggerian use of
      language that Heidegger himself expressly claims – at least in his most

recent writings. In fact, as we shall endeavour to show later, these bogus confessions are one aspect of the work of *Selbstinterpretation* and *Selbstbehauptung* to which the later Heidegger devotes his entire writing effort.

24   It is through strategies that are no less paradoxical – even though they take on the appearance of scientificity – that the 'political science' which identifies scientific objectivity with 'ethical neutrality' (i.e. the neutrality between social classes whose existence it denies anyway) contributes to the class struggle by providing all the mechanisms which help produce the false consciousness of the social world with the support of a false science.

25   Ultimately, there is no word which is not an untranslatable *hapax legomenon*: thus the word 'metaphysical', for example, does not have the same sense for Heidegger that it has for Kant, nor for the later Heidegger the sense that it has for the earlier. Heidegger simply pushes an essential property of the philosophical use of language to the extreme on this point: philosophical language as a sum of partially intersecting idiolects can only be adequately used by speakers capable of referring each word to the system where it assumes the meaning they intend it to bear ('in the Kantian sense').

26   E. Jünger, *Essai sur l'homme et le temps*, vol. 1: *Traité du Rebelle* (*Der Waldgang*, 1951) (Monaco: Rocher, 1957), pp. 47–8. On p. 66 there is a perfectly clear although implicit reference to Heidegger.

27   'Authentic Being-one's-Self does not rest upon an *exceptional condition* of the subject, a condition that has been detached from the "they"; *it is rather an existentiell modification of the "they" – of the "they" as an essential existentiale*' (Heidegger, *Being and Time*, p. 168; cf. also p. 223).

28   Ibid., pp. 341–8 and 352–7.

29   Ibid., pp. 380–1, 439–40 and 464–5.

30   F. Stern, *The Politics of Cultural Despair* (Berkeley: University of California Press, 1961).

31   W. Z. Laqueur, *Young Germany: A History of the German Youth Movement* (London: Routledge, 1962), pp. 178–87.

32   Stefan George's style was imitated by an entire generation, particularly through the influence of the 'youth movement' (*Jugendbewegung*), seduced by his aristocratic idealism and his contempt for 'arid rationalism': 'His style was imitated and a few quotations were repeated often enough – phrases about he who once had circled the flame and who forever will follow the flame; about the need for a new mobility whose warrant no longer derives from crown and escutcheon; about the Führer with his *völkisch* banner who will lead his followers to the future Reich through storm and grisly portents, and so forth' (Laqueur, *The Politics of Cultural Despair*, p. 135).

33   Heidegger explicitly evokes tradition – more precisely, Plato's distortion of the word *eidos* – in order to justify his 'technical' use of the word *Gestell*: 'According to ordinary usage, the word *Gestell* [frame] means

some kind of apparatus, e.g. a bookrack. Gestell is also the name for a skeleton. And the employment of the word *Gestell* [enframing] that is now required of us seems equally eerie, not to speak of the arbitrariness with which words of a mature language are so misused. Can anything be more strange? Surely not. Yet this strangeness is an old custom of thought' (Heidegger, *The Question Concerning Technology*, p. 301). Against the same accusation of imposing 'randomly arbitrary' meaning, Heidegger replies, in 'A letter to a young student', with an exhortation 'to learn the craft of thinking' (M. Heidegger, 'The things', in *Poetry, Language, Thought* (New York: Harper Colophon, 1975), p. 186).

34 E. Spranger, 'Mein Konflikt mit der nationalsozialistischen Regierung 1933', *Universitas Zeitschrift für Wissenschaft, Kunst und Literatur*, 10 (1955), pp. 457–73, cited by F. Ringer, *The Decline of the German Mandarins: The German Academic Community, 1890–1933* (Cambridge, Mass.: Harvard University Press, 1969), p. 439.

35 J. Habermas, 'Penser avec Heidegger contre Heidegger', *Profils philosophiques et politiques* (Paris: Gallimard, 1974), p. 90 (my emphasis). Cf. the revised version of this essay in English, 'Martin Heidegger: the great influence', in Habermas's *Philosophical–Political Profiles*, tr. F. F. Lawrence (London: Heinemann, 1983), pp. 53–60.

36 Ibid., p. 100.

37 Heidegger, 'Building, dwelling, thinking', p. 339.

38 M. Halbwachs, *Classes sociales et morphologie* (Paris: Minuit, 1972), p. 178. It goes without saying that such a phrase is excluded in advance from *any self-respecting* philosophical discourse: the sense of the distinction between the 'theoretical' and the 'empirical' is in fact a fundamental dimension of the philosophical sense of distinction.

39 It would be necessary – in order to bring out this implicit philosophy of philosophical reading and the philosophy of the history of philosophy which goes with it – to note systematically all the texts (commonly found in Heidegger and his commentators) which express the expectation of a pure and purely formal treatment, which demand internal reading, circumscribed by the text itself or, in other words, which express the irreducibility of the 'self-engendered' work to any historical determination – apart, obviously, from the internal determinations of the autonomous history of philosophy or, at the most, of the mathematical or physical sciences.

40 It is not the sociologist who imports the language of orthodoxy: 'The addressee of the "Letter on Humanism" combines a profound insight into Heidegger with an extraordinary gift of language, both together making him beyond any question one of the *most authoritative interpreters* of Heidegger in France' (W. J. Richardson, s.J., *Heidegger: Through Phenomenology to Thought* (The Hague: Nijhoff, 1963), p. 684, regarding an article by J. Beaufret); or: 'This sympathetic study [by Albert Dondeyne] orchestrates the theme that the ontological

difference is the single point of reference in Heidegger's entire effort. Not every *Heideggerian of strict observance* will be happy, perhaps, with the author's formulae concerning Heidegger's relation to "la grande tradition de la philosophia perennis" ' (ibid.).

41 M. Heidegger, *An Introduction to Metaphysics*, tr. R. Mannheim (New Haven: Yale University Press, 1973), p. 8.

42 M. Heidegger, *Nietzsche*, vol. 2, *The Eternal Recurrence of the Same*, tr. D. F. Krell (San Francisco, Ca.: Harper & Row, 1984), p. 17. The work, Heidegger says somewhere, 'escapes biography' which can only 'give a name to something that belongs to nobody'.

43 It is remarkable, knowing how tenaciously he rejected and refuted all external or reductive readings of his work (see his letters to Jean Wahl, Jean Beaufret, to a student, to Richardson, discussion with a Japanese philosopher, etc.), that Heidegger had no hesitation in using against his rivals (Sartre, in the case in point) the arguments of a 'clumsy sociologism'. Thus, if necessary, he was prepared to reinvest the topic of 'the dictatorship of the public realm' with the strictly *social* (if not sociological) sense which it undoubtedly had in *Being and Time*, and what is more, to do so in a passage where he is attempting precisely to establish that the 'existential' analysis of the 'they' 'in no way means to furnish an *incidental* contribution to sociology' ('Letter on humanism', in *Basic Writings*, p. 197). This recycling of Heidegger I by Heidegger II bears witness to the fact (underlined by the emphasis on 'incidental' in the sentence quoted) that, if everything is re-denied, nothing is renounced.

44 J. Beaufret, *Introductions aux philosophies de l'existence. De Kierkegaard à Heidegger* (Paris: Denöel-Gonthier, 1971), pp. 111–12.

45 O. Pöggeler, *La Pensée de M. Heidegger* (Paris: Aubier-Montaigne, 1963), p. 18.

46 From this point of view one might connect a certain interview with Marcel Duchamp (in *VH 101*, no. 3, *Autumn* 1970, pp. 55–61) with the 'Letter on humanism', with its innumerable refutations or warnings, its calculated interference with interpretation, etc.

47 One might object that this 'claim' is itself denied in the 'Letter on humanism' (pp. 215–17), but this does not prevent it from being reaffirmed a little later (pp. 235–6).

48 Richardson, *Heidegger*, p. 224 n. 29 (my emphasis); see also ibid., p. 410 on the distinction between 'poesy' and 'poetry'.

49 H. Marcuse, 'Beiträge zur Phänomenologie des historischen Materialismus', in *Philosophische Hefte*, 1 (1928), pp. 45–68.

50 C. Hobert, *Das Dasein in Menschen* (Zeulenroda: Sporn, 1937).

51 It is the same logic which has led, more recently, to apparently better grounded 'combinations' of Marxism and structuralism or Freudianism, while Freud (interpreted by Lacan) provided new support for conceptual puns like Heidegger's.

52 Cf. Heidegger in his 'Letter on humanism' (p. 212) for the refutation of

an 'existentialist' reading of *Being and Time*: the refutation of the interpretation of the concepts of *Being and Time* as a 'secular' version of religious concepts; the refutation of an 'anthropological' or 'moral' reading of the opposition between the authentic and the inauthentic (pp. 217–21); and the rather more laboured refutation of 'nationalism' in the analyses of the 'homeland' (*Heimat*), etc.

53 Heidegger, 'Letter on humanism'.

54 K. Axelos, *Arguments d'une recherche* (Paris: Minuit, 1939), pp. 93ff; see also K. Axelos, *Einführung in ein künftiges Denken über Marx und Heidegger* (Tübingen: Max Niemeyer Verlag, 1966).

55 What we see at work here – that is, in its practical truth – is the scheme of the 'ontological difference' between Being and beings: can it be a coincidence that it arises naturally when there is a need to emphasize distances and re-establish hierarchies, between philosophy and the social sciences in particular?

56 It is this blind understanding which is designated by the apparently contradictory declaration by Karl Friedrich von Weizsäcker (quoted by Habermas, 'Penser avec Heidegger contre Heidegger', p. 106): 'I began to read *Being and Time*, which had just been published, when I was still a student. Today I can state with a good conscience that at the time I understood nothing of it, strictly speaking. But I could not help feeling that it was there, and there alone, that thought could engage with the problems that I felt must lie behind modern theoretical physics, and today I would still grant it that.'

57 The same Sartre who would have smiled or been indignant at Heidegger's elitist professions of faith if they had come before him in the guise of what Simone de Beauvoir called 'right-wing thought' (forgetting, curiously, to include Heidegger), would not have been able to have the insight that he had into the expression which Heidegger's works gave to his own experience of the social world, expressed at length in the pages of *La Nausée*, if it had not appeared to him dressed in forms fitting the proprieties and conventions of the philosophical field.

7 On Symbolic Power

1 E. Cassirer, *The Myth of the State* (New Haven: Yale University Press, 1946), p. 16.

2 I have in mind the etymological sense of *kategorein* as noted by Heidegger (i.e. 'to accuse publicly'); and also the terminology of kinship, which is a prime example of social categories (terms of address).

3 The neo-phenomenological tradition (Schütz, Peter Berger) and certain forms of ethnomethodology accept the same presuppositions merely by omitting the question of the social conditions of possibility of the *doxic experience* (Husserl) of the world (and in particular of the

social world), that is, of the experience of the social world as being self-evident ('taken for granted' in Schütz's words).

4 The ideological stances adopted by the dominant are strategies of reproduction which tend to reinforce both *within* and *outside* the class the belief in the legitimacy of the domination of that class.

5 The existence of a specialized field of production is the precondition for the appearance of a struggle between orthodoxy and heterodoxy, which share the common feature of being distinguished from *doxa*, that is, from what remains undiscussed.

6 It also means we avoid the ethnologism (visible in particular in the analysis of archaic thought) which consists in treating ideologies as myths, that is, as the undifferentiated products of a collective labour, and thus in ignoring all the features they owe to the characteristics of the field of production (e.g. in the Greek tradition, the esoteric re-interpretations of mythic traditions).

7 The symbols of power (e.g. clothes, sceptre) are merely *objectified* symbolic capital and their efficacy is subject to the same conditions.

8 The destruction of this power of symbolic imposition based on misrecognition depends on *becoming aware* of its arbitrary nature, i.e. the disclosure of the objective truth and the destruction of belief. Heterodox discourse – in so far as it destroys the spuriously clear and self-evident notions of orthodoxy, a fictitious restoration of the *doxa*, and neutralizes its power to immobilize – contains a symbolic power of mobilization and subversion, the power to actualize the potential power of the dominated classes.

8 Political Representation: Elements for a Theory of the Political Field

1 M. Weber, *Economy and Society: An Outline of Interpretive Sociology*, vol. 2, ed. G. Roth and C. Wittich (Berkeley: University of California Press, 1978), pp. 1395ff., 1451ff.

2 Neo-Machiavellian theories take this division into account only to ascribe it to human nature. Thus Michels speaks of 'incurable incompetence' (R. Michels, *Political Parties: A Sociological Study of the Oligarchical Tendencies of Modern Democracy*, tr. E. and C. Paul (London: Jarrold and Sons, 1916), p. 421) or of 'the perrenial incompetence of the masses' (p. 424) and describes the relation between professionals and non-professionals in the language of *need* (the masses' 'need for leadership' (p. 54), the masses' need for an object of veneration (p. 69), etc.), or in the language of *nature* ('The apathy of the masses and their need for guidance has as its counterpart in the leaders a natural greed for power. Thus the development of the democratic oligarchy is accelerated by the general characteristics of human nature' (p. 217)).

3 See, in particular, P. Bourdieu, *Distinction: A Social Critique of the Judgement of Taste*, tr. R. Nice (Cambridge, Mass.: Harvard University Press, 1984), pp. 397–465.

4 This implies that the division of political labour varies with the overall volume of economic and cultural capital accumulated in a given social formation (its 'level of development') and also with the more or less asymmetrical structure of the distribution of this capital, especially the cultural capital. In this way, the spread of access to secondary education was the source of a set of transformations of the relation between parties and their militants or electors.

5 Wittgenstein, *Philosophical Investigations*, tr. G. E. N. Anscombe (Oxford: Basil Blackwell, 1958), para. 337, p. 108.

6 The relation between professionals and non-professionals takes very different forms for the dominant: since they are, most of the time, capable of producing their political acts and opinions themselves, it is never without a certain reticence and ambivalence that they resign themselves to delegation (imposed on them by the specific logic of legitimacy which, based as it is on misrecognition, condemns the temptation to celebrate one's own activities).

7 One can describe as a *party association* an organization whose almost exclusive object is to prepare for elections, and which derives from this permanent function a permanence which ordinary associations do not possess. Resembling an association by the limited and partial character of its objectives and of the commitment it requires and, thereby, by the thoroughly diversified social composition of its *clientele* (made up of electors and not of militants), it resembles a party by the permanence imposed on it by the recurrence of its specific function, namely, preparing for elections. (It is notable that the *ideal party* as described by Ostrogorski is precisely an association, in other words, a *temporary* organization, created *ad hoc* for the purposes of a given claim or a specific cause.)

8 A. Gramsci, *Selections from Political Writings (1921–1926)*, tr. Q. Hoare (London: Lawrence & Wishart, 1978), pp. 197, 12.

9 R. Luxemburg, *Masse et chefs* (Paris: Spartacus, 1972), p. 37; translated from the French.

10 A. Gramsci, *Selections from Political Writings (1910–1920)*, tr. J. Andrews (London: Lawrence & Wishart, 1977), pp. 330–9.

11 In this way, for example, the elitist theory of opinion, which is implicit in the elaboration or analysis of opinion polls or in the ritual lamentations over the high level of abstentions, betrays itself, in all innocence, in inquiries into the *opinion-makers* which, drawing their inspiration from an emanationist philosophy of 'diffusion' as analogous to the streaming of liquid, aim to follow opinions back along the networks through which they circulate to the source from which they seemingly spring – in other words, to the 'elite' of 'opinion-makers', whom nobody ever thinks to ask for a reason for their opinions. (See for example C. Kadushin, 'Power, influence and social circles: a new

methodology for studying opinion makers', *American Sociological Review*, 33 (1968), pp. 685–99.)

12 The fact remains that this evolution could be countered, to some degree, by the general rise in the level of education which, given the all-powerful importance of educational capital in the system of explanatory factors of variations in individuals' relation to politics, is probably of a kind to contradict this tendency and to reinforce, to different degrees depending on the apparatus involved, pressure from the base, which is less inclined to accept unconditional delegation.

13 The televised debate which brings together professionals chosen for their specific competence but also for their sense of political propriety and respectability, in the presence of a public reduced to the status of spectators, thus realizing class struggle in the form of a theatrical and ritualized confrontation between two champions, symbolizes perfectly the end of the process of autonomization of the political game properly speaking, one that is more than ever imprisoned in its techniques, its hierarchies and its internal rules.

14 On the logic of the struggle for the imposition of the principle of di-vision, see P. Bourdieu, 'Identity and representation', ch. 10 in this volume.

15 As proof of this, one need only cite the differences (which the necessities linked to the history and logic proper to each national political field bring out) between the different representations that the 'representative' organizations of social classes placed in equivalent positions, such as the working classes of different European countries, give of the interests of these classes. This is true despite all the efforts made to achieve a greater homogenization (such as the 'bolshevization' of the communist parties).

16 Weber, *Economy and Society*, vol. 2, p. 1447.

17 'Proletarian unity is blocked by opportunists of every hue, who defend the vested interests of cliques, material interests and especially interests derived from political power over the masses' (Gramsci, *Selections from Political Writings (1910–1920)*, p. 178).

18 The paradigmatic form of this structural duplicity is probably represented by what the revolutionary tradition of the USSR calls 'the language of Aesop', that is, the secret, coded, indirect language to which revolutionaries resorted to evade the Tsarist censorship and which reappeared in the Bolshevik party, on the occasion of the conflict between the supporters of Stalin and those of Bukharin, that is, when it was a matter of preventing, by 'party patriotism', conflicts within the Politburo or the Central Committee from leaking out of the party to the outside world. This language conceals, behind its anodyne appearance, a hidden truth which 'any sufficiently cultivated militant' can decipher, and it can be read, depending on its addressees, in two different ways. See S. Cohen, *Nicolas Boukharine. La vie d'un bolchevik* (Paris: Maspero, 1979).

19 Hence the failure of all those who, like so many historians of Germany

after Rosenberg, have attempted to define 'conservatism' absolutely, without seeing that its substantial content had to change continuously in order to conserve its relational *value.*

20 Gramsci, *Selections from Political Writings (1921–1926)*, pp. 139–40.

21 Among the factors creating this effect of closure and the very special form of esotericism that it generates, one must include the frequently observed tendency among the party officials of political apparatuses to restrict their sphere of social interaction to other party officials.

22 Gramsci, *Selections from Political Writings (1921–1926)*, p. 191 (my emphasis).

23 Failure to acknowledge what these concepts owe to history debars one from the one real possibility of freeing them from history. As tools of analysis but also of anathematization, instruments of knowledge but also instruments of power, all those concepts ending in '-ism' that the Marxological tradition eternalizes by treating them as pure conceptual constructions, free of any context and detached from any strategic function, are 'frequently linked to particular circumstances, tainted with premature generalizations, and marked by bitter polemics' and generated 'in divergence, in violent confrontations between the representatives of the various different currents' (G. Haupt, 'Les marxistes face à la question nationale: l'histoire du problème', in G. Haupt, M. Lowy and C. Weill, *Les marxistes et la question nationale, 1848–1914* (Paris: Maspero, 1974), p. 11).

24 It is well known that Bakunin, who imposed absolute submission to the leadership in the movements he constituted (for example the National Fraternity) and who was basically a supporter of the 'Blanquist' idea of 'active minorities', was led, in his polemic with Marx, to denounce authoritarianism and to exalt the spontaneity of the masses and the autonomy of the federations.

25 J. Maitron, *Le mouvement anarchiste en France* (Paris: Maspero, 1975), vol. 2, pp. 82–3.

26 The position (more or less central and dominant) in the party apparatus, and the cultural capital possessed, form the source of the different and even opposed visions of revolutionary action, the future of capitalism, relations between the party and the masses, etc., which confront each other within the workers' movement. It is, for instance, certain that economism and the propensity to accentuate the determinist, objective and scientific side of Marxism is more closely associated with 'scientists' and 'theoreticians' (for example, Tugan-Baranowski or the 'economists' in the social-democratic party) than with 'militants' or 'agitators', especially if their theory of economics is self-taught (that is doubtless one of the sources of the opposition between Marx and Bakunin). The opposition between centralism and spontaneism or, to put it another way, between authoritarian socialism and libertarian socialism, seems to vary in an altogether parallel way, the propensity to scientism and economism inclining people to entrust those who possess

knowledge with the right to define, in an authoritative way, the line to be followed (the biography of Marx is traversed by these oppositions which, as he grows older, are decided in favour of the 'scientist').

27 Voting strategies also have to face the alternative between an adequate but powerless representation, on the one hand, and an imperfect but, by virtue of that very fact, powerful representation, on the other. In other words, the very logic which identifies isolation with powerlessness forces one to make *compromise choices* and confers a decisive advantage on stances already confirmed with regard to the original opinions.

28 It is no coincidence if opinion polls demonstrate the contradiction between two antagonistic principles of legitimacy, namely technocratic science and the democratic will, by alternating questions that appeal either to the judgement of an expert or to the wishes of the militant.

29 The violence of political polemics, and the constant recourse to ethical questioning, whose weapons are most frequently *ad hominem* arguments, can also be explained by the fact that mobilizing ideas owe part of their credit to the credit of the person who professes them. Furthermore, it is not merely a question of refuting them, by means of a purely logical and scientific argument, but of *discrediting* them by discrediting their author. By giving a free rein to ways of combating adversaries not only in their ideas but also in their person, the logic of the political field provides a highly favourable terrain for strategies of resentment: in this way, it offers to the first-comer a means of attaining, most often by a rudimentary form of the sociology of knowledge, theories or ideas which he would be incapable of submitting to scientific criticism.

30 E. Benveniste, *Indo-European Language and Society*, tr. E. Palmer (London: Faber, 1973), pp. 94–100.

31 Ibid., p. 99.

32 Ibid., p. 143.

33 The extreme caution which defines the accomplished politician, and which can be measured in particular by the high degree of euphemization of his discourse, can doubtless be explained by the extreme vulnerability of political capital, which means that the politician's trade is a high-risk profession, especially in periods of crisis when, as can be seen in the case of de Gaulle and Pétain, small differences in the dispositions and values involved may be the source of totally incompatible choices. (This is because the essence of extra-ordinary situations is to abolish the possibility of compromises, ambiguities, double-dealing, multiple memberships, etc., authorized by the ordinary recourse to multiple and partly integrated criteria of classification, by imposing a system of classification organized around a single criterion.)

34 One result of this is that the politician is a close associate of the journalist, who holds sway over the mass media and who thus has power over every kind of symbolic capital (the power of 'making or unmaking reputations' which Watergate showed in full measure).

Capable, at least in certain political situations, of controlling a politician's or movement's access to the status of a political force really
counting for something, the journalist is, like the critic, bound to play
the role of someone who points out the qualities of someone or
something while being unable to do for himself what he does for others
(and the attempts he may make to mobilize in favour of himself or his
work the intellectual or political authorities which owe something to his
action as a favourable judge are condemned in advance). Thus he is
united to those he has helped to make (in proportion to his value as a
favourable judge) by a relation of deep *ambivalence* which leads him to
oscillate between admiring or servile submission and treacherous
resentment, ready to speak his mind the minute the idol he has helped
to produce commits some blunder.

35 Benveniste, *Indo-European Language and Society*, p. 324.
36 'Instead of leaders they have become bankers of men in a monopoly
    situation, and the least hint of competition makes them crazy with
    terror and despair' (Gramsci, *Selections from Political Writings, 1922–
    1926*, pp. 17–18). 'In many respects a union leader represents a social
    type similar to the *banker*. An experienced banker, who has a good
    business head and is able to foresee with some accuracy the movement
    of stocks and bonds, wins credit for his institution and attracts
    depositors and investors. A trade-union leader who can foresee the
    possible outcome as conflicting social forces clash, attracts the masses
    into his organization and becomes a *banker of men*' (ibid., p. 77).
37 The opposition between the two kinds of political capital is the source
    of one of the fundamental differences between elected representatives
    in the Communist Party and those in the Socialist Party: 'Whereas the
    great majority of socialist mayors refer to the fact that they are well
    known public figures, whether this is due to family prestige, profession-
    al competence, or services rendered in the course of some activity or
    another, two thirds of the Communists consider themselves first and
    foremost as delegates of their party' (D. Lacorne, *Les notables rouges*
    (Paris: Presses de la fondation nationale des sciences politiques, 1980),
    p. 67).
38 The reader will no doubt think of the Gaullist adventure. But one could
    also find an equivalent in an altogether different region of the social
    and political space. Thus Denis Lacorne observes that elected repre-
    sentatives in the Communist Party who enjoy a personal notoriety
    almost always owe their status as 'local personalities' to some 'heroic
    act' performed during the Second World War (ibid., p. 69).
39 That being said, a political mission can be distinguished, even in this
    case, from a mere bureaucratic function by virtue of the fact that it
    always remains, as we have seen, a personal mission, which involves
    the whole person.
40 This is not the only feature which suggests that the workers' movement
    fulfils for the working class a function homologous to that which the

2

Church fulfils for peasants and for certain fractions of the petite bourgeoisie.

41 Here one can quote Michels: 'The most tenaciously conservative members of the organization are, in fact, those who are most definitely dependent on it' (Michels, *Political Parties*, p. 124). And further on: 'A party which has a well-filled treasury is in a position, not only to dispense with the material aid of its comparatively affluent members, and thus to prevent the acquirement by these of a preponderant influence in the party, but also to provide itself with a body of officials who are loyal and devoted because they are entirely dependent on the party for their means of subsistence' (ibid., p. 129). Or Gramsci: 'Today, the representatives of established interests – i.e. of the cooperatives, the employment agencies, the shared land-tenancies, the municipalities and the providential societies – although they are in a minority in the party, have the upper hand over the orators, the journalists, the teachers and the lawyers, who pursue unattainable and vacuous ideological projects' (Gramsci, *Selections from Political Writings, 1921–1926*, p. 81).

42 Weber, *Economy and Society*, vol. 2, p. 1165.

43 These analyses also apply to the case of the Church: as the political capital of the Church is objectified in institutions and, as is the case in the recent period, in jobs controlled by the Church (in teaching, the press, youth movements, etc.), the Church's power tends to rest less and less on instilling doctrine and the 'cure of souls'; in this way, it can doubtless be better measured by the number of jobs and agents indirectly controlled by the Church than by the numbers of 'mass-goers' or 'Easter-worshippers'.

44 'The normal development of the trade union organization produced results that were the complete opposite of those that had been foreseen by trade unionism: the workers who had become trade union leaders completely lost their vocation as workers and their class spirit and acquired all the characteristics of the petty-bourgeois functionary, intellectually lazy, morally perverted or easy to pervert. The broader the trade union movement became, as it embraced great masses of people, the more officialdom took over' (A. Gramsci, *Écrits politiques*, vol. III (Paris: Gallimard, 1974), pp. 206–7; translated from the French).

45 'Town halls represent the essential base of the Socialist Party's means, men and influence . . . So long as there are town halls, the party will last, will survive, whatever happens. It is easy to understand why the town halls are the socialists' mainstay. You might even say they are the only really serious thing. Ideology, declarations of principle, plans for action, programmes, debates, discussions, dialogues, all that is important, of course . . . But on the local level, the party is in power, or at least has the illusion that it is. That is why all the playing around has to stop when municipal elections come up. You have to face up to

concrete problems. You defend your territory, without any theoretical prattling, strenuously, right up to the bitter end' (P. Guidoni, *Histoire du nouveau Parti socialiste* (Paris: Tema-Action, 1973), p. 120).

46 One can observe this in the apparently most unfavourable case, that of the Bolshevik Party: 'Behind the façade of declared political and organizational unity, known under the name of "democratic central-ism", there was no such thing as a uniform Bolshevik political philosophy or ideology in 1917 or even several years later. On the contrary, the party included a remarkable variety of points of view: differences extended from semantic points to conflicts over the most basic options' (Cohen, *Nicolas Boukharine*, p. 19).

47 If one remembers the place that the working-class system of values grants to virtues such as integrity ('being wholehearted', 'being cut and dried', etc.), keeping your word, being loyal to your own people, being self-consistent ('that's just the way I am', 'I'm not going to have my mind changed for me', etc.), all of them dispositions which, in other universes, would appear as a form of rigidity or even stupidity, it becomes easy to understand how the effect of loyalty to one's original choices – a loyalty which tends to make membership of a political party an almost hereditary property, one which is capable of surviving changes in condition within or between generations – is particularly powerful in the case of the working classes and benefits especially the parties of the left.

48 Although it includes invariant characteristics, the opposition between the party officials and ordinary supporters (or, *a fortiori*, occasional voters) can be interpreted in very different ways depending on the parties. The key factor here is the distribution of capital and, above all perhaps, of *free time* among the classes. (It is, after all, well known that if direct democracy cannot resist economic and social differentiation, this is because, through the unequal distribution of free time which results from it, administrative responsibilities are concentrated in the hands of those who have at their disposal the time necessary to fulfil these functions for little or no remuneration.) This simple principle could also help to explain the differential participation of the different professions (or even of the different levels of status within a single profession) in political or trade-union life and, more generally, in all semi-political responsibilities. Thus Max Weber notes that directors of great institutes of medicine and the natural sciences are neither particularly inclined nor suitable to occupy the post of rector, and Robert Michels points out that scientists who have taken an active part in political life 'find that their scientific faculties undergo a slow but progressive atrophy' (Michels, *Political Parties*, p. 221). If one also notes that the social conditions which favour or authorize people's refusal to give their time to politics or administration also frequently encourage a certain aristocratic or prophetic disdain for the *temporal* profits that these activities might promise or procure, it becomes easy

to understand some of the structural invariants of the relation between intellectuals in the different kinds of apparatus (political, administrative or other) and the 'free' intellectuals, between theologians and bishops, or between researchers and deans, rectors and scientific administrators, etc.

49 Lacorne, *Les notables rouges*, p. 114.

50 Weber, *Economy and Society*, vol. 2, p. 1149.

51 Robert Michels, who notes the close correspondence between the organization of the 'democratic party of combat' and military organization and the numerous respects (particularly in Engels and Bebel) in which socialist terminology is indebted to military jargon, observes that leaders, who, as he remarks, are closely attached to discipline and centralization (Michels, *Political Parties*, pp. 189, 208), never fail to appeal to the magic of common interest and to 'military-style arguments' every time their position is threatened: 'They maintain, for instance, that, if only for tactical reasons, and in order to maintain a necessary cohesion in the face of the enemy, the members of the party must never refuse to repose perfect confidence in the leaders they have freely chosen for themselves' (ibid., p. 237). But it is doubtless with Stalin that the strategy of *militarization* – which, as Stephen Cohen notes, is probably Stalin's sole original contribution to Bolshevik thought, and thus the principal characteristic of Stalinism – finds its fulfilment: sectors of intervention become 'fronts' (the grain front, the philosophy front, the literature front, etc.); objectives or problems are 'fortresses' that 'theoretical brigades' have to 'storm', etc. This 'military' thought is evidently Manichean, celebrating a group, a school of thought or a conception set up as an orthodoxy in order the better to destroy all the others (see Cohen, *Nicolas Boukharine*, pp. 367–8, 389).

52 Struggles within the communist party against the authoritarianism of the leaders, and against the priority they grant to the interests of the apparatus as opposed to the interests of those they represent, can clearly only reinforce the very tendencies they combat: the leaders need only mention, or even incite, political struggle, in particular against the most immediate competitors, in order to authorize an appeal to discipline – in other words, submission to the leaders – as is imposed in time of struggle. (In this sense, the denunciation of anti-communism is an absolute weapon in the hands of those who dominate the apparatus, since it disqualifies criticism, even objectification, and imposes unity in face of outside forces.)

53 See Cohen, *Nicolas Boukharine*, p. 185. An ethnographic study of practices of assembly would provide a thousand illustrations of these procedures of authoritarian imposition based on the practical impossibility of breaking, *without impropriety*, a unanimously cultivated unanimity (by abstaining in a show-of-hands vote, by crossing a name off a pre-established list, etc.).

9 Delegation and Political Fetishism

1 T. Hobbes, *Leviathan*, ed. C. B. Macpherson (Harmondsworth: Penguin, 1968), p. 227.
2 See L. Jaume, 'La Théorie de la "personne fictive" dans le Léviathan de Hobbes', *Revue française de science politique*, 33/6 (December 1983), pp. 1009–35.
3 See G. Post, *Studies in Medieval Thought, Public Law and the State, 1100–1322* (Princeton: Princeton University Press, 1964); also O. von Gierke, *Das deutsche Genossenschaftsrecht* [1868] (Graz: Akademische Druck- und Verlagsanstalt, 1954), especially vol. 3 (1881), para. 8, 'Die Korporationstheorie der Kanonisten', pp. 238–77 (I owe this reference to Johannes-Michael Scholz, whom I would like to thank); and P. Michaud-Quantin, *Universitas* (Paris: Vrin, 1970).
4 I. Kant, *Religion within the Limits of Reason Alone*, 2nd edn, tr. T. M. Greene and H. H. Hudson (La Salle, Ill.: 1960), p. 153.
5 F. W. Nietzsche, *The Antichrist*, tr. R. J. Hollingdale (Harmondsworth: Penguin, 1968), p. 167.
6 Ibid., p. 132.
7 Ibid., p. 133.
8 Ibid., p. 184.
9 Ibid., p. 184–5.

10 Identity and Representation: Elements for a Critical Reflection on the Idea of Region

1 The difficulty of conceptualizing the economy of the symbolic in adequate terms can be seen for instance by the fact that, while managing, exceptionally, to avoid the culturalist idealism that is so much the rule in these matters, and devoting attention to the strategic manipulation of 'ethnic' characteristics, Patterson reduces the interest he sees as being at the source of these strategies to a strictly economic interest, thus neglecting everything which, in struggles over classification, obeys the tendency to maximize symbolic profit. (See O. Patterson, 'Context and choice in ethnic allegiance: a theoretical framework and Caribbean case study', in N. Glazer and D. P. Moynihan (eds), *Ethnicity: Theory and Experience* (Cambridge, Mass.: Harvard University Press, 1975), pp. 305–49).)
2 E. Benveniste, *Indo-European Language and Society*, tr. E. Palmer (London: Faber, 1973), pp. 311–12 (and also, on *krainein*, as the power to predict, p. 332).
3 Ibid., pp. 422–3.
4 Cultural difference is probably the product of a historical dialectic of cumulative differentiation. As Paul Bois has shown for peasants of the

west of France whose political choices defied electoral geography, what makes the region is not space but time and history (P. Bois, *Paysans de l'Ouest. Des structures économiques et sociales aux options politiques depuis l'époque révolutionnaire* (Paris and the Hague: Mouton, 1960). The same thing could be shown with regard to Berber-speaking 'regions' which, at the end of a different historical evolution, were sufficiently 'different' from Arab-speaking 'regions' to give rise, on the part of the colonizer, to treatment that was very different (as in the case of education, for instance), and thus bound to reinforce the differences that had served them as a pretext and to produce new ones (those differences which are linked to emigration to France, for example), and so on. Even the 'landscapes' or 'native soil' so dear to geographers are in fact inheritances, in other words, historical products of social determinants. (See C. Reboul, 'Déterminants sociaux de la fertilité des sols', *Actes de la recherche en sciences sociales*, 17–18 (November 1977), pp. 85–112. Following the same logic, and in opposition to the naïvely 'naturalist' usage of the notion of 'landscape', one would have to analyse the contribution of social factors to the processes by which a region is turned into a desert.)

5 The adjective 'Occitan' and, *a fortiori*, the noun 'Occitanie' are *recent* and *scientific* words (coined by *Latinizing* the *langue d'oc* into *lingua occitana*), designed to designate scientific realities which, for the time being at least, exist only on paper.

6 In fact, this language is itself a social *artefact*, invented at the cost of a decisive indifference to differences, which reproduces on the level of the 'region' the arbitrary imposition of a unique norm against which regionalism rebels and which could become the real source of linguistic practices only at the price of a systematic inculcation similar to that which has imposed the generalized use of French or any other 'national' language.

7 The founders of the Republican school system explicity adopted the aim of inculcating, among other things, by the imposition of the 'national' language, the common system of categories of perception and evaluation capable of establishing a unified vision of the social world.

8 The link, everywhere attested, between regionalist movements and feminist (and also ecological) movements stems from the fact that, being directed against forms of symbolic domination, they presuppose ethical dispositions and cultural competences (visible in the strategies employed) which tend to be encountered in the intelligentsia and in the new petite bourgeoisie (see P. Bourdieu, *Distinction: A Social Critique of the Judgement of Taste*, tr. R. Nice (Cambridge. Mass.: Harvard University Press, 1984), pp. 265–6, 357–63, 365–9).

9 How else can one understand, other than as so many compulsive assertions of the claim to the magical *auctoritas* of the *censor* as described by Dumézil, a claim which is part and parcel of the

sociologist's ambition: namely, the obligatory recitations of canonical texts on social classes (ritually contrasted with the statistical *census*) or, at a higher level of ambition and in a less classical style, the prophecies announcing 'new classes' and 'new struggles' (or the inevitable decline of 'old classes' and 'old' struggles), two genres which occupy a large place in so-called sociological production?

10   The reasons for the spontaneous repugnance felt by 'scientists' for 'subjective' criteria would deserve a long analysis: there is the naïve realism which leads one to ignore everything that cannot be pointed to or touched; there is the economism which leads to a failure to recognize any determinants of social action other than those that are visibly an integral part of the material conditions of existence; there are the interests attached to the appearances of 'axiological neutrality' which, in more than one case, constitute all the difference between the 'scientist' and the militant and which forbid questions and notions contrary to the proprieties from being introduced into 'scientific' discourse; there is, last and by no means least, the scientific *point of honour* which leads observers – and this is probably all the more the case the less sure they are of their science and their status – to multiply the signs of a *break* from the representations of common sense and which condemns them to a reductive *objectivism*, which is perfectly incapable of including the reality of common representations in the scientific representation of reality.

11   Marxist research into the national or regional question has been blocked, probably right from the start, by the combined effect of international utopianism (supported by a naïve evolutionism) and of economism, not to mention the effects of the strategic preoccupations of the moment which have often predetermined the verdicts of a 'science' oriented towards practice (and lacking both a true science of science and a science of the relations between practice and science). The effectiveness of these factors taken as a whole can be seen particularly clearly in the typically performative thesis of the primacy – which is so often contradicted by the facts – of class solidarities over 'ethnic' or national solidarities. But the inability to *historicize this problem* (which, to the same degree as the problem of the primacy of spatial relations or social and genealogical relations, is raised and answered in history) and the constantly asserted theoreticist pretention to designate 'viable nations' or to produce scientifically validated criteria of national identity (see G. Haupt. M. Lowy and C. Weill, *Les marxistes et la question nationale* (Paris: Maspero, 1974)), seem to depend directly on the degree to which the regal intention to rule and direct serves to orient the royal science of frontiers and limits: it is no coincidence that Stalin is the author of the most dogmatic and most *essentialist* 'definition' of the nation.

11 Social Space and the Genesis of 'Classes'

1 One can imagine that one has broken away from substantialism and introduced a relational mode of thought when one is in fact studying real interactions and exchanges. (In fact, practical solidarities, like practical rivalries, linked to direct contact and interaction – proximity – may be an *obstacle* to the construction of solidarities based on proximity in the theoretical space.)

2 Statistical investigation can grasp this relation of power only in the form of *properties*, sometimes legally guaranteed by *titles* of economic property, cultural property (educational qualifications) or social property (titles of nobility). This explains the link between empirical research into classes and theories of social structure as a system of *stratification* described in the language of distance from the instruments of appropriation ('distance from the focus of cultural values', in Halbwachs's terms), that Marx himself uses when he speaks of the 'mass deprived of property'.

3 In certain social universes, the principles of division which, like the volume and structure of capital, determine the structure of the social space, are reinforced by principles of division that are relatively independent of economic or cultural properties, such as ethnic or religious affiliation. The distribution of agents appears in this case as the product of the intersection of two spaces which are partly independent of each other, since an ethnic group situated in an inferior position in the space of ethnic groups can occupy positions in all the fields, even the highest, but with rates of representation that are inferior to those of an ethnic group situated in a superior position. Each ethnic group can thus be characterized by the social positions of its members, by the rate of dispersion of these positions and finally by its degree of social integration despite dispersion. (Ethnic solidarity may have the effect of ensuring a form of collective mobility.)

4 The same would be true for the relations between geographical space and social space. These two spaces never coincide completely; however, a number of the differences which are usually associated with the effect of geographical space, for example with the opposition between the centre and the periphery, are the effect of distance in social space, i.e. of the unequal distribution of the different kinds of capital in geographical space.

5 General Pershing's remark on landing in France in 1917 (tr.).

6 This *sense of realities* in no way implies a *class consciousness* in the social–psychological sense, which is the least unreal sense one may give to this word, i.e. an *explicit representation* of the position occupied in the social structure, and of the collective interests that are correlative with it; even less does it imply a *theory of social classes*, i.e., not only a system of classification based on explicit and logically coherent princi-

ples but also a rigorous knowledge of the mechanisms responsible for the distributions. In fact, to put an end to the metaphysics of the 'awakening of consciousness' and 'class consciousness', a sort of revolutionary *cogito* of the collective consciousness of a personified entity, we need only examine the social and economic conditions which make it possible for this form of distance from the present moment of practice to exist, a distance presupposed by the conception and formulation of a more or less elaborate representation of a collective future. (This is what I sketched out in my analysis of the relations between temporal consciousness, including the aptitude for rational economic calculation, and political consciousness among Algerian workers; see P. Bourdieu, *Algeria 1960*, tr. R. Nice (Cambridge: Cambridge University Press, 1979).)

7   In this case, the production of common sense consists, essentially, in the constant re-interpretation of the common stock of sacred discourses (proverbs, sayings, gnomic poems, etc.), in 'purifying the language of the tribe'. By appropriating the words in which everything recognized by a group is deposited, one gains a considerable advantage in struggles for power. This is clear in struggles for religious authority: the most precious word is the sacred word and, as Gershom Scholem observes, it is because mystical opposition to established religion has to re-appropriate established symbols in order to achieve recognition that it is 'recuperated' by the tradition. As stakes in different struggles, the words of the political lexicon carry a polemical charge in the form of the *polysemy* which is the trace of the antagonistic usages that different groups have made, or make, of these words. One of the most universal strategies resorted to by the professionals of symbolic power – poets in archaic societies, prophets, politicians – thus consists in putting *common sense* on your side by appropriating the words that are invested with value by the whole group because they are the repositories of its belief.

8   As Leo Spitzer has clearly shown with regard to *Don Quixote*, in which the same person is given several names, *polyonomasia* – the plurality of names, nicknames and sobriquets attributed to the same agent or the same institution – together with the polysemy of words or expressions designating the fundamental values of different groups, is the visible trace of struggles for the power to name, struggles which occur in all social universes (see L. Spitzer, 'Perspectivism in Don Quijote', in Linguistics and Literary History (New York: Russel and Russel, 1948)).

9   F. Kafka, *The Trial* (Harmondsworth: Penguin, 1953), p. 197.

10 The directory of trades and occupations is the realized form of that social neutralism which cancels out the differences constitutive of the social space by treating uniformly all positions as *professions*, at the cost of a constant shift from the definitional point of view (titles and qualifications, nature of the activity, etc.). When people in the Anglo-

Saxon world call doctors 'professionals', they are emphasizing the fact
that these agents are defined by their profession, which is for them an
essential attribute; on the other hand, someone who hitches carriages
together is hardly defined at all by this attribute, which designates him
only in so far as he performs a certain kind of work. As for the teacher
who has passed the *agrégation* exam, he or she is qualified, like the
hitcher of carriages, by a task, an activity, but also by a qualification
and title, like the doctor.

11   Entering a profession with a title is increasingly dependent on the
possession of an educational qualification, and there is a close relation
between educational qualifications and professional remuneration. The
situation is quite different in untitled occupations in which agents
performing the same work may have very different educational qualifications.

12   Those who possess the same title tend to constitute themselves as a
group and to provide themselves with permanent organizations (the
association of doctors, associations of alumni, etc.) aimed at ensuring
group cohesion (with periodical reunions, etc.) and at promoting the
group's material and symbolic interests.

13   The most perfect illustration of this analysis can be found, thanks to the
fine work done by Robert Darnton, in the history of that sort of cultural
revolution that the dominated figures within the emergent intellectual
field – people such as Brissot, Mercier, Desmoulins, Hébert, Marat,
and so many others – carried out within the Revolutionary movement
(destruction of the Academies, dispersion of the salons, suppression of
pensions, abolition of privileges). This cultural revolution sprang from
the status of 'cultural pariahs' and its first priority was to attack the
symbolic foundations of power, contributing, by its 'politico-
pornography' and its deliberately scatalogical lampoons, to the task of
'delegitimation' which is doubtless one of the fundamental dimensions
of revolutionary radicalism. (See R. Darnton, 'The high Enlightenment
and the low-life of literature in pre-revolutionary France', *Past and
Present*, 51 (1971), pp. 81–115; on the exemplary case of Marat, who,
as people often forget, was also – or initially – a bad physicist, see also
C. C. Gillispie, *Science and Polity in France at the End of the Old
Régime* (Princeton: Princeton University Press, 1980), pp. 290–330.)

14   For a similar analysis of the relation between the kinship group 'on
paper' and the kinship group in practice as 'will and representation',
see P. Bourdieu, *Outline of a Theory of Practice*, tr. R. Nice (Cambridge: Cambridge University Press, 1977) and *The Logic of Practice*,
tr. R. Nice (Cambridge: Polity Press, 1990).

Index

communism
  and political dispossession 26
  and political parties 187, 189, 200–1
communism, linguistic 5, 43–4
community, linguistic 40, 45–6, 53
competence
  acquisition 82
  communicative 257 n.4
  cultural 287 n.8
  generative 4, 7, 37, 66
  linguistic; and authority 6, 19, 69–70,
    76; and education 61
  and performance 5, 7, 37–9, 43–4, 55
  political 175–80
  popular 71, 85, 89
  practical 7–8, 18
  rare, *see* distinction
  social 41, 70, 173, 262 n.16
competition
  between political professionals 177,
    183, 187, 188–90, 196, 199, 247
  linguistic 56, 62, 64
compromise
  formation 78–9, 137
  political 179–80, 189–90
Comte, A. 43
condescension, as strategy 1, 29, 68–9,
    71, 78, 124
Condillac, E. B. de 6, 47
conflict, linguistic 259 n.17
conformism, logical 166
conformity
  linguistic 94, 152
  social 22, 124
connotation 39–40, 109
consciousness
  awakening 204, 233, 243–4, 289 n.6
  class 289 n.6
consecration 118–19, 125–6, 134, 151, 195
  of self 209–14, 219
consensus 40–1, 49, 105–6, 126, 130–1,
    164–6, 236, 239
constitution, act of 119, 123, 135
consumer, political 172, 173
consumption, conspicuous 55–6, 237
convention, social 9, 102
convergence of social conditions 72
correctness 79, 93
  and bourgeoisie 21, 62–3, 83
  and literary professionals 60–1
  see also hypercorrection; hypocorrection
credentials, *see* credit
credit 24, 28, 119, 192–3, 281 n.29
crisis, and heretical discourse 128–9
culture
  esoteric 27, 184

  popular 91–2
custom, linguistic 265 n.8

Darnton, Robert 291 n.13
Dasein in Heidegger 141, 143, 145–7,
    149–50
Davy, Georges 48–9
De Gaulle, Charles 281 n.33
delegation 75, 107–16, 168, 173, 193, 194,
    196, 199
  and apparatus 216–19
  and dispossession 26–7, 171, 174
  and naming 239–40
  and political fetishism 27, 203–19
  and representation 107, 203–4, 248–9
  and self-consecration 209–14
  see also spokesperson
demonstration 224, 249, 251
deprivation, language 53
Derrida, Jacques 225 n.26
determinism
  economic 182, 280 n.26, 287 n.9, 288
    n.11
  social 139, 144, 164
deviation
  and social value 53–7, 60, 62–5, 94
  system 184–8
dialect, and official language 6–7, 19, 45,
    46–9
dictionary
  and language standardization 6, 48
  and popular speech 90–2
difference
  consecration 118–20, 123–4
  social/linguistic 54–6, 57, 93, 222, 237–
    8, 245–6
diffusion, cultural 62–4
discipline, in political party 200–1
discourse
  dominant 169
  esoteric 41
  exoteric 154
  heterodox 128–31, 213, 277 n.8
  and linguistic market 38–41
  political 27–9, 183, 190–1
  reactionary 131–2
  ritual 107–16
  value 77, 82
discourse analysis 28, 76
disinterestedness 16, 193
dispositions 12–13, 17–18, 33, 88, 126
  ethical 287 n.8
  linguistic 17, 37–8, 51–2; and popular
    speech 93–7
  political 133, 200–1
  see also inculcation

dispossession
  and delegation 204, 206
  economic 172, 244
  linguistic 52, 59
  political 26–7, 131, 169, 171–2, 174–7, 249
dissimilation 63–4
distance
  from production 85, 87
  social 79, 232
distinction
  and bourgeoisie 21, 62–4
  and communication 167
  and deviation 21, 22, 55, 62–5, 94–5, 120, 177, 265 n.7
  and literary professionals 59–60
  philosophical 143–4
profit of 18–19, 34, 55–6, 65, 73
  and social world 237–8
  see also vulgarity
domination
  by symbolic productions 166–8
  language 5–6, 44–9, 59–60, 69
  market 69
  mediated 197
  symbolic 50–2, 72, 93
  and symbolic violence 23–4
dramatization 129
Duchamp, Marcel 154, 275 n.46
Ducrot, O. 75
Dumézil, G. 287 n.9
Durkheim, Emile 49, 120, 123, 167, 203, 212
  on social structures 31, 164, 166, 251

economy, *see* determinism, economic; field, economic
education
  and cultural capital 14, 24–5, 55–6, 62, 97, 241
  and labour market 6, 49
  and language dominance 6–7, 48–9, 59–61, 264 n.29
  and value of language 22, 57
elites, in Heidegger 143, 149, 151, 276 n.57
empiricism
  and knowledge 164
  and language acquisition 259 n.19
Encrevé, Pierre 259 n.18, 260 n.26
Engels, Friedrich 166–7
enunciation, labour of 129
epistemology 11–12, 164–6
essence, social 102, 121–2
ethnicity 30, 95, 220, 223
ethnologism 276 n.6

ethnomethodology 147–8, 276 n.3
euphemization 80, 84–5, 132, 170, 266 n.17
  and censorship 19–20, 22, 78–9, 137
  and philosophical language 20, 142, 144, 148
  and politics 169, 281 n.33
evaluation of language 23, 53–4, 70, 77, 82–4, 259 n.21
examination, competitive 120
exchange
  as economic 66, 67–72
  goals 66–7
  private 71, 84, 98–101
  ritual 72–3
  as socially structured 2, 4, 8
  symbolic 23, 37, 107
existence
  authentic/inauthentic 143, 149–50, 155
  and symbol 249–51
exorcism 134
expression, instruments 172–3

factionalism 208
family, and linguistic competence 62, 71, 82
Farias, Victor 255 n.26
felicity conditions 8–9, 73–6, 116
Ferro, Marc 218
fetishism
  of legitimate language 52–3, 151
  political 27, 203–19, 249
fides 192
fides implicita 174, 199, 206
field 14–17, 25, 57–8, 215
  economic 15–16, 25, 227, 229, 244
  homologies 29, 41, 168–9, 182, 187, 214–16, 243–8
  intellectual 20, 189–90, 216
  linguistic 57; dynamics 61–5
  literary 16, 57–61
  political 25–9, 41, 127–36, 243–8; and apparatus 199–202; and expression 137–8; and social field 28–9, 183; theory 171–202
  social 183, 229–31, 238, 242, 244, 247
  see also space
filler phrases 85
force, illocutionary 9, 75, 80, 107–9, 125, 129, 170, 191
form
  of classification 164
  and content 20–1, 79–80, 139, 151
  and function 85–6, 113
  imposition 137–59, 153
  respect for 20, 151–9

296   *Index*

form – *cont.*
  and social relations 80–1
  and substance 141–3
  symbolic 164
formalism 28–9, 80, 147, 147–8, 153,
    213–14
formality
  and bourgeois usage 84–5
  and censorship 137–8
  and linguistic dominance 69–71, 78–9, 81
Foucault, Michel 31
freedom, obligatory 95
Frege, Gottlob 41
French, and language dominance 5–6, 19,
    43–9, 68, 78
Freud, Sigmund 143
frontier, and regional identity 222–3, 227
functionalism, and symbolic productions
    166–7

game
  double 180–3
  investment in 180–1
  see also field
game theory 16
Garfinkel, Harold 254 n.14
Geertz, Clifford 254 n.14
gender relations, neglected 30
generation, and dominant market 95, 97
George, Stefan 150, 273 n.32
gift exchange 23–4
Goffman, Erving 235
government, political power 182
grammar
  incorporated 61
  and language as code 59, 258 n.12
  and legitimation of language 58–9, 60–1
  and meaning 38
grammaticality 41, 76
Gramsci, Antonio 174–5, 183, 184, 187,
    194, 219, 282 nn.41,44
group
  and delegate 26, 106, 203–9, 211–14,
    248–50
  ethnic 233, 237, 289 n.3
  exclusion from 138, 195–6
  identity 221, 223–4
  instituted 130, 133–4, 174, 205, 206–7,
    221, 236, 250
  political 181–2, 186, 188–90
  and social space 30, 232–3
  see also class
Guidoni, P. 283 n.45
Guiraud, Pierre 17, 86, 264 n.26

Habermas, Jürgen 10, 31, 107–9, 152,
    257 n.4

habitus 12–14, 17–18, 50
  class 83
  formation 123, 248
  linguistic 18, 21–2, 37–8, 46, 48, 77, 79,
    81–9; dominated 71–2, 95; formation
    17, 51–2, 81; *see also* hexis
  political 27, 176, 188, 200
Halbwachs, M. 288 n.2
Haupt, G. 280 n.23
hedge, linguistic 85
Hegel, G. W. F. 213, 233
Heidegger, Martin 20–1, 139, 140–51,
    152–8, 276 n.2
  Being and Time 152, 157, 274 n.43, 275
    n.52, 276 n.56
  'Letter on humanism' 154, 156, 275
    n.46
  Time and Being 157
Helvetius, Claude Adrien 214
Heusch, Luc de 118
hexis, bodily 13, 17, 81–9, 92, 123
hierarchy
  of discourses 152, 238
  linguistic 17, 68–9
  of principles of division 245–6
  social 1, 22–3, 54–5, 68, 88, 167–8, 240
Hirschman, Albert 208
history, and political thought 269 n.3
Hobbes, Thomas 208–9
Hobert, C. 156
Hoffman, S. *180*
Holbach, Baron d' 214
homology, *see* field
Hugo, Victor 59
Humboldt, W. von 49, 164, 258 n.11
Husserl, E. 235, 276 n.3
Hymes, Dell 253 n.9
hypercorrection 21, 62–3, 83, 125
hypocorrection 63, 125

iconology/iconography 166
ideal speaker 5, 7, 10, 44
idealism
  cultural 98, 125, 286 n.1
  and knowledge 164, 169
identity
  institution of 120–1, 124–5
  professional 240–2, 248
  regional 220–8
  sexual 17–18, 88
  social 18, 87–8, 98, 130–1, 234, 236,
    247–8, 259 n.17
  see also naming
ideology
  and philosophical discourse 152–3
  political 27–8, 143–4, 167, 168–70

immigrants, and working class 91, 95, 97, 266 n.14
imperialism, intellectual 3–4
imposition of power 41, 71, 72–3, 84, 90, 96, 212, 239
imposture 76, 109, 214
inculcation 12, 59–61, 62, 90, 122–3, 168, 264 n.29
information, in linguistic exchange 66–7, 107
initiation
 and politics 176, 195
 and suffering 123
injunction 122
institution
 and language dominance 45–6
 and performatives 8–10, 73–4, 109–16
 and politics 173, 174–5, 177, 186, 195–7, 248
 rites 117–26
 as social fiction 251
 and symbolic violence 24–5, 50
 see also authority; group; rites of institution
insult 75–6, 105, 121, 239, 243
integration
 linguistic 46
 social 166–7, 289 n.3
intellectualism 37, 229, 235
intention
 performative 105
 political 172–3
interactionist theory 64–5, 167
interest
 and action 16, 127, 175
 expressive 37, 137, 139, 142, 159, 172
 and ideology 167
 political 175, 182–3, 188, 202, 215–16, 246–7
internalism 109, 153
interpretation 153–8, 210
intimidation 51–2, 99
investigation, linguistic 71–2, 83
investiture 119, 121–2, 195–6
investment in field 14, 178, 195, 197
irony 94, 96, 262 n.18

Jaspers, K. 141
journalism
 as field 216
 and symbolic capital 281 n.34
Jünger, Ernst 20, 142, 149

Kabyle society 23–4, 118–19, 236
Kafka, Franz 240
Kant, Immanuel 32, 42, 149, 209–10

Kantorowicz, E. H. 75, 124, 248
Kautsky, Karl 191
knowledge
 and political action 127, 132, 136
 practical 92–3
 and recognition 62, 164–6, 168, 242
 sacred/profane 145, 154

labour
 division 169–70
 domination *165*, 244
 intellectual division 4
 political division 171–202
 religious division 168–9
 sexual division 50, 83, 88, 100–1
Labov, W. 18, 52–3, 83, 85–6
Lacan, Jacques 146
Lacorne, D. 200, 282 nn.37,38
Lacoue-Labarthe, Philippe 255 n.26
Lakoff, G. 84–5
Laks, Bernard 87–8
language
 autonomy 41, 107, 140–2
 elevated 152
 generative capacity 4, 37, 41–2
 legitimate 6, 69, 113, 129, 170; and literary field 57–61
 official; and dialects 6, 19, 45, 46–9; and political unity 5–7, 44–6, 50–1, 53, 287 n.7
 originative capacity 42
 regional 261 n.2
 as social 1–2, 4–10, 33–4, 38, 41, 53–5, 61, 67–8, 105–6, 287 n.6
 specialized 137, 140–51
 as structured system 166
langue d'oïl 6, 46
langue and *parole* 4, 7, 33, 37, 44, 44–5, 107, 166
langues d'oc 6, 47, 258 n.9, 287 n.5
Laqueur, W. Z. 273 n.32
Lattimore, Owen 122
law, and language 41–2, 49, 173
Lefebvre, Henri 157
left/right oppositions 185–6
legitimacy
 cultural 98
 imposition 69, 72–3
 of language, *see* language, official
 of power 23, 238, 242, 278 n.6
leisure, and political action 172, 284 n.48
Lelong, R. P. *108–14*, 116
Lévi-Strauss, Claude 3, 4, 11, 23, 30
linguistics
 critique 2–10, 18, 32–4, 37–8, 43–4
 structural 11, 33–4

Index compiled by Meg Davies (Society of Indexers)